SATURDAY NIGHT SOLDIERS

Saturday Night Soldiers

The 4th battalion of the Lincolnshire Regiment
in World War II

John Benson

2002
RICHARD KAY
80 SLEAFORD ROAD • BOSTON • LINCOLNSHIRE PE21 8EU

ISBN 1 902882 51 2
© John Benson
AD 2002

The main body of the text prepared for printing on a home personal computer in Georgia 10 pt. typeface by John Benson.

Printed and bound in England by Foxe Graphics Ltd.
Enterprise Road, Golf Road Industrial Estate, Mablethorpe, Lincolnshire LN12 1NB

For the men of the 4th battalion of the Lincolnshire Regiment, and particularly for those who did not return.

Contents

Illustrations

vii

Photographs reproduced by permission of:
¶ Trustees of the Imperial War Museum.
* Trustees of the Lincolnshire Regimental Museum.

The pictures which appear on pages 80, 83, 84, 85, 86, 132 and 134 are from The History of the 79th Armoured Division, written anonymously and privately printed and published in 1945. The picture of the Germans leaving Holland (page 190) was supplied by Bernard Sluiter. All the other photographs have been supplied by and reproduced with the kind permission of former members of the 4th battalion or their relatives. Although the present ownership of the photographs is known, in some cases the actual copyright is not. If copyright has inadvertently been infringed we shall be grateful if the copyright owner will contact the publisher.

Maps

By permission of the Public Record Office.

Maps re-drawn and amended by John Benson from a number of different sources.

The cover is by Kevin Smith of Lincoln, telephone 01522 530713.
Nothing is known about the soldier of the 4th Lincolns who is depicted on the cover except that his name was Harold.
The website for the Saturday Night Soldiers is at www.4thlincolns.co.uk.

Acknowledgements

This book could not have been completed—nor even started—without the assistance of many people. Former members of the 4th Lincolns and their relatives willingly consented to being interviewed. They told me their stories, lent photographs and press cuttings and put me on to others who could—and did—help. For instance, through Sid Hall—the first person I went to see—I was able to trace Mrs Rosemary Gawthorn, who gave me photographs and a wealth of information about the battalion and her father, Major Don Stokes. Mr and Mrs Fred Lawson let me borrow some pictures and advised me to contact Jack Hardy and Gordon Bone, who were both very helpful. Mrs Grace Banks and Fred Burton responded to my appeal for help in the *Lincolnshire Echo,* and from Cheshire Tom Hassall sent me the photograph of him helping to milk a goat. In the Boston area, Norman Barber, Tom Adamson, Mrs Sylvia Graveling and Captain O R Giles gave me a great deal of help. Arthur Turner in Bradford told me about the mortar platoon, which he eventually commanded, and put me on to Stan Masters in London who sent me several photographs which have been included in the book. The late Captain Anthony Hay Bell from High Toynton, who was with 'B' Company until he was commissioned into the 6th Lincolns in 1942, lent some photographs and gave me permission to draw upon his lively, unpublished account of his time with the battalion. Although Major J O Flint DSO MC of Barholme modestly claimed that he didn't think he would be able to help a great deal, he did in fact give me quite a lot of information and let me borrow a couple of very good pictures. Ernest Taylor of Scunthorpe was in the Royal Lincolnshire Regiment and although he was not in the 4th battalion he was nevertheless able to let me copy some photographs from his collection and Charlie Denton also helped. I was grateful to Steve Vernon who, at the very last moment, sent me a photograph of his grandfather with the pre-war machine gunners and another one of Major Don Stokes. Captain John Lee of the Royal Lincolnshire Regimental Association read the initial draft of the book, as did several of those already mentioned above, and they all made helpful comments and suggestions.

I spent several days at the Public Record Office at Kew reading the battalion's War Diaries. I also visited the Imperial War Museum and am grateful to the Trustees for permitting me to reproduce pictures from their Photographic Archive. Major-General Dick Gerrard-Wright gave permission for me to reproduce photographs from the Lincolnshire Regiment's Museum. All the staff of the Lincolnshire Life Museum in Lincoln were extremely helpful, as always, in pointing me in the right directions.

I'm very grateful to everyone who helped. And that of course includes my wife Linda and my two sons, Matthew and Simon, for their support and patience. My apologies to anyone I've inadvertently missed out.

John Benson
Burton
Lincoln

September 2002

Before the War

At the outbreak of the Second World War there were two Regular Army battalions of the Lincolnshire Regiment. The 1st battalion was in India and it remained in the Far East for the rest of the war. The 2nd battalion, stationed at Portland Bill, went to France shortly after the war started, was evacuated from Dunkirk, landed in Normandy on D-Day and was in Bremen when the war ended.

There were also two Territorial Army battalions of the Lincolnshire Regiment, the 4th and the 6th. There was no 3rd battalion and the 5th battalion—Territorials from the north of Lincolnshire—had become a searchlight unit (in those days, Royal Engineers) in 1937.

Men of the 4th battalion at the camp in the Isle of Man, July 1939. All of them worked for the Post Office. Left to right: Privates J Hughes, G C Elliott, E Forman, K Still, K Dodds and W Prestwood.

During the First World War someone had the idea of forming local volunteer battalions of 'Pals', or 'Chums'—friends and brothers could join up together and stay in the same regiment. But when the men went into action and were

1

slaughtered in their hundreds, the loss to local communities, streets and even families was so tragic that it was decided afterwards they would never be raised again. But the inter-war Territorial Army units which were in every town of any size were unaffected by this decision. They still comprised local young men who knew each other well from work, schooldays, a football team or even a pub. A few of them were brothers.

The men in the Territorial Army (the TA) were volunteers—civilians who trained for one or two nights a week and at weekends. They were known as the 'Terriers' or, more humorously, the 'Saturday Night Soldiers'. Everyone knew each other pretty well. Many of them were friends who'd decided to join the TA together for a bit of fun. It was the thing to do—a bit of a lark. At Lincoln, some of the men had joined so that they could be in the 4th battalion's band.

The band of the 4th battalion outside their headquarters, the Drill Hall in Broadgate, Lincoln.

The highlight of the year was the fortnight's training camp, usually held at a different place every year—an enjoyable working holiday with plenty of free time off duty which everyone looked forward to. It was the only holiday which many of the men were likely to have in those days, and some had joined the TA just so that they could go to the camp.

Depending upon how many times they attended, the Territorials received between three pounds ten shillings and five pounds a year—the equivalent of a couple of weeks' extra wages to most of the men. When they went to the annual camp, privates received army pay of fourteen shillings a week, but of course in many cases they didn't receive any wages from their employers whilst they were away.

Men of the 4th battalion off-duty at Douglas, Isle of Man, in 1939.

Territorial Army units were run on a less rigid, more informal, basis than the regular army. It was all rather friendly and a bit amateurish. They were a bit like a peace-time—and younger—version of the Home Guard which was formed later, in 1940. The amount of training which the Terriers received wasn't much different in nature and duration to the Home Guard and although the officers and NCOs did their best the equipment they had to use was not only old but in short supply. It was all done on the cheap. Nevertheless, in Whitehall, the Territorial Army was—quite unrealistically and unfairly—down on paper as a reserve which would immediately be mobilised in the event of a national emergency and take its place alongside units of the regular army.

The officers were drawn from the middle-class—professional people or local businessmen. Many of them had been to public school. Donald Stokes, standing on the extreme left in the picture below, was in the family business (Stokes' café and coffee shop on the High Bridge in Lincoln), whilst Reginald Tweed (standing third from the left) was a solicitor in Horncastle.

Some of the 4th battalion's officers at camp in Horncastle, about 1926. It is interesting that two of the officers were still wearing their 'pips' on their sleeves.

The 6th battalion had only been formed a few weeks before the outbreak of war. In March 1939, the government had doubled the establishment of the Territorial Army hoping to attract over 200,000 more volunteers. The band of the 2nd battalion came from Portland to help recruiting drives in Lincolnshire towns and there was such a ready response that by May recruitment to the only existing battalion, the 4th, had to be stopped. At the same time, the government had also introduced conscription and young men aged 21 were called-up. They would have to do six months' full-time training and then a further period with their local Territorial Army unit, but there was also another option. Rather than doing the six months full-time training men could opt to join the TA for a longer period of four years. Realising that if they waited to be called-up they could be sent anywhere, several men chose this latter option and enlisted in the TA with their friends so that they could at least be together.

Friends, colleagues and brothers often joined the Territorial Army together. In this group from 'B' Company at Douglas, Tony Bell (extreme left) and Bob Bell (3rd from the

left) were brothers. Sergeant Alway, (3rd from the right) was a schoolteacher and was later commissioned. Not all of the men had been issued with the new battle-dress, and some of those who had were still wearing peaked caps. There had been other innovations a few months earlier. Puttees no longer had to be worn and the men now marched in threes rather than fours.

Right: Men from the Signals Section at the annual camp.

Machine gunners. This photograph must have been taken at an earlier camp because the Vickers guns were taken from them in 1938. Donald Stokes, then a captain, is in 'civvies'.

Another group of men from 'B' Company at Douglas in July 1939, some in the old-style uniform and some in battledress.

There were now so many Territorials in the 4th Lincolns that in July 1939, just after they'd been to the Isle of Man for their annual training camp, there was a reorganisation on a geographical basis. A new battalion, the 6th, was formed from the companies at Grantham, Spalding, Holbeach and Stamford. The headquarters of the 6th battalion were at Grantham and they became part of the 46th (North Midland) Division. They also were at Dunkirk and later fought in North Africa and Italy.

The 4th battalion, with headquarters at the Drill Hall in Broadgate at Lincoln, was left with 'B' Company at Horncastle, 'C' Company at Boston, 'D' Company at Spilsby and Alford and 'A' Company at Lincoln, and formed part of the 49th (West Riding) Division.

This book is about the 4th battalion, the Territorial Army volunteers who were destined to become the first soldiers of the Lincolnshire Regiment to see action in the Second World War.

Private Tom Adamson.

Church Parade.

17 Platoon from Alford.

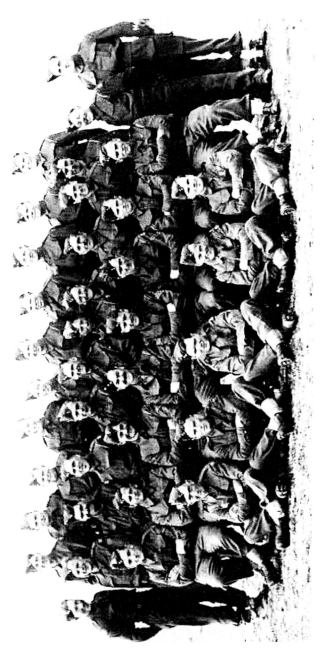

18 Platoon from Spilsby.

Called-up

The Territorial Army was mobilised on Friday the 1st September 1939, the day that Hitler invaded Poland. Throughout the country, the civilian part-time soldiers of the Territorial Army, mechanics, shop assistants, bank clerks, postmen, butchers, solicitors, bricklayers, farm workers, schoolteachers, delivery men—every conceivable trade and profession—reported to their depots in response to instructions broadcast on the wireless and printed in the evening newspapers. In some parts of rural Lincolnshire messages had to be sent by men on bikes to tell farm hands working in the fields. The men put down their tools and their pens, said goodbye to their workmates, went home, got changed into their uniforms, said goodbye to their families and went off to war.

'A' Company and 'HQ' Company of the 4th (Territorial) battalion of the Lincolnshire Regiment reported to their depot at the Drill Hall in Broadgate, Lincoln.

Although there were only about 300 men at the Lincolnshire Regiment's depot at the New Barracks on Burton Road, there was no accommodation for them there as regular army reservists had also been called-up and were expected to arrive within a day or two. (In fact overflow accommodation had to be found for the troops who soon started to pour into Lincoln, and this was about a mile away from the barracks at Stores Park on Longdales Road—large, high and very cold store huts which had been used by the RAF in the 1914-18 war).

So the Territorials just had to stay where they were and sleep on the floor at the Drill Hall. Over the next few days, wives, parents and girlfriends kept coming to find out whether they were still there and what was happening.

The Drill Hall, Lincoln.

After a time the men were allowed to go home in the evening but they had their meals at the Drill Hall, prepared on the premises by some of the men who had volunteered for the job and whose results, to put it kindly, showed their inexperience.

This happened at Boston and Spilsby too, but after 'B' company had reported to their Drill Hall in Boston Road, Horncastle they were immediately taken that evening by buses to Scunthorpe. They were billeted in the Palais de Dance and arrangements were made for them to have their meals at the Co-op café. It was feared that the large steel works and glowing slag heaps at Scunthorpe would be an immediate prime target for the Luftwaffe and 'B' company's task was to help the police and the air raid wardens as and when the raids occurred. But there were no air raids and those who had worked on farms were temporarily released for the harvest. Scunthorpe Corporation let the men use the swimming baths free of charge, they were given free tickets to the cinemas and theatre and many of the men were welcomed in people's homes. A bus company laid on a special coach on Sundays so that relatives and friends from Horncastle could visit them.

Four small Scunthorpe boys wonder why these men of 'B' Company are filling
sandbags. Perhaps the men do too.

It wasn't long before a number of reservists arrived to join the battalion. Most of them were men who had served in India with the regiment as regular soldiers but had been called-up because they were still on the reserve list. As old soldiers they knew every trick in the book about how to avoid duty. But they were also experienced and some were very quickly promoted as NCOs.

A batch of young men also arrived from the New Barracks—the very first of the conscripts who had completed their full-time training. Most of them were from Lincolnshire but about thirty of them came from the Leeds area. Arthur Turner, who had just finished his apprenticeship as an ornamental plasterer, was one of them. As his work was likely to take him all over the country the option of training for a couple of days a week with a TA unit in Bradford was just not practical. So he'd opted for the six months full-time training, after which he'd expected to return home and go back to work. But now that war had been declared he was in the army full-time. His six months in the army actually became seven years.

Private Arthur Turner.

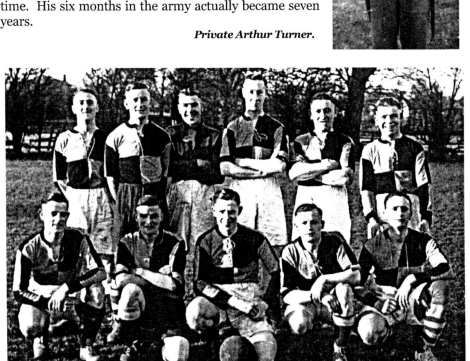

'B' Company football team on a rare sunny day in Ripon.
Standing: Sid Hall, K Hogg, Patterson, Britton, Patrick, Stones.
Front: Gibson, J Clark, H Hart, J Mallett and J Thornton.

Late in October 1939, the whole battalion was sent to Ripon where some of the officers and men were billeted in private houses. Others had the good fortune to be billeted in a pub. The battalion trained around Fountains Abbey, but this consisted mainly of drilling, saluting and marching under the newly-promoted NCOs. Some of the men had only fired five rounds of ammunition on a range and there was virtually no training in tactics. Even the marches and drills became difficult to carry out, for very soon the country was gripped in one of the most severe winters of the century. A major pre-occupation for the men was the business of just trying to keep warm. To make matters worse, an epidemic of measles swept the country that winter and quite a number of men caught it.

In the second week of December all the battalion, except for 'C' Company, went on leave but the men had to return to spend Christmas at Ripon. Those in 'C' Company were more fortunate. By the luck of the draw they went on leave when the others got back to Ripon and were able to spend Christmas at home in Boston.

The weather became even colder. They didn't know it, but it was a foretaste of what was to come.

'A' Company pose outside the 'Black Dog' pub at Ripon.

Norway

Three-quarters of Germany's iron ore came from Sweden. Millions of tons were imported every year and without it German industry would grind to a halt. In the winter, when the Gulf of Bothnia was frozen up for months, the ore could only be exported through the Norwegian port of Narvik, less than twenty miles from the Swedish frontier and north of the Arctic Circle on the North Atlantic coast.

Both Winston Churchill and Hitler realised the strategic importance of Norway. Churchill—at that time the First Lord of the Admiralty—was worried that ships carrying iron ore for Germany were beating the British naval blockade by hugging the thousand miles of Norwegian coastline from Narvik, keeping within the territorial waters of a neutral country. This was an intolerable state of affairs. Germany was taking advantage of Norway's neutrality whilst Britain—respecting that neutrality—was allowing the traffic to proceed. Churchill wanted to mine the Norwegian waters, and in September 1939 he put forward this proposal in a paper presented to the War Cabinet. This put the Cabinet in a quandary. Although there was agreement about the need there was reluctance to infringe Norwegian neutrality and in the end nothing was done.

Norway was also on Hitler's mind. He too had realised that the British could seriously threaten the supply of iron ore from Sweden by mining Norwegian waters. If the Allies went further and actually *occupied* Norway they would be able to command the Baltic. Not only would all supplies from Scandinavia be threatened but the German navy would be bottled up. Hitler also reminded himself that Britain and France had declared war over Poland. Germany had neither troops nor coastal defence fortifications on their Baltic coast and a landing by the Allies—or perhaps worse still by the Russians—would not only cut off their Army in Poland but would also lead straight to Berlin, less than a hundred miles away. (Hitler needn't have worried about this possibility as it hadn't crossed the minds of the Allies. The navy would have been vulnerable to air attack). On the other hand, Hitler saw that if the German navy had bases in Norway his ships and submarines would have many outlets and could control the North Atlantic. Whilst the British War Cabinet agonised over mining the territorial waters, Hitler gave orders for plans to be prepared to invade Norway.

Meanwhile, an unexpected development occurred. When the Russians feel threatened they take steps to occupy the adjacent country to act as a sort of 'buffer'. Their minds were also on the Baltic. They swiftly signed agreements with Estonia, Latvia and Lithuania to garrison Red Army troops at key bases. With Leningrad only twenty miles from the Finnish border they also sought a similar arrangement with Finland. The Finns were unable to agree to all the Russian demands, the negotiations broke down and on the 30th November 1939 the Russians invaded Finland and bombed Helsinki.

The Finns did surprisingly well against the Russians. Their troops were well equipped with skis and warm clothing. The Russians had neither. The Russian artillery was inadequate, their tanks were light and their advances were attacked from the flanks and cut to pieces. After about a month the fighting died down, with the Finns so far victorious. This made everyone think, including the Germans.

The Finnish government appealed for aircraft and war materials. Many nations felt sorry for the gallant Finns and wanted to help them. But there was only one possible route into Finland and that was through Narvik in neutral Norway and then through neutral Sweden.

So Churchill's mind returned once more to Norway. If only the Allies could set up a base in Narvik it would not only cut off Germany's iron ore from Sweden (it could be sent to Britain instead) but it could also be used to supply the Finns. Churchill proposed that Britain should occupy key bases in Norway such as Narvik and Bergen, by force if necessary. Regarding the moral issue of occupying part of a neutral country, he persuaded himself that we had a right—more, a duty—to set aside for a time the very laws which we were fighting to re-affirm. Small nations should not tie our hands when we were fighting for their rights and freedom.

The Finns stood firm throughout January 1940 but the Red Army brought up a mass of artillery and heavy tanks and mounted a huge offensive early in February. By the end of the month the Finns were exhausted. Both the French and the British thought that it was very important for Finland to be saved. The French decided to send fifty thousand volunteers and a hundred bombers to Finland. Two British divisions due to be sent to France were held back. The Cabinet instructed the Chiefs of Staff to prepare a plan to land forces in Narvik to go to the aid of the Finns. Strangely, they were still opposed to the idea of mining Norwegian territorial waters.

In Ripon, all leave was cancelled when the 4th battalion of the Lincolnshire Regiment received an order to 'stand-by'.

There was now a dramatic incident. In December 1939 the German pocket battleship *Graf Spee*, disabled following action with British and New Zealand warships, was scuttled at Montevideo in Uruguay. But her supply ship, the *Altmark*, was still at large and in mid-February she was sighted returning to Germany through Norwegian territorial waters. On board there were British seamen from the merchant ships which had been sunk by the *Graf Spee*, on their way to imprisonment in Germany. The British saw the *Altmark* as violating Norwegian neutrality. HMS *Cossack* intercepted her in a fjord at night and 299 British seamen were released and transferred to our destroyers. The Norwegians protested to the British government about the violation of their territorial waters.

The *Altmark* incident made Hitler sit up, for this was the first intimation that the British were prepared to violate neutrality. He decided that the occupation of both

Denmark and Norway should have priority over his plans to invade Belgium and France.

The German pocket-battleship 'Graf Spee'.

Meanwhile, the Russian terms for an armistice were accepted by the exhausted Finns on the 12th March. The British plans for military landings were shelved and some of the troops which had been allocated were sent to France instead. The 4th Lincolns' 'stand-by' order was cancelled.

The Allied politicians had failed to give any substantial aid to the Finns, and in retrospect this was just as well. Simply 'helping the gallant Finns' was one thing, but what the consequences of this action might have been was another. Curiously, the politicians do not seem to have made the connection that by helping the Finns they might have had us at war with Russia as well as Germany. But as things were, the politicians had lost face and the defeat of Finland was fatal to the French Prime Minister, Daladier. He was replaced by Reynaud who was keen on the idea of mining Norwegian territorial waters, and so at long last, seven months after he had first proposed it, Churchill was given the go-ahead. As the mining might provoke action by the Germans, the Supreme War Cabinet also agreed to send a British brigade and a French contingent to Narvik to occupy the port, advance to the Swedish border and, if necessary, occupy the Swedish iron ore fields. Other forces would possibly be landed in neutral Norway at Bergen and Trondheim to deny these ports to the Germans.

The 4th Lincolns suddenly received another 'stand-by' order and on Sunday the 7th April 1940, leaving their carriers and transport behind, they left Ripon by train for the Royal Naval Dockyard at Rosyth and boarded a cruiser, HMS *Berwick*. After dinner on board, the Commanding Officer, Lieutenant-Colonel R W Newton, held a meeting of his officers and disclosed that they were bound for Bergen the following day.

Norway

But momentous events were occurring elsewhere. A plane had spotted a German fleet moving across the mouth of the Skaggerak. At about the same time as Colonel Newton was finishing his dinner, the Home Fleet (*Rodney, Repulse, Valiant* with two cruisers and ten destroyers) was leaving Scapa Flow and by 10.00 pm the Second Cruiser Squadron (a further two cruisers and fifteen destroyers) had left Rosyth. The First Cruiser Squadron, also at Rosyth and busy embarking the Lincolns and the other troops, was ordered to put them ashore immediately and join the rest of the Fleet. Meanwhile British destroyers were busy laying mines in Norwegian waters.

The 4th Lincolns hastily disembarked from HMS *Berwick*. They were given an hour to take off the stores and equipment which had taken them eleven hours to load, and despite their frantic efforts some of it was still on board the *Berwick* as she sailed to join the Fleet, the Royal Marines band playing on deck as she left. From the Rosyth quayside the men gave her three cheers and then marched seven miles to a camp near Dunfermline. They were under canvas and it was raining.

The Norwegian government again protested strongly to London, this time about the mine-laying. But to the astonishment of the Admiralty, some of the German warships had now been sighted heading for Narvik. By an amazing coincidence Hitler's occupation of Denmark and Norway was taking place.

The British were very hopeful of success as there were superior naval forces both to the north and the south of the Germans. But four cruisers and seven destroyers were on their way to Bergen when a plane reported that two German cruisers were already there. Destroyers ordered to seize Narvik and prevent a German landing also found German destroyers there already. The Germans—in the face of overwhelming British superiority at sea—had swiftly occupied all the major ports on the Norwegian coast. It was believed that some of their troops must have been hidden in the holds of empty freighters returning for more ore through Norwegian waters, escorted, ironically, by ships of the Norwegian navy. The Germans had also used paratroops. Churchill, bitterly disappointed, said that we had been forestalled, surprised and outwitted.

Churchill still wanted Narvik very much. Roads and railways in northern Norway were few and it was thought that if Narvik could be seized it could be defended and reinforced from the sea. Possibly the King of Norway could even set up a government there.

On Thursday the 11th April the 4th Lincolns left their camp at Dunfermline and went by train to Gourock, where they joined the other two Territorial battalions which made up the 146th Brigade, the 4th King's Own Yorkshire Light Infantry (KOYLI) and the Hallamshire (City of Sheffield) battalion of the York and Lancaster Regiment. The Lincolns boarded a luxury liner, the *Empress of Australia*. This ship, built in Germany during the First War, had originally been called the *Tirpitz* and, brand new, had been seized by the British as war reparations in 1919. She had been given to the P & O line which had then sold her

18

on to the Canadian Pacific line. In May 1939 she had been chosen to take the King and Queen on their visit to Canada. To the delight of the troops they found that this luxury liner still retained its pre-war standard in food and accommodation. They set off the following morning and zig-zagged to Scapa Flow where they joined other liners, including the *Monarch of Bermuda*, the *Rio de Pacifico* and the Polish *Chobry*.

The 'Empress of Australia'.

The convoy, escorted by four cruisers and ten destroyers, sailed confidently into the Atlantic on Friday the 12th April. There was a destroyer either side of the *Empress of Australia* and warships as far as the eye could see. In addition to the numerous boat drills the troops were kept occupied with lectures on health and sanitation under Arctic conditions. One of the Lincolns, a regular, could read Morse Code and he had an attentive audience when he deciphered messages flashed between the ships.

During the voyage each man was issued with two extra kitbags of clothing, including two thick white woollen pullovers, a leather jerkin, snow boots, sun goggles, a fur cap and a sleeping bag—almost enough gear for a polar expedition.

But they were not so well-equipped for fighting. There was no transport (although some did arrive later) and the carrier platoon didn't have any carriers as they had also been left behind. Even some of the rifles which had been taken were 'DP'—for 'Drill Purposes' only, because they didn't have a firing pin. There were only two or three Bren guns for each company. The Lincolns had had heavy Vickers machine guns for many years and in 1937 had actually won the Territorial Army Vickers Cup, firing against 114 other units. But towards the end of 1938 the Vickers guns had to be handed in when battalions were reorganised into four 'rifle' companies which would have 2-inch mortars instead. The problem was that although the Lincolns did possess a few 2-inch mortars they only had smoke bombs and the base-plates for their two 3-inch mortars (which had just been issued a few days earlier) were amongst the equipment which had been left behind

19

on the *Berwick*. Without their base-plates, the mortars couldn't be fired. There were no anti-tank or anti-aircraft guns. Worst of all, there was no air cover.

The convoy crossed the Arctic Circle, sailing north-east for Narvik. Meanwhile, on Saturday the 13th April, the battleship HMS *Warspite,* together with nine destroyers, went into action at Narvik and scored a remarkable victory. Without any losses they sank all eight of the German destroyers which were in the harbour, together with some supply ships. For good measure, the *Warspite's* Walrus aircraft bombed and sank a submarine. Of the German naval forces in Narvik, only a submarine, the U51, survived by escaping to sea. Two days later, on Monday the 15th April, the *Empress of Australia*, the *Chobry* and some of the destroyers left the rest of the convoy and changed course to the south-east. This was partly because of the *Warspite's* victory at Narvik but mainly due to a change of plan in London.

At the same time as the *Warspite's* 15-inch guns were wreaking havoc at Narvik there was a meeting of the War Cabinet and it was decided that Trondheim should also be taken as well as Narvik. This seemed to make sense. Once Trondheim was captured, the excellent harbour there could be used to disembark thousands of troops. Fighter squadrons could be flown in to the nearby airfield to establish air superiority. Allied troops and supplies could be taken to Trondheim by sea far quicker than German reinforcements, who would have to slog and fight their way there overland. The Germans could be delayed—or even prevented—from advancing north towards Narvik. And if enough Allied troops could be landed at Trondheim then—who knows—there was even the possibility that the Germans could be driven out of Norway altogether. The Chiefs of Staff made plans for a full-scale frontal attack on Trondheim, code-named 'Hammer', which would take place on the 22nd April. The Royal Navy, assisted by the Fleet Air Arm and the RAF, would land a regular brigade which would be sent from France together with French troops and a thousand Canadians, and there would be a Territorial Army brigade in reserve. The airfields at Stavanger and Vaernes, now in German hands, would soon be put out of business by RAF bombers and the Fleet Air Arm, assisted by bombardment with high explosive from HMS *Suffolk's* 8-inch guns. Subsidiary landings would also be made in conjunction with the main attack both to the north and the south of Trondheim to secure the area around the port. In fact the navy was already putting seamen and marines on shore at the small port of Namsos, about a hundred miles to the north of Trondheim, to await the arrival of the 8th Sherwood Foresters and the 5th Leicesters, the two battalions of Territorials which comprised Brigadier Morgan's 148th Brigade.

Shortly afterwards this plan was also changed and instead of going to Namsos the 148th Brigade was diverted to another small port, Andalsnes, about a hundred and fifty miles to the south of Trondheim. The 147th Brigade, also Territorials and still in Britain, would join them later.

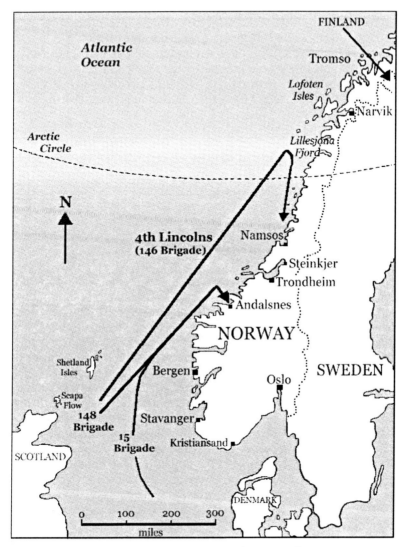

Map 1. The Lincolns were diverted from Narvik to Namsos.

So whilst the rest of the convoy continued to Narvik, the 4th Lincolns—with the other two Territorial regiments of the 146th Brigade—were diverted to Namsos to take the place of the 148th Brigade. The 5th Demi-brigade of Chasseurs Alpins (French) set sail from the Clyde to join them. Under the overall command of Major-General Carton de Wiart VC they were to advance towards Trondheim as

21

quickly as possible. The forthcoming assault on Trondheim would be supported by a pincer movement from the Territorial Army forces at Namsos and Andalsnes, Operations 'Mauriceforce' and 'Sickleforce' respectively.

When the men left their stuffy quarters and went on deck early in the morning of Tuesday the 16th April they were greeted by the shock of a blast of icy air. They found that the *Empress of Australia* had anchored in Lillejonas Fjord, a hundred miles north of Namsos, together with the *Chobry* and some destroyers. Major-General Carton de Wiart had arrived at Namsos in a Sunderland flying boat the previous evening in the middle of a heavy air raid and his Staff Officer had been wounded. In his view it was far too risky for the crowded troopships to go any further because of all the German air activity. It was decided that the troops would have to be transferred to destroyers. The Hallamshires transferred from the *Chobry* to destroyers and the Lincolns started to board HMS *Afridi* and HMS *Sikh* which were to put them ashore at Namsos. Except for a plane which droned backwards and forwards very high overhead, everything was peaceful—the fjord, beautiful snow-covered mountains on either side and neat houses scattered here and there. Suddenly the tranquil scene was shattered when German planes came screaming in from nowhere.

This was the men's very first introduction to the harsh reality of war, and it came as a sudden and very nasty shock. Anti-aircraft guns and pom-poms blasted away at the German planes, whose bombs were falling much too close for comfort to the ships. Most of the men had never heard big guns firing before and the terrific din was frightening in itself. Although only half of the Lincolns had so far boarded, the destroyers didn't wait for the other half but set off at full speed for Namsos to avoid the German bombs. They were dive-bombed incessantly on the way there. Troops down in the hold of the *Afridi* were very scared when there was an extremely loud bang and all the lights went out—one of several near misses. Nevertheless, they survived and the destroyers managed to disembark all the troops safely.

Namsos was only a small port with a stone quay and two wooden wharves. Most of the buildings in the town were made of timber and the population of around four thousand was employed mainly in the timber trade. The troops arrived there at about 9.00 pm and by midnight they were on a special train which took them to Grong, a town about twenty-five miles away and on the main railway line to Trondheim. In the moonlight they could make out the snow-covered mountains and the countryside seemed wild and rugged. The troops, very tired, were billeted in the local school.

Fortunately, none of the ships still in Lillejonas Fjord had been seriously damaged during the attack by the German bombers. But because the destroyers had come under heavy air attack on the way to Namsos the admiral was worried about losing them. He reversed the decision of the previous day. The rest of the troops still on board the *Empress of Australia* in Lillejonas fjord would have to be transferred to the Polish liner *Chobry* which would go to Namsos and disembark them as quickly as possible.

This was in fact achieved without much difficulty, but the result of the transfer of the troops from ship to ship over both days was that much of their equipment was left behind.

Namsos.

For some reason or other Brigadier Phillips, the officer commanding the 146th Brigade, was still on board a ship heading for Narvik. In his absence, Lieutenant-Colonel Newton of the 4th Lincolns was put in temporary charge of the brigade.

The remainder of the Lincolns, who had now arrived at Namsos on the *Chobry*, joined the rest of the battalion at Grong on Thursday the 18th April. The snow was four feet deep in places and it was only possible to get anywhere by walking along the slushy and icy roads. The landscape looked cold, bleak, desolate and cheerless.

Meanwhile, HMS *Suffolk* had bombarded Stavanger airfield with her 8-inch guns as planned, but had come off the worst. She had caused some damage but evidently not nearly enough, for she was bombed continuously for seven hours. Some of the bombs found their target and the *Suffolk* had to limp back to Scapa Flow with her quarterdeck awash.

Possibly this had some influence upon the Chiefs of Staff in Whitehall for on the following day, the 18th April, they changed their minds. They'd gone off the idea of a frontal assault on Trondheim. It was too risky. The War Office was worried that even if the Royal Navy managed to disembark the army successfully, the troops would be under constant air attack until the airfield at Stavanger could be seized for the RAF fighters. Furthermore, as a result of speculation in the press, everyone—including the Germans—now expected that the British would be landing at Trondheim. The Admiralty, pointing out that almost the whole Home Fleet would have to be used to support the direct attack on Trondheim, was also worried about the Luftwaffe and didn't want to run the risk of heavy air attacks.

This was indeed a very significant development. Before the war the Admiralty had dismissed the danger of air attack on warships. It was nothing to worry about. But the menace from the air had quickly become apparent, and it was formidable. For the first time in history, the sea-power of the mighty British Navy had been curbed, its strength challenged and threatened from the air. Things would never be the same again. It was a bitter pill for the Royal Navy and there were some who found it difficult to swallow.

So, much to the disappointment of the politicians, the Chiefs of Staff called off the proposed frontal attack on Trondheim. Mind you, they were still in favour of taking Trondheim, but by other means. Rather than running the risk of a direct, opposed, landing a pincers movement could be developed by heavily reinforcing the troops which had already landed at Namsos and Andalsnes. Trondheim could be blockaded from the sea, so it could still be taken (they argued) with much less risk than by a direct assault on the port. On paper this seemed to be the best option.

Incredibly, no-one thought of notifying Major-General Carton de Wiart, commanding the Allied forces at Namsos, that the plan to make a direct assault on Trondheim was off and that the main effort was now to be made from Namsos and Andalsnes. He still believed that his small, ill-equipped, half-trained force was a diversion, to be synchronised with the main attack on Trondheim, due on the 22nd April, and that he had to press on with all speed. Neither had anyone yet given much thought to the likelihood that the force at Andalsnes, rather than attacking Trondheim to the north, might first have to defend itself from the Germans advancing from the south. Furthermore, Namsos and Andalsnes were only minor ports. Would they be able to handle the large number of men and the amount of military stores necessary in the build-up for a major operation? And until the airfields had been taken the Allied troops—and shipping—would be subject to heavy air attack. RAF bombers could reach Norway from Britain but what was needed were long-range fighters. There weren't any. So we could only counter the threat from the air if we ourselves had bases in Norway for fighter planes, but we couldn't establish any because the Germans had air superiority. It was a vicious circle. It was beginning to dawn on Whitehall what they had let themselves in for. Still, something—anything—had to be done to help the Norwegians, although Churchill had begun to realise glumly that we had 'only a choice of unpleasant courses before us'.

Early on Friday the 19th April, the day after the Lincolns had got themselves together at Grong, they moved by rail to Steinkjer—immediately called 'Stinker' by the troops— a small town built of timber at the end of Trondheim Fjord. It was bitterly cold, particularly at night. Steinkjer was an important position, for it was on an isthmus between the fjord and Lake Snaasa and covered the approach to Namsos. But until the Royal Navy controlled the fjord there was not only the danger that German troops from Trondheim would be able to reach Steinkjer by sea, but the right flank of any Allied troops advancing beyond Steinkjer would be extremely vulnerable. Because of the deep snow they could only travel along the road and this ran very close to the fjord. Consequently, they could come under fire at close quarters from the sea. However, this didn't seem a great danger for the moment because the fjord was still frozen.

The Hallamshires moved into positions to the north, between Steinkjer and Namsos. Whilst the KOYLI moved forward by train to positions between Steinkjer and the bridge at Verdal, twenty miles to the south, the Lincolns took up positions in and around Steinkjer. 'B', 'C' and 'HQ' companies remained in the town, billeted at the school, whilst 'A' company under Captain Gregory went three or four miles north to Egge and 'D' company under Captain Staniland travelled about five miles to the south-west to Vist to prevent the Germans from landing in the bays. German reconnaissance planes, flying low, went about their work unhampered. The troops had landed at Namsos in the dark and all their stores had been swiftly removed from the quay before it was light, so the Germans were still unsure about the strength of the British force. Camouflage in the snow was impossible and so everyone was ordered to keep under cover during the day and not to fire at the German planes as it would disclose their positions. Nevertheless, they all realised that their tracks in the snow would be plainly visible to the German aircraft. It was impossible to dig-in because the ground was frozen. Hardly any adequate maps had been issued. One enterprising officer found a map of Norway on a poster advertising holidays, at a railway station, and Captain Dick Giles took one which showed all the towns and villages in central Norway off a classroom wall. (He returned it to the school whilst on holiday thirty-two years later.) No-one was clear about where they were or what they were supposed to do next.

Meanwhile, three battalions of the French mountain troops, the Chasseurs Alpins, had landed at Namsos. Shortly after they arrived it was found that their skis had been left behind in Scotland. When the first German reconnaissance plane arrived at dawn it spotted the French stores and equipment which were still scattered on the quay. Now that they were sure that more Allied forces were arriving at Namsos, German planes, in waves of fifteen, started to bomb the port and by nightfall on Saturday the 20th April the railway station and the tracks were in ruins, and the school and the hospital had been destroyed. Captain Giles was ordered to take a crew from Movietone News to film the German planes bombing a road bridge. Although the quay was still intact it had now become very clear that there could be no further substantial build-up of forces or their supplies through the port of Namsos.

Early on Sunday morning the 21st April, Corporal Sid Hall, on look-out at Steinkjer school, was amazed to see a German warship some distance away in the supposedly frozen fjord and there were reports shortly afterwards that enemy soldiers had landed.

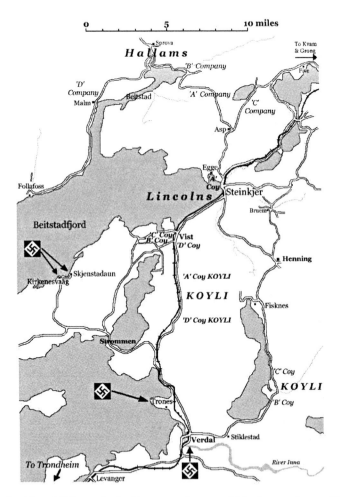

Map 2. *Brigadier Phillips, who had managed to get off the boat going to Narvik and had arrived at Steinkjer, saw immediately that now the fjord had started to thaw the whole right flank of his brigade was very vulnerable.*

In any previous campaign, the Royal Navy would have made short work of any enemy shipping in the fjord, but the sad lesson had been learned that it was the aeroplane which now ruled the waves and the Germans seemed to have plenty of them. It was too risky for the navy to go into the fjord and there was nothing they could do to help. So Brigadier Phillips withdrew the KOYLIs who had reached the bridge at Verdal and when he did so any hope of a further advance towards Trondheim vanished.

All the same, the situation was not quite as bad as it might have been. The Germans could have made their landing at Steinkjer. As it was they had landed troops at Skjenstadum (who were now heading for Vist) and more troops at Kirkenesvaag who were travelling south-east towards Strommen. Troops which had been landed at Trones were heading for Verdal to meet yet more Germans who were advancing northwards along the road from Trondheim. It was only necessary for the British to hold the causeway at Strommen and the narrow isthmus at Vist. A company of the KOYLI was sent to Strommen.

Nevertheless, the British troops were at a disadvantage. Whereas they were confined to the roads, the enemy soldiers, Austrian mountain troops complete with skis and snowshoes, could infiltrate our positions simply by travelling across open country. The British had no snowshoes and even if they had had them no-one would have known how to use them. The enemy had heavy mortars, light field guns and machine guns mounted on sleds, the British had neither mortars nor artillery. Moreover, the Germans not only had complete air superiority but were bombarding the roads and the British positions from the sea.

Back at Steinkjer, there was pandemonium. Orders were shouted, then countermanded and then changed again. Although everyone had heard the rumour that a German warship had been seen coming up the fjord no-one seemed to know much more. The troops were standing to in 'fighting order' and were all keyed up with waiting, wondering what was happening. In the end eight Bren guns from the carrier platoon were sent by lorry to reinforce 'A' Company at Egge, whilst 'B' company from Horncastle, under Captain Tweed, was hurriedly transported from Steinkjer in civilian lorries and buses to support 'D' company at Vist. Major Black, the second-in-command, travelled with them to take charge of both companies.

'B' company joined 'D' company at Vist at 9.00 am. It was snowing heavily. Lieutenant-Colonel Newton had intended 'B' company to take up a position to the left of 'D' company, but for some reason—perhaps because of the inadequate maps—they were sent by Major Black down a narrow road, little more than a track, which ran through a forest to the west and to the right of 'D' Company. The snow was five feet deep on either side of the track. It was thought that the enemy were at least six miles away so it came as a shock when shots rang out from some high ground after the 'B' Company had gone only about two miles. The two men in the lead dropped, bleeding, in the snow. Shortly afterwards mortar bombs exploded with a terrific crash only yards away. More pandemonium. An officer yelled: 'Take cover!'—an order which was quite unnecessary as all the men had already dived into the deep snow at the side of the road. The best they could now do was to crawl or roll in the snow. Another officer shouted: 'Fix bayonets!' Bloody hell, thought some of the men, first time in action and within seconds its 'fix bayonets' already. A German reconnaissance plane flew back and forth overhead.

Captain Reggie Tweed, a Horncastle solicitor, led the men towards a nearby clearing in the forest where there was a farmhouse and some wooden outbuildings on the right hand side of the track and some other buildings on the left. Once inside these shelters the Lincolns came under machine gun, small arms and mortar fire from the Austrians concealed amongst the pine trees less than a hundred yards away. Amidst the din and the sound of falling tiles and breaking glass the men could hear the Austrian officers shouting orders. To some, the proximity of the enemy was perhaps more frightening than anything else. Meanwhile, Major Black had returned to Vist to send up a section of 'D' Company under Second Lieutenant Flint to keep in touch with 'B' Company.

Bullets ripped through the buildings, but somehow no-one was hit. Captain Tweed, under fire the whole time, calmly visited the men who were in the farmhouse. Bullets smacked into the doorway all around him but failed to hit him. Shortly afterwards he came out again, and this time the Austrians didn't even bother to open fire.

A few of the men found a loft in one of the buildings which gave a good field of fire. They knocked through the wooden wall and returned fire with a Bren gun but they were soon spotted and a line of bullets holes suddenly appeared in the wall about six inches above their heads. Lance-Corporal Jacklin got a piece of shrapnel in his eye and another man yelled for his mother when he was wounded in the leg by a tracer bullet. At about 6.00 pm tracer bullets set a pile of hay alight and within moments the loft was ablaze. With tears in their eyes from the smoke the men scrambled frantically one at a time through the only exit, a trap door, taking the wounded with them.

Before long all the wooden buildings were ablaze and the order was given to withdraw to some woods about half a mile to the west of Vist station. Two small sections—about twenty-five men altogether—didn't receive the order to retire and continued firing at the enemy until they ran out of ammunition, using the snow to keep their Bren guns cool. Eventually they were cut off and were all taken prisoner, as were three others who were looking after the wounded men who had been taken from the blazing barn. The Austrians couldn't believe that there wasn't an officer in charge and kept asking Lance-Corporal Jack Wynn, a bank clerk from Horncastle, where he was. The men were treated well by the Austrians, but sadly three of them were to die during the long forced marches in the winter of 1944/5, when the Germans moved the prison camps in Poland because of the advancing Russians.

With the smoke from the burning buildings acting as a very effective screen, the rest of 'B' company floundered through the thick snow, covered by fire from Lieutenant Pattin's platoon who were in some houses to the rear. When they arrived at their new position in the early evening one or two fell asleep, exhausted, in snowdrifts, oblivious to the spasmodic fire from both sides which was still going on. When night fell they withdrew to a farmhouse. Although very tired, no-one could sleep because by this time it was so bitterly cold. At around midnight there was a scare as it was thought that the house had been surrounded by an Austrian patrol. Outside, the men could just make out some dark blobs in the snow about fifty yards away and riddled them with bullets. They were bushes. Corporal Sid Hall heard someone about thirty yards away behind some trees, took aim with his Bren gun and squeezed the trigger. Nothing happened. Perhaps the gun had frozen—which was very fortunate for Second Lieutenant Alex Greenwood who emerged, white-faced, from the trees.

The Territorial Army men from Horncastle in 'B' company had been the very first unit of any battalion of the Lincolnshire Regiment—perhaps of any regiment—to come into close action against the enemy in the Second World War. It had not been without cost. Privates Prike and Smith had been killed and Privates Humphrey and Roe, who had been wounded and taken prisoner, died later. In fact, Private Roe died that evening and the Austrians allowed one of his comrades to say a few words at the funeral before they buried him by the side of their own dead and fired three volleys over the graves.

Meanwhile, at Steinkjer, the Germans had dropped leaflets advising the civilian population to evacuate the town. Lieutenant-Colonel Newton, puzzled and concerned when he heard where 'B' Company was, sent Major Stokes and the reserve of 'HQ' Company to Vist to join 'D' company and to take up the position which he'd originally intended 'B' company to take. 'C' company, under Captain Cragg, was also sent to a position just north of 'HQ' Company at Vist. They arrived at about 8.00 pm but were unable to contact the men of 'B' Company, who by now had withdrawn to their new position.

The Austrians, who had been advancing towards Strommen, had seen that the KOYLI were already there so they were directed northwards to join their other troops at Vist, which had now become a vital position. If the enemy captured Vist the KOYLI further south would be cut off.

'HQ' and 'C' companies of the Lincolns left just before Steinkjer was heavily bombed with high explosives and incendiaries. Soon every building was on fire. A second raid destroyed the brigade's supplies, including the Lincolns' stores and spare clothing. Battalion headquarters had to move several times, and with the destruction of the town's telephone system it was no longer possible to communicate with Brigade HQ—although 2nd Lieutenant Newsum managed to get through twice on a motor bike.

Brigadier Phillips decided to withdraw the KOYLI and as there was no transport he had to depend upon a few requisitioned lorries to move them. The Lincolns would have to bear the brunt of the fighting and hold Vist until the KOYLI had been withdrawn.

At the end of a very confusing and anxious day, 'A' Company plus eight Bren guns were just south of Egge, 'D' Company (less one platoon) were in the area of Vist station, 'B' Company were 700 yards west of Vist station, 'HQ' Company (plus one platoon of 'D' Company) were astride a crossroads outside Vist and had 'C' Company just to the north of them. Battalion HQ was in a house in some woods 200 yards north of the school at Steinkjer.

The following morning (Monday the 22nd April) most of the men had managed to get a cup of tea and some breakfast before the expected enemy attack. At about 10 o'clock, 'D' Company and number 10 platoon of 'B' Company came under fire from machine guns, mortars and light artillery and were shelled by the warship from the sea and machine-gunned from the air. Little response could be made as there was no artillery or mortars. An Austrian patrol appeared and was dispersed by Bren gun fire, but bullets from a sniper hidden in the woods cracked into the walls, much too close for comfort. From about a thousand yards away the Lincolns watched helplessly as the Austrians captured two platoons of the KOYLIs, whose transport had got stuck in the snow. They were marched over the top of a hill with their hands up. The Lincolns thought that the KOYLIs had been on their way to reinforce them, but they were actually withdrawing from their positions further south and were on their way to Steinkjer.

Major Black had been instructed by Lieutenant-Colonel Newton to hold on until it was dark but in the early afternoon he ordered 'B' and 'D' companies to withdraw to Steinkjer, covered by a Bren gun post under Lieutenant Alway. German reconnaissance planes overhead watched the progress of the Lincolns all the time, and soon they were joined by bombers. Their main target was Steinkjer, already in ruins, and the men could hear the explosions and crashes ahead of them. Every few minutes they had to take cover in the deep wet snow when a bomber flew over very low. It was a nightmare.

Steinkjer, a health resort, was now certainly an unhealthy place to be. Bombed and machine-gunned, the men trudged through the blazing ruins of the town. It had been obliterated. All the wooden buildings had been set alight and there were bomb craters everywhere. Although the road bridge over the river had been destroyed, they were able to cross by the railway bridge which was still more or less intact. Then a Stuka blew it up and the last few men had to swim for it in the freezing river. A few Norwegian troops helped to pull them out when they reached the other side. After what seemed to be an eternity, the men were able to have a short rest at a village called Asp, about three miles to the north of Steinkjer. Meanwhile 'A' company, which had been at Egge and out of the action, joined 'B' and 'D' companies at Asp. From some high ground overlooking Steinkjer they had seen the Austrians advancing into the town with their guns and mortars on sledges.

Lorries were hired at Asp to take the troops to the village of Elden, fourteen miles away, where they arrived at four o'clock on the morning of Tuesday the 23rd April, utterly exhausted, hungry and freezing. It had been a very eventful twenty-four hours. They were found barns to sleep in and they stayed there, under cover, throughout the day. At nightfall the troops moved ten miles north to the village of Rodhammer.

Most of the men had moved through Steinkjer by 6.30 pm but the Commanding Officer had stayed with his batman and the Regimental Sergeant Major until almost nine o'clock, waiting in vain for 'C' and 'HQ' Companies to arrive. Lieutenant-Colonel Newton picked up a few stragglers as he dejectedly made his way through the night, eventually arriving at Folling, where he found the KOYLI. Captain Dick Giles of 'C' Company had been sent to Steinkjer by Major Black to make contact with battalion headquarters but when he couldn't find the HQ he commandeered a bus and filled it with stragglers on their way out of Steinkjer. They hadn't gone far when they came under fire from some Norwegian troops and the man sitting in front of Captain Giles got a bullet in his arm. The bus skidded into a snowdrift and was damaged, so the men had to get out and walk the rest of the way. A Norwegian officer explained that he had thought that they were Germans.

Meanwhile, Major Black had sent a message at 11.30 on the Monday morning to 'C' and 'HQ' Companies at Vist saying that the KOYLI were withdrawing and that they should follow them to Steinkjer. This order to withdraw wasn't received until the late afternoon of Monday because the company runner, Private Ronnie Roach, had become mixed-up in the action when the KOYLIs had been captured. Somehow he had managed to get away, under fire all the time, by crawling through the deep snow. By the time he arrived the Austrians were firing from the left and the left rear. The German planes were still droning back and forth overhead, directing the fire from the warship in the fjord. Major Stokes and Captain Cragg did not have much difficulty in deciding that the sooner everyone left the better. The problem was that it was still daylight. Nevertheless, Major Stokes decided to withdraw quietly at once into some woods on the right, where he hoped to find 'B' Company. He ordered his men not to fire unless they were attacked. It was decided to leave heavy equipment and twenty boxes of ammunition as they would be too heavy to carry through the deep snow.

The men (there were almost two hundred of them) trickled into the wood, just before a farm building which some of them had been occupying was blown up. Some Norwegian civilians told them that Steinkjer was now in German hands. There was a brief conference between the officers and the senior NCOs. Captain Cragg, a regular army officer, thought that the men should separate and try to reach Sweden, every man for himself. But Major Donald Stokes decided that rather than the men making their own way separately it would be better for everyone to stay together. He waited until it was dark and then ordered the men to link hands and set off in single file. Led by Sergeant-Major Cannon and Sergeant Isaac with fixed bayonets and followed by Major Stokes and Captain Cragg with revolvers and knives, the men moved quietly in the darkness through the waist-deep snow, treading in the footsteps of the man in front, perhaps to save energy or perhaps just to leave a single track to confuse the reconnaissance planes the following day. Lieutenant Tunnard was at the rear to keep the men moving. The men crossed an open valley near Vist station and after a time they came across a farm where there appeared to be some Germans. They moved silently along the side of a hedge, the farm to their left, but just then a vehicle started up, its big headlights lighting up everything in front of it. It was moving along the track leading from the farm to the main road. If it turned left when it reached the road all would be well, but if it turned right everyone would be illuminated as if caught in a spotlight. Everyone watched the vehicle as it slowly made its way to the road, scarcely daring to breathe. It turned left.

After they had crossed the valley the men had to stagger and crawl up the side of a mountain in three or four feet of snow. Throughout the night they could see a glow in the sky—Steinkjer burning. Eventually they found a barn where they were able to snatch a little sleep. By this time it was three o'clock in the morning and so far they had only covered a mile and a half. They were still in danger.

Fortunately the resourceful Private Roach (he was later commissioned) had managed to find both a compass and a map the previous day. The men set off again at 7.00 am heading east in the hope of finding the KOYLI at a village called Henning. It was snowing heavily, but this was a blessing in disguise as the German reconnaissance planes were grounded. To lighten the load of the exhausted men, respirators were now discarded. Steel helmets had already been left behind the previous day (they made too much noise when the men brushed against the branches of the trees) and some of the men had also ditched their haversacks. When they arrived at Henning at around noon it was found that the KOYLI had left during the night.

After a quick meal (they found some food which the KOYLIs had abandoned in a barn) they headed towards Grong as it was thought that the rest of the battalion might have gone there. Moving mostly through forests in two feet of snow, and keeping well clear of Steinkjer where the Germans had now landed troops, they moved safely through the isthmus until they eventually arrived at a small village called Sunnan. By this time it was 7.30 pm and the men, almost out on their feet, were looking forward to resting in the village. It was not to be. There were some Norwegian soldiers there who told them that the Lincolns were not at Grong, but had taken the westerly road in the direction of Namsos. The Norwegians also said that they were on the point of blowing the bridge up as the Austrians were close behind, approaching the village along the railway line. Major Stokes' party had arrived in the nick of time and everyone had to dash across the bridge just before the Norwegians blew it up. They trudged wearily through the darkness until one o'clock in the morning when they found a large barn at a village called Five. They snatched a few hours sleep before starting off again at eight o'clock in the morning. It was now Wednesday the 24th April.

Everyone was dead beat and morale was low. Lance-Corporal Arthur Turner of the mortar platoon overheard Major Stokes and Captain Blackstone discussing the low spirits of the men. Captain Blackstone remarked: 'If only we had some cigarettes—that might help.'

'I've got some cigarettes, sir,' Lance-Corporal Turner offered.

'That's good of you, Corporal,' Captain Blackstone said, 'but a few cigarettes amongst all these men wouldn't be much help.'

'But I've got three hundred and fifty,' Lance-Corporal Turner said, 'and I don't want anything for them—I'll give them to you.' Although he didn't smoke he'd bought them, unbelievably cheaply, on the *Empress of Australia* and still had them in his haversack.

'But we must give you something for them,' Major Stokes insisted. Both officers searched their pockets and Captain Blackstone finally found two pieces of Wrigley's chewing gum which he handed to Lance-Corporal Turner.

The men set off again. The going was tougher—more hilly and thicker snow. Luckily they came across a Norwegian missionary who spoke perfect English and he guided them to a village where they arrived at 4.00 pm. The missionary found a horse and dray and a driver here for Captain Cragg, who set off to try and find the battalion. After some miles he came across the Hallamshires and he continued his journey by bike and then by car until he reached the headquarters of the KOYLI.

The men arrived at the village where the Hallams were posted and slept in a barn. They were dead beat, for they had been on the move for 47 hours with only a total of 12 hours rest. The following morning they were given a little stew, the first hot food they'd eaten since Monday morning. Later that day, Thursday the 25th April, lorries were sent to fetch Major Stokes and the two hundred men he had led in the freezing temperature and they were reunited with the rest of the regiment at Rodhammer. It was estimated afterwards that they must have trekked through the deep snow for about forty-five miles. The men had been wearing wet boots and socks for days and the feet of most of them were in a terrible state. Their kitbags of Arctic clothing had been destroyed at Steinkjer so they had no dry clothes to change into. Major Stokes was still wearing his pyjamas under his battledress, for he hadn't had time to dress properly when the enemy had first been sighted on the Sunday morning. His men were full of praise about his leadership and the way he had calmly guided and encouraged them through all the difficulties. Although they had been given up for lost Major Stokes' party arrived without having lost a man or even a rifle.

Major Don Stokes and Captain Jack Cragg.

Capt Cragg and some of the men from 'C' Company have a breather after their long trek.

Meanwhile, the Commanding Officer and his small party of 22 stragglers had also moved with the KOYLI until they had come across the HQ of the Hallams. A lorry had taken them to join the rest of the battalion at Rodhammer.

Nevertheless, the battalion was not quite complete for some of 'B' company had become separated during the withdrawal through Steinkjer. Private Tony Bell, who had been one of the section which had stayed behind covering the withdrawal of the company, found himself alone and carrying two Bren guns. He managed to get through Steinkjer but just outside the town there was a shot and a bullet whizzed past his head. A Norwegian officer holding a smoking revolver appeared and apologised for mistaking him for a German. Tony Bell gave him one of the Bren guns and climbed into a passing lorry where he found a sergeant from the Lincolns. The truck took them to a farmhouse where they had a drink and something to eat and they dried their wet socks and boots by the fire. Soon they were off again, this time on foot, and eventually they came across a Norwegian outpost at about 2.00 am. They managed to get a couple of hours sleep here before setting off again. After a few miles they met up with a section of the KOYLI who were also in retreat, and were joined later that day by Lieutenant Alway, Corporal Waddingham and Private Turner. They had all got wet through when swimming the river at Steinkjer and had replaced their battledresses with anything dry which they could get hold of. Private Turner was wearing a dinner jacket and a skiing cap.

The party decided to make for Grong. It had started to thaw and they trudged along the tracks, through the mud and slush, past frozen lakes, snow-covered mountains and unending pine forests. Here and there they came across kindly Norwegian people who gave them food and shelter so that they could snatch a few hours sleep. After two days and nights they arrived in Grong and found that it was a mass of smouldering ruins. The population was living in a railway tunnel for safety but they gave the soldiers something to eat and a lorry to take them to Namsos. When they arrived at Namsos, Lieutenant Alway found that some of the battalion's transport had landed from England. A truck took him to the battalion which by this time had moved a few miles north to the village of Ranem. The rest of the party were given the job of working at the brigade ration dump. They were not short of food or cigarettes. This didn't last long however for after a day or two a German plane bombed both the ration dump and the ammunition dump. Travelling after dark, for German bombers were constantly in the air throughout the day, this small party from the Lincolns rejoined the rest of the battalion on the 28th April.

Corporal Sid Hall and two other men from 'B' company had gone into the hills near Vist and had come across a farmhouse. The farmer put them into a loft which was lined with sheep skins and said he would let them know if he heard any Germans coming. Eventually some enemy troops arrived but they didn't find the British soldiers as they were in a small room which they had found at one end of the loft. The door to this room was hidden by the sheep skins. After the Austrians had gone, the farmer told Corporal Hall and the others that they would have to leave. After several hours the soldiers met two British officers and stayed with them until they eventually found the rest of the battalion.

By this time, the 4th Lincolns were living a thoroughly miserable existence. Everyone had to stay in hay lofts throughout the day as enemy bombers were still very active overhead. Transport to and from the dock at Namsos was being constantly bombed and machine gunned. The nights were extremely cold. Only a few men had greatcoats and all the blankets had been destroyed when the battalion's stores had been bombed at Steinkjer. Everyone was fed up.

In Boston, nineteen-year old Sylvia Graveling, the wife of Private Sid 'Chuck' Graveling, became very worried when her mother-in-law ran into the house shouting: 'The Germans have got all of the Lincolns—all of them! Lord Haw Haw's just announced it on German radio!'

On Sunday the 28th April, just one week after the enemy had been first sighted, the Lincolns received orders to move to Namsos. They reached a village called Skage where they relieved some French Chasseurs Alpins troops and stayed for four days. On Thursday the 2nd May they moved to Namsos, passing through road-blocks manned by Norwegians and arrived just before midnight. All of the town's wooden houses had been burnt to the ground; only the brick-built chimney stacks remained. Although the

Cpl Sid Hall (left) and Private Tony Bell.

36

quay had been very badly damaged and was in flames, HMS *Afridi* had somehow managed to come alongside. The Lincolns hurriedly went straight on board and shortly afterwards set sail. As they left Namsos, the *Afridi* shelled the line of parked transport which the British had to leave behind.

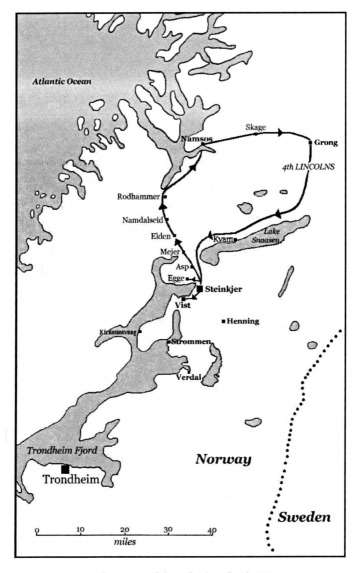

Map 3. The route of the 4th Lincolns in Norway.

No-one knew where they were going to but most of the men thought that they were bound for Narvik. Someone said it was England and everyone laughed, but he turned out to be right.

It had been decided in Whitehall to evacuate central Norway. In the half-light before dawn (it didn't get fully dark at this time of year in Norway) the men were transferred from HMS *Afridi* to a French armed merchant cruiser, the *El Kantara* (26,000 tons), which was waiting a little way up the fjord, and they learned that they were bound for Scapa Flow and home. Brigade HQ and about 700 Chasseurs Alpins were also on board the ship. A few men from the battalion were on other ships.

The convoy—two transport ships, two cruisers and four destroyers—put to sea at dawn and were immediately spotted by a German reconnaissance plane. Shortly afterwards about fifty Stukas arrived. Altogether the Stukas made four separate attacks on the convoy between 8.00 am and 3.00 pm and despite very heavy ack-ack fire they scored a direct hit on the French destroyer, the *Bison*, which blew up and sank almost immediately. HMS *Afridi* went alongside and picked up survivors but an hour later she herself was hit. Her steering gear was put out of action and, ablaze, she raced round in circles until she was stopped. Another destroyer, HMS *Griffin*, pulled alongside and amid screeching sirens and the screams of the wounded, the men jumped from the *Afridi* onto her decks. Private Simpson, who was on board the destroyer, was killed, but John Melbourne from Napier Street, Lincoln—a seaman on the *Afridi*—survived. The burning *Afridi*, still afloat, was finally torpedoed and sunk by one of the British cruisers. It was exactly two years—to the day—since she had been commissioned.

A big cheer went up from the *El Kantara* when British fighter planes flew very low over the convoy the following day. The rest of the journey was uneventful and the convoy arrived at Scapa Flow just as the sun was rising over the mountains on Sunday the 5th May. The Lincolns disembarked from the *El Kantara* that afternoon, and with Brigade HQ and the KOYLI they boarded the SS *Reina del Pacifico*, a luxury liner of 15,000 tons and were soon speeding at 20 knots down the west coast of Scotland. Everyone was pleased to have left the *El Kantara* as there was a worrying shortage of lifebelts on board and no proper sleeping accommodation. The only drink had been *vin ordinaire* and the food had been French army biscuits, spaghetti and tinned meat (alleged to have been monkey). Nevertheless, everyone had nothing but praise for the French seamen and the ack-ack gunners for the way they had defended the ship.

Escorted by a cruiser and six destroyers and with the *Duchess of Atholl* carrying the Hallamshires, the *Reina del Pacifico* took the Lincolns and the KOYLI from Scapa to Glasgow where, on Wednesday the 8th May, they received new uniforms and kit in exchange for what was left of their Arctic gear. They were cynically amused when comparing the press accounts of their exploits in Norway with what had actually happened, were surprised by the warmth of the welcome which they received and astonished when the Chief of the Imperial General Staff, General Sir Edmund Ironside, came personally to inspect the whole Brigade in a transit shed. He told them that man for man, under proper conditions, they were a match for the Germans and that they had come back with their tails up. He regretted that it had not been possible to send them the guns and air support they needed. A telegram was also received from the Secretary of State for War expressing his appreciation of the splendid efforts which had been made in face of great difficulties. He said that the success of the withdrawal in particular reflected great credit on all concerned.

So at least the withdrawal had been a success. But successful withdrawals don't win wars. The Norwegian campaign was a fiasco, a disaster from start to finish. The Germans had acted boldly and swiftly, occupying all the major ports in Norway in the face of the overwhelming superiority of the Royal Navy. The reaction of the Chiefs of Staff to this first campaign of the war had been muddled. Insufficient thought and preparation had been devoted in peace-time to the threat to conventional forces which was now coming from the air, and both the navy and the army had found themselves unable to move in the face of German air superiority. In fact the aeroplane had altered the whole aspect of conventional warfare. For instance, it had been assumed (and it had certainly once been true) that Allied troops could have been moved to Trondheim by sea quicker than the Germans could have reached there by land—but the Chiefs of Staff had completely overlooked the possibility that German troops could be transported there by air. In fact, the Germans increased the number of troops garrisoned at Trondheim from 1,800 to 5,000 in just four days. The Allies were also baffled by the speed of the well-trained German forces. It was to take the British some years to realise that the Germans had ripped up the book about conventional warfare and had written a new one.

Half-trained young Territorials with inadequate and insufficient weapons—little more than regiments on paper—had been sent to Norway. This might have been understandable had they been part of a hastily-improvised force hurriedly put together as an urgent response to the German invasion, but this was not the case, for the original intention had been for these soldiers to seize important ports in Norway, by force against the Norwegians if necessary. And even before that they had been earmarked to fight the Russians in Finland.

Afterwards it seemed to some of the soldiers who had taken part that the Allied expedition to Norway had been merely a half-hearted gesture—a sideshow, not taken seriously by military minds fixed upon the Maginot line and the Belgian frontier. But both Churchill and Hitler had appreciated the importance of Norway from the very beginning and subsequent events showed how right they were. German occupation of Norway brought them uninterrupted supplies of iron ore from Sweden, bases for their submarines and control of the north-east Atlantic—particularly important later on in the war when convoys attempted to reach Russia.

Success in Norway would also have been important both politically and psychologically for the Allies, for it would have been the first set-back for the Nazis. As things turned out, Steinkjer, Namsos, Grong and Vist had been totally destroyed and thousands of people had been made homeless. The British had not only lost lives and equipment but prestige in the eyes of other nations—particularly the neutral nations we were trying to persuade to enter the war on our side. Certainly, the Norwegians had been dismayed when the Allies had left.

Whilst most of the men got away from Namsos it was a different story at Andalsnes. Brigadier Morgan's 148th brigade got as far as Lillehammer where they joined exhausted Norwegians. On the 24th April General Paget's 15th brigade arrived from France to join them. The British soldiers with their rifles and Bren guns were up against three German divisions, equipped with 5.9-inch howitzers, mortars and tanks. Seven hundred of the young Territorials in Morgan's brigade were lost, but General Paget skilfully managed to get his own troops back to Andalsnes and together with some Norwegians and the remnants of the 148th brigade they embarked on cruisers and destroyers for an uneventful journey home. The 148th brigade never saw active service again.

At Narvik, things had been held up for weeks, for although General Mackesy had been told by General Ironside that 'boldness is required', he refused to move until the snow had melted. No-one, including Winston Churchill, could get him to budge. In the meantime the Germans had managed to reinforce their small garrison there—1100 miles from Germany—and for weeks their force, six thousand strong, held at bay a static Allied force of twenty thousand troops. General Auchinleck had to be sent to take charge. In the end Narvik was taken with very few casualties within a day by a Norwegian battalion and two battalions of the French Foreign Legion. A shore-based squadron of Hurricanes gave protection from the air.

But Narvik wasn't taken until the 28th May, by which time the British Expeditionary Force in France was on the beaches of Dunkirk. The Navy was needed elsewhere. No sooner had Narvik been taken at last than the Allied forces had to be withdrawn, leaving on shore a few thousand scattered and disorganised—but victorious—Germans. The Gladiators of 263 Squadron and the Hurricanes of 46 Squadron, which had been landed on airstrips from carriers, were successfully flown onto the deck of the carrier HMS *Glorious*—the first time that this had ever been attempted by the RAF. But this daring achievement was in vain. For some inexplicable reason the *Glorious* didn't remain under the protection of the main convoy but steamed ahead. Unfortunately she met the German battle-cruisers *Scharnhorst* and *Gneisenau* and within two hours she was sunk, together with both of her escorting destroyers, with the loss of 1,474 men of the Royal Navy and forty-one of the RAF. Only forty-five men survived. The Norwegian campaign had been a dreadful fiasco to the very end.

Iceland

The failures in Norway led to a rumpus about the way the war was being run and on the day the 4th Lincolns arrived at Glasgow the House of Commons was in the second day of a debate about the war situation. Although it was Winston Churchill, as First Lord of the Admiralty, who had played a prominent part in directing the Norway campaign it was the Prime Minister, Neville Chamberlain, who got the blame. Two days later he resigned and Churchill got his job. This day, the 10th May 1940, was a memorable day in world history, for it was also the day the Germans launched their attack on the Western Front, invading Belgium, Luxembourg and Holland. And then, within a matter of weeks, it seemed likely that the Germans would be invading Britain. Every soldier, every warship and every aeroplane was needed at home.

So in the end, in the light of these momentous events, it turned out to be extremely fortunate that the British were no longer committed in Norway. And although the Allies had lost a number of warships during the campaign they had sunk or heavily damaged many ships in the German Fleet—a vital factor when Hitler pondered the possibility of invading England.

The 4th Lincolns arrived at Stobs Camp, near Hawick in Scotland, on Thursday the 9th May and despite the fact that all leave had been stopped for everyone else because of the German invasion on the Western Front, a special train left for Lincolnshire the following Sunday to take them on ten days leave.

'B' company was met at Woodhall Spa railway station by a bus and private cars and when they arrived at Horncastle Market Place shortly after six o'clock there was a short speech of welcome and cheers from the crowd. The following Monday the Urban District Council gave them supper at the Ship Hotel and they received presents from the Horncastle Comforts Fund. At Boston, 'C' Company was welcomed home as the train drew into the station by the Mayor, Councillor P Clarke, and the men then marched to the Assembly Rooms in the Market Place, headed by the British Legion and Kirton brass bands playing the regimental march, the 'Lincolnshire Poacher'. At Lincoln's LNER station the Mayor (Councillor A L Bower), the City Sheriff and the Town Clerk and their wives were with hundreds of excited people who had been waiting on the platform for up to two hours to greet the men. As the train came over the level crossing there were waving, shouting khaki-clad figures at every carriage window. Perhaps the Mayor had intended to give a speech, but such a cheer went up when the train pulled into the station that he wouldn't have been heard and he had to content himself with expressing the city's greetings to Major Don Stokes. The soldiers then carried Major Stokes shoulder-high out of the station.

In some homes there was no-one to welcome. Nine men had been killed and five had been wounded. A further twenty-three men were missing and it was to be some weeks before anxious families heard that they had been taken prisoner. But considering what they had been through and the odds which had been stacked against them, the Lincolns could perhaps count themselves lucky that they had got away so relatively lightly.

Spending a few days of his leave in London, Captain Giles visited the News Theatre in Piccadilly Circus and saw the film of the German bombers attacking the road bridge at Namsos which the crew from Movietone News had made.

On Thursday the 23rd May the special train returned the men to Stobs Camp where they found that all the huts had been broken into and that personal possessions were missing. The battalion quickly settled down to routine army life—drill, route marches, dental inspections, lectures, PT and company training. A draft of new men arrived and an ENSA concert party visited. 'A' company had been ordered to stack all their rifles on the quayside before leaving Namsos, for use by the Norwegian Army so it was said, (in fact they were stored and used later by the Norwegian resistance) and so they had to be issued with new ones. But there were fears of a German invasion and a few days later the rifles were taken from them to be sent to the south of England. The men had to wait for several weeks before they received replacements. In view of the events in France, officers reconnoitred the area around Hawick to prepare local defence schemes in case German paratroops landed.

Major Black, the second-in-command, left the battalion to take up a post at the War Office and on the 7th June the Commanding Officer, Lieutenant-Colonel Newton—who had completed the usual three years in command—handed over the battalion to Lieutenant-Colonel R L de Brisay, a regular army officer who had just returned from service with the 1st battalion in India. Major Donald Stokes was

Lt-Colonel Newton with his wife.

42

the new second-in-command. Captain N Round-Turner from 'D' company took over as officer commanding 'B' company in place of Captain Tweed who, released on compassionate grounds, eventually became the officer commanding the Horncastle Home Guard.

On Tuesday the 18th June, Royal Army Service Corps buses moved the 4th Lincolns from Stobs Camp to Dunkeld and then, five days later, the battalion went by rail to the Clyde where they boarded the brand-new 21,000 ton liner RMS *Andes*. They set off the following day, Monday the 24th June, and the *Andes* headed up the west coast of Scotland, escorted by an aircraft carrier and two destroyers. It was less than seven weeks since the Lincolns had returned home from Norway. This time they were heading for Iceland.

*   *   *   *   *

Iceland used to belong to Denmark, but in 1918 a separate state had been set up—still under the Danish Crown—responsible for its own affairs except for international relations. Iceland had always had quite good relations with Germany. Most Icelandic doctors and scientists had received at least part of their education in Germany, and German universities had spent money researching Icelandic history and culture.

For a year or two before the war the Germans had increased their efforts to establish good relations with Iceland, particularly with the younger people. They arrived with an aeroplane and gliders and gave free instruction in gliding, they sent instructors in skiing and rock climbing and invited football and athletic teams to Germany where they were offered lavish hospitality.

Commercial trade between the two countries also increased. The British found all this rather suspicious and alarming but did nothing to try to foster increased friendship with Iceland. And then, when the war broke out, the Royal Navy blockaded exports from Iceland to Germany, one of their valuable customers.

Suddenly, with the German conquest of Denmark and their invasion of Norway—and its thousand miles of Atlantic coastline—the spotlight was turned upon Iceland and its important strategic position along the North Atlantic sea lanes. At the Admiralty, Winston Churchill saw that if the Germans invaded Iceland as well they could set up air and naval bases and control the entrances and exits of the Atlantic. It was essential for the British to establish a presence in Iceland before the Germans got there first. The Foreign Office tried to negotiate along these lines, but Iceland declined and re-affirmed its neutrality.

On Wednesday the 8th May over eight hundred Royal Marines sailed from Greenock in two cruisers, HMS *Berwick* and HMS *Glasgow* which, with two destroyers, entered Reykjavik Bay two days later—the same day that Germany launched their attack on Holland, Belgium and Luxembourg. Iceland had no armed forces of any kind and it was a simple task for the Marines, guided by local British residents, to secure key locations. The German consulate was seized and German residents were taken into custody. No-one did any work in Reykjavik that day. Everyone seemed to be out in the streets and down by the harbour watching the Marines, unafraid, excited and curious. The Icelandic government made a formal protest at the British infringement of their country's neutrality and although some people gave the Marines a cool reception almost everyone accepted that the occupation was a wise and necessary step. The Icelandic Prime Minister asked his people to see the British as guests.

The following week the 147th Brigade arrived to relieve the Marines, who then returned home. This Territorial Army brigade had been in readiness to go to Namsos as reinforcements when the decision was taken to withdraw from Central Norway. It comprised the 6th and 7th battalions of the Duke of Wellington's Regiment and the 5th West Yorkshire Regiment, and they had the job of defending all of Iceland—a country slightly larger than Ireland and with a coastline of over 3,000 miles—against a German invasion. The Brigadier soon realised that this was an impossible task and it wasn't long before he was sending urgent messages asking for reinforcements. London sent the 146th Brigade.

During the voyage the men were told that they were heading for Iceland. Those who had thought that they were quite seasoned travellers by now soon revised their opinion, for despite it being mid-summer, the Atlantic was rough. Not many were looking forward to going to Iceland but quite a number were very pleased when after two days sailing the coast came into view.

No-one really knew what to expect in Iceland. The very name of the place caused a shiver and there were some who were expecting to find igloos and Eskimos. From the deck of the *Andes*, the men looked glumly at the snow-covered mountains and the uninviting bare landscape, without even so much as a tree in sight.

The *Andes* docked at Reykjavik and the sick were taken to hospital. Reykjavik was a modern town with wide roads, a couple of cinemas and an excellent taxi service. What seemed strange was that there was no black-out and that it didn't really get dark at night. Although it was the largest town in Iceland, the population of Reykjavik in those days was only about 30,000—a quarter of the population of the entire country. It was a slightly larger port than Boston. The 4th Lincolns didn't get the opportunity for sightseeing in Reykjavik for they put to sea again the following day. After a journey which lasted almost a day, they arrived at Akureyri on the north coast of Iceland and disembarked from the *Andes* into small boats which took them into the port.

Akureyri had a population of around 6,000—a little larger than Horncastle—and was Iceland's second largest town. It wasn't many miles away from the Arctic Circle. The Lincolns were billetted in the local school and the reception they received from the inhabitants was cold and aloof, although not openly hostile. Despite Denmark having been invaded by the Germans, the Icelandic people resented the British intrusion and the war being brought to their neutral country. Besides, you only had to look at what had happened in Norway—the arrival of Brit-

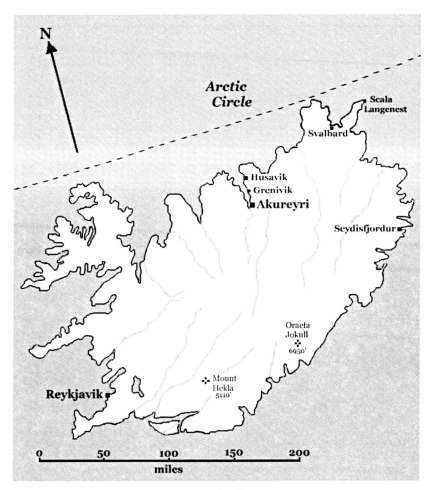

Map 4. Iceland.

ish troops had resulted in peaceful towns such as Steinkjer being completely flattened, causing misery to hundreds of local civilians.

The 4th Lincolns had been given the job of defending the north-eastern sector of Iceland, and this meant that they had to do what all soldiers spend much of their time doing—digging-in. Here, in Iceland, this wasn't easy. In some places the ground was waterlogged whilst in others the ground was volcanic rock. There was no timber to shore up trenches.

It took quite a long time for the men to become acclimatised to life in Iceland. Almost all of the population of this remote, barren, volcanic land lived on the coast in fishing villages and two or three coastal towns. There was no railway and the only decent road was impassable for eight months of the year.

HQ Company officers, summer 1940.

Standing (l to r): 2nd Lt A J Scruby, 2nd Lt Gordon Newsum, Major Don Stokes, 2nd Lt Dick Newsum, Lt G Fairbairn, Lt T Joyce. Seated: 2nd Lt Toby Jessop and Lt Christie. All were Territorial Army soldiers with the exception of the Quarter Master, Lt Joyce, a regular soldier who had risen from the ranks. The Intelligence Officer, 2nd Lt Scruby, ended the war as a Colonel, although not with the Lincolns.

Fishing and, to a lesser extent, sheep-rearing were the main occupations. There were some wild ponies but what they lived on was anyone's guess as very little could be grown in this desolate country. Apart from a few scrub bushes, the only things which seemed to grow here were some small silver birches which were being cultivated. No fruit and virtually no vegetables were grown. There were a few potatoes, but they were small and usually black and frost-bitten. So the basis of the troops' diet was tinned and after ten men had been admitted to hospital suffering from scurvy everyone had to take a vitamin pill each morning. The men were told that they were to make up for the lack of fruit and there was a standing joke when they got their morning pills whether they were going to be apples or pears that day.

There was an acute shortage of timber and even bits of old worthless wood were highly prized by Icelanders. Virtually everything had to be imported, from coal to tinned food. To their dismay, the troops found that there was no beer as the Icelanders were apparently not allowed to brew it. There was the danger that the morale of the men would become very low, but fortunately there was plenty of work to keep them occupied.

The CO, Lieutenant Colonel de Brisay was advised by the Brigadier to use his car rather than his Icelandic pony. 'We're not in India now', the Brigadier reminded him.

It was thought that the Germans might invade Iceland at any time and arms were carried by the men even when off duty. With a number of key points and such a lengthy coastline to cover, it wasn't long before the men were detached into small groups. 'A' Company was sent to guard a nearby airfield whilst a platoon from 'B' Company did port control work at Akureyri. Other platoons were sent to set up observation posts at various points. Number 10 Platoon of 'B' Company, for instance, was sent to Husavik, almost fifty miles from Akureyri. The road was little more than a track and the countryside was bare and desolate. There were huge lakes and rivers and lava fields which stretched for miles and looked like the surface of the moon. Occasionally there were signs of human habitation—

primitive shacks built with sods of earth and so small that it was difficult to imagine that people could possibly live in them.

Akureyri in the winter...

...and in the summer.

Husavik was a small fishing village. Miles away from the rest of the regiment, the task of the few men in this isolated platoon was to defend the area against an invasion by the Germans. The men set up observation posts along the coast and dug some trenches on the tops of the cliffs and wondered what would happen if the Germans actually arrived. It was summer and the weather was quite warm, which was just as well for they were living under canvas, beside a small stream on the outskirts of the village. They kept themselves busy and even worked on Sundays for there was nothing to do in their spare time. A few of the men made fishing rods and tried fishing for catfish and cod. Occasionally they had a spot of luck.

They were not short of fish. All the men in the village were fishermen and at night they went to sea in small motor boats, returning the next morning with their holds full of cod and halibut. One or two of the fishermen at Husavik kept a cow and a few sheep as a sideline.

Akureyri.

Meanwhile, more troops had arrived in Iceland, this time three battalions of Canadians. Work was also started in building naval facilities—a camp, a pier and jetties, warehouses and even a bakery. The Fleet Air Arm brought a squadron, soon to be replaced by RAF Fairey Battle light bombers. Some of the pilots were Australians and one of their favourite pastimes was to fly between the twin towers of Akureyri church. A new draft of 6 officers and 153 men also arrived for the 4th

Lincolns, and for a time became 'F' Company under the command of Captain Dick Giles, a solicitor from Boston.

The main recreation for the men in these summer months was football. There were platoon matches, inter-company matches and games when the Lincolns met other battalions. Efforts were also made to establish better relations with the Icelanders and a football match was arranged between the battalion and a local team which the Lincolns won 2-0. The football match was a great success and another game was played ten days later. This time the Lincolns were heavily beaten, 9-2. A representative match between Iceland and the Army was arranged, which Iceland won 2-0.

The camp at Akureyri.

The Icelandic people were becoming more friendly. No doubt this was partly in response to the friendly attitude of the soldiers, but it may also have had something to do with the fact that the British were providing work and a good income for many of the local people. But there was a set-back in the relationship with the Icelanders when two women were assaulted one night in the street, one seriously injured in the head. A communist newspaper, the *Verhamaturium*, took the opportunity to condemn the British occupation and issued pamphlets urging people to take reprisals. The young lady recovered and the whole thing blew over but for a time it was feared that the incident would have grave repercussions. As well as the communists there were others who took every opportunity to stir up trouble. The Icelandic Nazi Party which the Germans had set up was still in existence and they spread anti-British propaganda. For instance they claimed that if the Germans *did* invade it would be all the fault of the British, for if they'd stayed away the Germans would never have thought of violating Icelandic neutrality. Sometimes soldiers were attacked or spat on by youths in the streets and cafés, and although some people couldn't stand the sight of the British, by and large the longer they stayed the friendlier the Icelanders became.

The warm weather didn't last long, the nights started to draw in very quickly and the men were still living in a camp under canvas, where the aptly-named Sergeant Bogg was in charge of the latrines. They began to worry about the prospect of spending the Icelandic winter under canvas. A mobile cinema showed George Formby in a film called 'I See Ice'—a prophecy which didn't escape the notice of some of the troops. Nissen huts arrived for the Lincoln's main camp at Akureyri, but there was a shortage of timber and cement for the foundations and not much progress was made. By the time the cement finally arrived in September there had already been one or two sharp frosts—which themselves caused delays because of the problem of setting the concrete—and there had been two quite heavy downfalls of snow. Lieutenant Fairbairn, who had been an architect in 'Civvy Street', was given the job of planning the camp—ablutions, the guard room, headquarters, the cookhouse, sewers—and the men had to put the Nissen huts together themselves. By the time General Gort visited the Lincolns in late October most of the huts had been erected.

Erecting a Nissen hut.

Two Lincoln lads—Fred Lawson and Colin Hockney

Major Donald Stokes.

The Signals platoon and their equipment in Iceland.

By this time the NAAFI had opened a canteen at Akureyri where the lads could buy cups of tea and buns—and sometimes beer—and a shop which sold cigarettes, tobacco, sweets and tinned fruit. The YMCA arrived and set up a canteen, and Toc H and the Salvation Army opened centres. The soldiers received their pay in kroner and could buy things in Icelandic shops (which they found a little expensive). Bookshops were full of English books. The kroner were, incidentally, printed at New Malden in Surrey!

Although it was still autumn, the north winds were piercing on this northern coast of Iceland. The troops had been issued with leather jerkins, fleece-lined coats and fur caps but they still appreciated the scarves, gloves and jerseys which Lincolnshire women had knitted and 'Comforts Fund' organisations had sent out. About six hundred items had been sent by the *Lincolnshire Echo* Comforts Fund alone. Those still living in tents envied those who had moved into the comparative comfort of Nissen huts. All of the Nissen huts were lit with electricity—still unfamiliar to many of the lads from rural Lincolnshire. Electricity, generated by the torrents which raged down from the glaciers, was cheap and readily available in Iceland.

A number of bus trips were arranged to the many spectacular waterfalls in the area and to the hot volcanic geysers. Pipes from the geysers ran into open-air bathing places and the men just dived straight into the hot water. The changing rooms were also centrally-heated by the warm pipes. There was never a lack of volunteers for swimming parades, although unfortunately on one visit Private George Burden had a heart attack when he went into the pool and died.

Outdoor swimming pool. Brrr...

Maintaining the morale of the men during the long, dark nights was going to be a problem. There was a cinema in Akureyri which showed quite recent American films with Icelandic sub-titles. A newspaper for the British Forces was started. Called the *Midnight Sun*, it was printed by an Icelandic firm, gave the news in English and encouraged articles written by the troops.

Skaters.

The fjord froze and the Lincolns negotiated the hire of 25 pairs of skates on three days a week. At night, floodlights from the hospital ship *Leinster* lit the fjord for the skaters. A recreation hut was built which had a wireless sent by the Mayor of Lincoln and a shop which sold light snacks. The pictures on the walls were railway posters which someone had got from the LNER, including the poster for Lincoln with a painting of the cathedral. Much of the furniture in the hut was made by the men themselves.

A mobile cinema visited the hut once a week and showed talkies to packed houses. A library was started and was augmented by a supply of books sent by Lincoln Public Library. Corporal Basil Rose, who owned a music shop on the corner of Tentercroft Street and High Street in Lincoln and could play almost any instrument, organised and led a band. All the instruments had to be borrowed from local Icelanders who asked for nothing in return except for the occasional tin of fruit or bar of chocolate. The arrangement made for the big drum was a tin of pineapple chunks a month. Soon there was a search for talent amongst all platoons when the battalion organised a concert. With the band playing a prominent part, it turned out to be a very good show and a few Icelanders who attended as guests enjoyed it so much that three repeat performances had to be given at their request for local people, even though some of them did not understand English. But many of the Icelanders could speak very good English—

and two or three other languages as well. Later, Corporal Bas Rose organised and led a band with men from some of the other units in Iceland called 'The Northern Lights' which frequently broadcast on Icelandic radio.

Corporal Basil Rose (left) and his band.

Quite a number of the reservists—the regulars who had served their time but had been recalled when war had broken out—had served in Shanghai and Hong Kong with the 2nd battalion and had learned how to play mah jong. After Major Stokes had sent an appeal to the *Echo*, several readers sent mah jong sets to Iceland.

The CO decided that during the long dark nights every man would be *made* to have a hobby. The results of the hobbies would be entered in a competition at the end of March. Bearing in mind the shortages of materials, his orders stressed (in capital letters): 'NO GOVERNMENT MATERIAL OTHER THAN WASTE WILL BE USED'. He also ordered the officers to prepare lectures to be given to the men for their entertainment in their off-duty hours. He suggested that the subjects of the lectures might be along the lines of 'How Britain Came to be at War', 'German War Aims' and 'Why France Failed'. Clearly, the troops were going to have some entertaining, fun-filled evenings to look forward to!

The arrival of winter played havoc with the training programme. Route marches had to be cancelled because of dangerous icy conditions and firing practices on the range frequently had to be put off due to strong gales. The waterlogged ground was a slushy, muddy mess. To add to the CO's problems, his right hand man, Regimental Sergeant Major Bostock, was taken ill and had to be admitted to the

Leinster. Much to everyone's surprise, he died of a stroke shortly before Christmas.

Shovelling the snow off the ice to prepare a skating rink.

Floodlights from HM Hospital Ship 'Leinster' were switched on at night for the skaters. Before the war the 'Leinster' had been in regular use as an Irish Sea ferry, and was converted into a hospital ship whilst in Iceland.

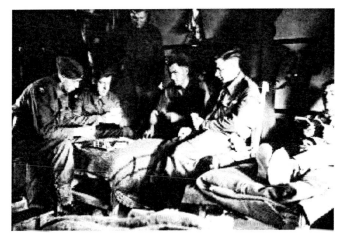

Crib school.

Officers getting up a fug in their Nissen hut.

By Christmas it didn't get properly light until around 10.00 am and it was dark again soon after 2.30 pm. Geese were bought locally and served for Christmas

dinner and each man had two bottles of beer. In the New Year, a contingent of Norwegian soldiers suddenly arrived and it was then that the Lincolns learned that a ski platoon was being formed. Men were selected from all companies and the Norwegian instructors took them off for training, which included learning how to use sledges and manage dog teams. It was enjoyable and most of the men learned to ski quite quickly. Later, the scheme was expanded until there was one ski platoon equipped and trained in each company.

Learning how to ski.

The battalion got up a concert party to help to cheer up the long Icelandic nights .

By this time, the winter had really set in on the northern Icelandic coast. There were some very heavy falls of snow and at times there were thirty degrees of frost. It was impossible for any transport to move. Food supplies couldn't get through and for a time the battalion had to exist on compo rations. Even the supply of blanco ran out, so webbing equipment had to be scrubbed. Then a severe flu epidemic broke out and all places of public entertainment in Akureyri were closed. Eventually transport was able to get through—but with difficulty, for the thaw severely damaged the roads. Some places were almost impassable and once again training programmes had to be cancelled because the men had to become road-menders. This went on for weeks and it was not until the middle of May that the roads were fully repaired. There had been one piece of good news however—UK leave. A scheme had started to allow men home, by rota, for 21 days leave and the first lucky ones left for Lincolnshire in March 1941.

Not all of the Lincolns were at Akureyri. A platoon still took it in turns to man the post at Husavik, and other small observation posts had been established elsewhere. Tony Bell of 'B' Company, now a Corporal, was put in charge of five men and sent to Scala Langenest, a small village right on the north-eastern tip of Iceland, to set up an observation post. There weren't any roads, or even a track, and the only way of getting there was either by sea or on horseback through the mountains. They were given seventy days rations, and a rowing boat from a coaster, the *Lochnagar*, dropped them off. They looked around for the village, but saw only four houses and a wild, rocky mass of mountains. That was it. The men felt incredibly lonely and their hearts sank as they watched the *Lochnagar* disappear over the horizon. It was almost as though they had been marooned on some remote island. The inhabitants of the houses came out and stared at them curiously. One of them, a ginger-haired chap, could speak a little English. Tony explained that they had come to stay for a while and needed somewhere to live and eventually the villagers agreed that they could use a small wooden hut above a barn on top of the cliff, overlooking the sea.

Corporal Tony Bell with his Tommy gun.

There were no beds, so the men had to make some bunks. There was no stove either, so cooking had to be done outside on an open fire until the men built a fireplace out of some old bricks which were lying about. They even built an oven, made from biscuit tins, which smoked a lot but worked quite well until it had to be abandoned after it had set fire to some hay in the barn beneath the hut. Fortunately, one of the men, Private Shackleton (said to be a distant relative of the explorer) was an excellent cook and could make cod taste like salmon. Tony had to keep a log book, reporting everything that happened and everything they saw. Outside, the wind whistled and great rollers crashed onto the surf a few yards away. The men saw quite a lot of shipping, mostly small fishing craft from the Faroe Islands, and sometimes the seamen came ashore for water. Tony's men were getting short of tobacco (they were saving their cigarette ends in a tin, ready to be used in case they ran out altogether) and on one occasion they traded a tin of bully beef with one of the seamen for half a pound of tobacco. Sometimes the seamen brought them news of the war, for they were out of touch with the outside world as the ginger-haired Icelander's radio was frequently out of order.

A nature-lover would have been in his element at Scala Langenest. There were scores of Arctic terns and if you got too near to their nests they would scream in a frightening way as they dive-bombed you. There were thousands of wild duck, mostly mallard, and the many seals which lived around the coast amused the men when they dived and then re-appeared yards away some time later. There were two lakes in the mountains about a mile away, connected by a small stream which was alive with trout. They made a pleasant change from the diet of cod.

Towards the end of September the *Lochnager* returned for Tony and his men. It was very rough and in the Denmark Strait the waves were as big as houses. The *Lochnager* stopped dead, shuddering from bows to stern each time it hit a wave, and then lurched forward, the propellers spinning madly when they came out of the water.

A few weeks later, Tony Bell headed off in a fishing boat about 25 miles up the fjord from Akureyri to take over another observation post which had been set up at a village called Grenavik which had a population of about 120. He and his men spent the whole winter there in a two-roomed shack. They used to go to the weekly village dance, rowed in the fjord and when it froze they spent a lot of time skating on a nearby lake. They even taught the Icelanders how to play ice hockey. Sometimes they would go with the fishermen in their small motor boats. By and large, it wasn't a bad sort of life. They hired a stove for the hut and when a wireless set arrived from England they felt very cosy. But sometimes there were blizzards so fierce that it was impossible to stand up and they had to stay indoors, listening to it howling outside. One morning they woke to find that the hut had been almost entirely covered with snow. They couldn't see out of the windows and had to be dug out by a neighbouring farmer. Nevertheless, when spring arrived, one or two of the men felt quite sorry when they had to return to the battalion at Akureyri.

Bleak scenes at Akureyri.

Spring turned into summer. The Canadians had left Iceland in the autumn and had been replaced by the 70th Brigade—Territorial Army Geordies from the 10th and 11th battalions of the Durham Light Infantry and the 1st Tyneside Scottish. Another infantry battalion and a further artillery battery arrived in June, and by this time there were over twenty-five thousand British servicemen in Iceland, for naval and air bases had also been built and there were coastal guns, anti-aircraft guns, and radar installations. Iceland was now fully operational as a base for the warships carrying out escort duties.

'It ain't half cold, mum'. Captain Cragg and some men from 'C' Company look rather chilly.

There was a short, but major, alert during the hunt for the *Bismark* because for a time it was thought that she might be heading for Iceland. There, waiting for her in defensive positions facing the Denmark Strait, were the men of the Pioneer platoon of the 4th Lincolns, armed with their spades and pickaxes. On another occasion there was a scare that U-boats might be using some of the fjords and Captain Giles was detailed to take a party—half mounted on Icelandic ponies and half on foot—to look for them. After a diligent reconnaissance by his mixed force of cavalry and infantry, Captain Giles was able to report that there was no sign of any.

*   *   *

Iceland's foreign interests were the responsibility of Denmark, which was now occupied by the Germans. So the Icelandic government decided to open their own legation in America and in July 1940, a couple of months after the British had first landed, Iceland asked the United States for protection. Although nothing was done at the time, the matter was raised again in 1941. America was edging closer to war and, in May 1941, President Roosevelt offered to garrison Iceland. This offer was immediately welcomed by Winston Churchill. Britain was still alone in the fight against the Nazis and our troops could be released from Iceland to fight elsewhere.

Not only that, the offer seemed to draw the Americans closer to entering the war, even though the mood in the United States was against American intervention. For that reason, Roosevelt had to tread carefully and he said that Iceland, like America, was still a neutral country—America would merely be a large neutral country protecting a smaller one. Diplomatic niceties had to be observed—Iceland would have to invite the United States to send troops and there would have to be a written agreement that they would leave immediately the war was over. (Actually, they're still there.) On the 7th July 1941, two American battleships, two cruisers and more than a dozen destroyers escorted the US Marines (complete with band) to Reykjavik. The following month they were followed by an infantry division and thirty fighter planes. In time, thousands of American troops were to follow. The first the Lincolns knew about this development was when they heard it on the BBC nine o'clock news and naturally there was speculation and wild rumours about being home within weeks. But the Americans still had to build-up their forces, the excitement died down and the men set about enjoying the long summer days when it never seemed to get dark. ENSA concert parties arrived from England. (ENSA stood for 'Entertainments National Service Association' but the troops reckoned, rather unfairly, that it stood for 'Every Night Something Awful.')

Corporal Rose's band attracted many spectators when they played in the local park, and football matches were arranged against all possible opposition, including HMS *Devonshire* which paid a visit to Akureyri.

Now that people were about in the streets, restaurants and dance halls, some of the lads started dating local girls who all wore modern dress and had their hair permed, just like the girls at home. But on Sundays, many families dressed in national costume to go to church. Older women wore black silk dresses, tightly girdled at the waist, with richly embroidered aprons. They wore small black skull-caps on their heads and their hair was plaited, two lengthy plaits being joined by a tubular piece of brass. Most of the Icelandic people belonged to the Lutheran Church and seemed to be very religious.

Another newspaper in English had been started, the *Arctic News*. An Icelander printed it, but it was produced by the army. It kept the troops up-to-date with how the war was progressing, but also contained snippets of 'news' which must have been hard to swallow, even in those days. For instance there was a piece which read: 'Gangsters' guns are to be used by the Home Guard. Sawn-off shot guns,

Lugers and Mausers, confiscated from the gangsters of America, are being shipped to England for use by the Home Guard'. Another read: 'The railings round the King's Palace have now been removed. They will later appear as a tank, which it is hoped to call "Buckingham Palace" '.

There could have been few grumbles when these ENSA girls arrived, having braved the danger of U-boats and the rough Atlantic seas to entertain the troops at Akureyri.

The 49th Division now had its own insignia. It was a polar bear and looked for all the world like an advert for Fox's Glacier Mints. There were no polar bears in Iceland—nor any other animal for that matter, except for ponies, rats and a few white foxes—but that didn't seem to matter. The 49th Division kept the polar bear insignia throughout the war, although it was to be amended as we shall see.

'Eyes right!' The 4th battalion parades through Akureyri on St George's Day, 1941.

There was an unexpected development one day when eight Vickers machine guns arrived. A new machine gun platoon was now formed and many of the old one—disbanded in 1938 when they had had to give up their Vickers guns—volunteered to join it, some taking a reduction in rank to do so.

Although more American troops had landed in Iceland, there was still no word about the Lincolns returning home. Pessimists said that they were there for the duration and even the optimists began to wonder if they were in for another long Icelandic winter. By September, when the fourth leave party of ninety men left for their 21 days UK leave, the battalion was definitely getting ready for winter. Fuel was issued on the basis of five pounds of coal and ten pounds of coke per man per day. Then it was heard that the Lincolns were to start training to become an alpine battalion as part of a Mountain Division, and that clinched it. Apparently this had been the idea of Winston Churchill, when he had visited Iceland on the way home from a meeting with President Roosevelt.

For many men, the prospect of mountain training in an Icelandic winter wasn't a very attractive one. It certainly wasn't everyone's cup of tea, for it was bound to be arduous, to say the least. All ranks had to undergo a medical examination and about a hundred men were deemed to be unfit for various reasons.

Captain Jack Staniland (seated fourth from the left) in Iceland with some of the members of 'D' Company, which he commanded.

The midnight sun in Iceland

Some well-known mountaineers and explorers arrived to start a training school. Amongst them was a naval officer, Peter Scott, the naturalist and the son of Scott of the Antarctic. 'B' and 'D' Companies were the first to started Arctic training. They were kitted out with special equipment, the string vests causing some amusement. The men learned mountain-climbing, how to mend skis and they practised firing Bren guns mounted on sledges. There were combined exercises carried out in conjunction with the Artillery and the men marvelled at the accuracy of the gunners' 25-pounders.

4th battalion officers in Iceland.

There were formidable mountain bivouac schemes which lasted for several days when the men slept in two-man tents in the snow and learned survival techniques. If the weather conditions became bad, for instance, the men had to tie themselves together and wait until it improved. They trudged their way in Arctic kit through snow and climbed rocks during the day and slept in their tents at night. On one occasion they spent the night in a large ice cave and then crossed a glacier, each party having three men ahead roped together, looking for crevasses.

Camping in the snow.

When the training was over there was special praise for the Lincolns for their enthusiasm. All in all it hadn't been a bad life for young men with a sense of adventure. Most of the men felt fitter and they were certainly now more confident. And there was a sense of pride and achievement.

Alpine troops.

The Norwegians' skiing school.

Mountain troops.

Akureyri camp in winter.

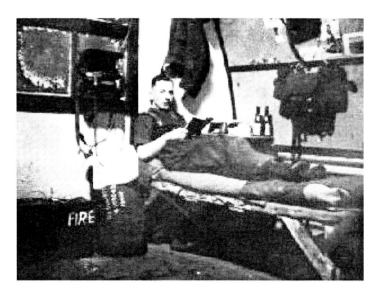

Duty Office, Christmas Eve, 1941.

The Icelandic winter wore on. The cold and the snow were as bad as the previous winter. The 70th Brigade escaped the worst of it, for in December 1941 they were the first British troops to return home from Iceland. There were a few grumbles as they had also been the last brigade to arrive (in October 1940).

In the spring, Private Sam Andrews, who had been a painter at Ruston's, became the first British soldier to marry an Icelandic girl. Captain Tunnard also married a local girl and Major Stokes was the best man when Captain Round-Turner got married.

Captain Round-Turner's wedding.

By now, America was in the war and more of their troops were arriving in Iceland. In April 1942 the British 147th Brigade and the HQ of the 49th Division returned to the UK. This just left the Lincolns and the rest of the 146th Brigade and they now came under American command.

4th battalion officers.

Standing at the rear: Frank Jackson, Edward Cook, John Flint, Dick Newsum, Dick Francis.
Centre row: Mrs and Captain Round-Turner, Donald Stokes, Jack Staniland, Mrs and Captain Tunnard, Lt-Col R L de Brisay (Commanding Officer)
Front: Dick Giles, 2nd/Lt J D Gaunt, —, —.

In July 1942 the Lincolns moved to the east coast of Iceland to Seydisfjordur, where the Royal Navy assembled convoys for Russia. But they weren't here long, for in August the advanced party left for home, followed by the rest of the battalion in September on HM Troopship *Duchess of Bedford*, which in pre-war days had been a luxury liner on the route to South Africa. The Lincolns had occasionally seen enemy aircraft and patrol vessels whilst they had been in Iceland but strangely it was only when they were leaving that they actually came under attack from some German bombers. The attack was unsuccessful and the Lincolns landed in Liverpool on the 9th September, 1942.

It was learned after the war that the Germans had had no intention of occupying Iceland after all. It was only after the British had landed that Hitler, enraged, gave orders for invasion plans to be made. But the logistics of invading—and then of supplying—were simply impossible and the idea was dropped.

But the occupation of Iceland by the British and then the Americans was vital in helping to win the Battle of the Atlantic in 1942 and 1943—and for Britain's survival.

The Midnight Sun.

Normandy

As soon as the 4th Lincolns returned from Iceland they were given fourteen days leave. They were now based at a camp at Hereford and all three battalions of the 146th Brigade were in that area. There were two other brigades in the 49th Division, and they were also in the West Country and Wales.

Perhaps it would be as well at this point to remind you of the three Territorial Army infantry battalions which were in the 49th (West Riding) Division. They were:

146th Brigade: 4th Lincolns, 4th King's Own Yorkshire Light Infantry (KOYLI), and the Hallamshire (City of Sheffield) battalion of the York and Lancaster Regiment. They were based at Hereford and Ross-on-Wye.

147th Brigade: The 6th and 7th battalions of the Duke of Wellington's Regiment. The 5th West Yorkshire Regiment left the brigade at this point and was replaced by the 11th Royal Scots Fusiliers. The brigade was based in Chepstow and Monmouthshire.

70th Brigade: This brigade had replaced the 148th Brigade, which had been decimated at Andalsnes, and comprised the 10th and 11th battalions of the Durham Light Infantry (DLI) and the 1st Tyneside Scottish (originally the 12th battalion of the DLI). This brigade was in Carmarthenshire.

For a time it was thought that the 4th Lincolns would continue training in their role as mountain troops, but this was 1942 and we had entered the fourth year of the war. British troops were fighting in the jungles of Burma, the 8th Army was in the desert and very soon the 1st Army would also land in North Africa. It seemed that there wouldn't be much call for ski-troops after all. Whilst the Lincolns and the other battalions had been in Iceland new weapons and new military methods had evolved and it was realised that there was quite a lot of catching-up to do. They were out-of-date—'snowbound' as one senior officer put it. Officers and NCOs were sent on courses at battle schools to learn the latest tactics. These were then introduced in the battalion's training programmes and gradually the role of mountain troops was abandoned.

Some of the men left the Lincolns at this stage. Sergeant Gordon 'Ginger' Bone, who had been a printer at the *Lincolnshire Echo*, went with Fred Lawson and half a dozen others on a 6-months engineering course to the Rolls-Royce works at Derby and when it was over they were transferred to the Royal Electrical and Mechanical Engineers (REME). Ginger was a good pianist and when they were short of a bit of money he would play the piano, which most pubs seemed to have in those days, and Fred would then go round the customers with a hat. Whilst they were on the course at Derby—only an hour and a half away from Lincoln—they were stationed at Normanton Barracks and although they had no duties at weekends they were only allowed home once a month. A very frustrating state of affairs. It was on one of these weekends at home that Ginger visited his colleagues at the *Echo*, and asked if it would be all right to show Fred around. Ginger showed how he set up type and Fred asked if he could reproduce an army leave pass. This was very easy. Some buff-coloured paper was found and Ginger ran off several hundred. Queues formed at Normanton Barracks on Fridays, Fred Lawson having the knack of signing the passes with an indecipherable scrawl which might just have passed for an officer's signature. They charged sixpence each.

A cold and wet winter of strenuous training culminated in Exercise Spartan which lasted nearly a fortnight and involved all units in the 49th Division. The 'enemy' was the Canadian army (which the Lincolns were later to get to know very well) who managed to capture the divisional headquarters. Captain Giles and the padre escaped from the compound they were placed in at Thame in Oxfordshire, and by taking a roundabout route in the padre's car they were able to rejoin what was left of the division.

There were now around eight hundred men in the battalion. Each of the four rifle companies comprised around 110 men and there were also the specialist platoons—carriers, mortars and anti-tank platoons. Some of the men went for specialist training when the anti-tank platoon was formed and 6-pounder anti-tank guns arrived. There were now over forty men in the mortar platoon which had trebled in size, now having three sections which each had two 3-inch mortars.

In July 1943, Lieutenant-Colonel de Brisay ('Breezy' to the troops) handed over command of the 4th Lincolns to Lieutenant-Colonel W E Carrick of the Northamptonshire Regiment. The 49th Division also had a new GOC when Major-General E H Barker took over. He was a lot like 'Monty' in many ways. He had the same manner and voice, and even looked a bit like him. Nicknamed 'Bubbles' because of his effervescent and vigorous nature, he instilled a new aggressive spirit throughout the division. One of his first acts was to change the division's emblem, for he thought that the polar bear, looking down, seemed to be too droopy and submissive. He wanted a more defiant, ferocious-looking bear with a snarl on its face. 'Lift its head up and make it roar,' he ordered. Actually, the artist who had drawn the original emblem had probably got it right, for polar bears apparently lower their heads when about to attack!

The new 'aggressive' polar bear.

The 49th Division became part of I Corps in the spring of 1943, and in the summer the 4th Lincolns moved to Scotland to begin training in combined operations and assault methods. This could only mean one thing—the invasion of Europe. The battalion moved from Comrie in Perthshire to Rothesay, Isle of Bute, where they practised landing from mock (and later real) landing craft and storming pill-boxes and blockhouses made from canvas and wood under a hail of fire from artillery, mortars and machine guns using live ammunition. They got used to the noise of war. The beaches had been made to look like those they might expect when landing in France, complete with barbed-wire and mines. The Lincolns got very wet in Scotland too—wet from the rain which seemed to be incessant and wet from constantly getting out of the landing craft into the sea.

In December 1943, the 4th Lincolns moved with the rest of the 49th Division to East Anglia and were transferred from I Corps to XXX Corps. A young Brigadier, Andrew Dunlop, took over command of 146th Brigade. The divisional headquarters was at Norwich and the Lincolns were billeted in a holiday camp at Kessingland, near Lowestoft, where there was neither heating nor lighting. They hastily indented for stoves.

Many Territorial regiments were inclined to be more informal—less rigid—than regular battalions, and the 4th Lincolns were no exception. Although some men had left the battalion and had been replaced by men from other parts of the country, there was still a large proportion of the Territorials from Lincolnshire who had been together since before the war. These included many of the officers.

Major Don Stokes from HQ Company was the second-in-command and the Officer Commanding 'A' Company was Captain Flint from Belmesthorpe, which although only a couple of miles from Stamford, was in Rutland. He had started the war as a Second-Lieutenant in 'D' Company at Alford, where he worked in Barclay's bank. Major Staniland, who had originally commanded 'D' Company, was from Toynton, near Spilsby, and he was now in charge of 'C' Company, whilst Major Pattin from Woodhall Spa commanded 'B' Company, in which he had been a Second-Lieutenant when the war started. Major Gordon Newsum from Lincoln was still with the battalion and his brother, Dick, was in charge of the Bren gun carriers. Major Blackstone, who had originally been the Adjutant, now commanded 'S' (Support) Company, where Captain 'Soapy' Waters was in charge of the mortar platoon—('Waters of the Mortars').

Shortly before Christmas 1943, General Dwight D Eisenhower was appointed as Supreme Commander for the Allied invasion of France. On Christmas Eve, General Sir Bernard Montgomery, then with the 8th Army in Italy, heard that he was to return to England to command the 21st Army Group—the British Home Forces which had been designated as the invasion force. Montgomery was appointed to take charge of the initial assault, commanding not only the British and Canadian troops, but also the American army until a sizeable bridgehead had been established after the landings on the Normandy beaches.

Montgomery had clear ideas of what he wanted—and what he didn't want. Officers with battle experience replaced many of the senior officers at 21 Army Group headquarters who had been there a long time and had become set in their ways. He had an aversion to officers who had spent many years in India and he got rid of them too. Many Commanding Officers over the age of forty were replaced. The Lincolns had a new CO when Lieutenant-Colonel Peter Barclay from the Royal Norfolk Regiment arrived in April 1944 to take over command. Educated at Harrow, he had been the first British officer to be decorated in the war, having been awarded the MC early in 1940 for leading a successful patrol in front of the Maginot Line. Connected to the Barclays of Barclay's Bank, he had been a regular officer with the Norfolks since 1929 and had been badly wounded before being evacuated from Dunkirk. He had been running a battle school in Norfolk before his appointment as the CO of the 4th Lincolns, and he was thirty-five years old.

Then it was learned that Montgomery had chosen his old regular 3rd Division and the experienced 50th Northumbrian (Tyne and Tees) Division for the assaults on Gold and Sword beaches. The 50th Division had been with Monty in North Africa and had landed on the beaches of Sicily. So this meant that after a year of training as assault troops, the role of the 4th Lincolns and the rest of the 49th Division had changed. They wouldn't be used in the assault on the beaches after all, but were to be follow-up troops, landing soon after D-Day.

Intensive training continued at Kessingland and there were many exercises carried out in co-operation with the artillery, tanks, signals and the RAF, some of them lasting for several days and involving troops from other formations such as the Canadians and the Tyneside Scots. Although the Lincolns would not be in the first wave of troops to land on D-Day they would still be landing on the beaches and all vehicles had to be water-proofed and then tested, tested and tested again by driving through deep water. There was instruction and exercises using flame-throwers, clearing mines and street-fighting. In Exercise 'Remedy', the battalion practised the evacuation of casualties, including vehicle 'casualties' by the REME. In May, the Lincolns were issued with cycles, and in Exercise 'Shishah' they practised taking up positions quickly after landing, using their bikes. Sometimes the exercises were watched by Major-General Barker and Brigadier Dunlop. Monty also made a point of visiting all his troops so that they could take a good look at him, and he visited the battalion, followed shortly afterwards by the King, who inspected the 146th Brigade at Somerleyton Park. Montgomery told the troops that should any of them be wounded they would be sent to the hospital nearest their home town.

During General Montgomery's visit there was a sharp brush with the CO. Monty always liked the troops to take a good look at him, and jumping onto the bonnet of a jeep he asked Lieutenant-Colonel Barclay to order the men to gather round. Barclay refused, saying that it was a tradition in the Lincolnshire Regiment that men didn't face each other. Montgomery got his way in the end, (after all he was a

Officers of the 4th battalion in March, 1944 at Kessingland, just before the arrival of Lieutenant-Colonel Peter Barclay MC, their new Commanding Officer.

<u>*Rear*</u> *(ranks not known): Knight, Odom, Metcalfe, Dawson, Gordon, Ed Cooke, Hargreaves, Orme, Gaunt, Ainger, Wallage.*

<u>*Centre:*</u> *Waters, 'Doc' Atherton, Golding, Demery, Paulger, Maskey, Nurser, Den Cook, Hartley, Alston, Fowler, 'Tubby' Walker, Francis.*

<u>*Front:*</u> *QM (Wadsworth?), Codd, Dick Newsum, Flint, Blackstone, Stokes, Carrick (CO), Staniland, Pattin, Cauduell, Corben, Hardcastle, Sparks.*

General) and the CO was told that he was 'a very obstinate young man.' It was a strange incident, for it was the first time anyone in the battalion had heard anything of this 'tradition'. Lieutenant-Colonel Barclay had been taking the mickey out of Monty. Some months later he was asked by Monty to write a pamphlet on the maintenance of morale, but he refused. Apparently, Barclay had often been in trouble with senior officers in his early days in the army and had invariably got away with it, but perhaps these two incidents explain why his promotion to Brigadier took a little longer than might have been expected.

Security was tightened as D-Day approached. All civilian travel was stopped between the UK and the neutral Irish Republic, and it is rather surprising that this had not been done earlier, for the Germans had a very active embassy in Dublin. There was a coastal belt, ten miles wide, from the Wash to Land's End which civilians were not allowed to enter. Censorship of soldiers' mail was introduced.

In Bradford, Sergeant Turner's first child, Stephanie, was born on the 25th May, but it was to be months before he would be able to see her. Just before leaving for Normandy, Sergeant Fred 'Tiny' Peacock married a girl he'd met whilst stationed at Hereford and Private George 'Monty' Banks also suddenly felt that he had to marry his fiancée Grace as soon as possible.

He nearly didn't make it, for the train had just started to leave the station when a sergeant dashed onto the platform shouting: 'All leave cancelled, all leave cancelled.'

George and the others who had 36-hour passes took no notice as the train slowly gathered speed and steamed out of the station. Grace, who had fallen for George before the war when she'd seen him in his red bandsman's uniform, nearly didn't make it either. She was a Leading Aircraftwoman, working in the kitchen at the requisitioned Casino at Skegness, and her sergeant had refused to let her have time off to get married. A WAAF officer saw her working and said: 'I thought you were supposed to be getting married today?'

She overruled the sergeant and gave Grace seven days' leave. Grace hastily prepared for her wedding. She got one of her friends to be the best man, giving

George 'Monty' Banks (standing, third from left) in his red bandsman's uniform had caught Grace's eye.

him a photograph of George so that he would recognise him when he met him off the train at Skegness station and she had to borrow money from the padre's wife to pay for the special licence. Grace was given away by a ginger-haired RAF corporal, the padre took the service at Skegness parish church, the wedding photographs were taken by Wraite's in the Tower Gardens and the reception was held in the café under the pier. One of Grace's colleagues in the cookhouse produced a cake. George and Grace then caught the Road Car bus to Lincoln, where they stayed the night with relatives and the following day they went to Kessingland because George had to report back. After George had reported in at the guard room he was given permission to sleep out, but they couldn't find anywhere to stay that night and after borrowing some greatcoats they huddled together in a nearby wood, smoking Woodbines. Grace was later able to find accommodation with a kindly local family, the Millers, and she and George were able to meet every evening after he had come off duty.

Pages of instructions arrived at Kessingland. It seemed as though every last detail had been thought of. Special equipment was issued. This included a Mae West life jacket for every man, who also carried two empty sandbags folded over his web belt. There were yellow celanese strips measuring 10 by 3.5 feet which could be put together to form a triangle for Ground to Air recognition. Each man was issued with two 24-hour rations (for the first two days after landing) together with one emergency ration, a tin of self-heating soup, a packet of twenty cigarettes, a water-sterilising outfit, 200 French francs (about one pound) and twelve hexamine (anti-seasickness) tablets. And in case the tablets didn't work, everyone was issued with three bags, vomit.

On the 28th May the 4th Lincolns were put on six hours notice to move but nothing happened for several days. Then, at last, orders were received. The vehicle party under Major Blackstone left Kessingland for London docks on the 2nd June and the rest of the battalion (with their bikes) set off from Lowestoft by train on Sunday morning, the 4th June, for a marshalling area near Lewes in Sussex.

The marshalling area was 'sealed'—no-one was allowed to leave. Everything was already laid on. There were two large briefing huts with maps and sand models of the area which they were expected to cover. All the troops were told where they were going, what was going to happen and what they were expected to do. The Lincolns, with the rest of the 49th Division, were to land on Gold Beach as the follow-up to the 50th Northumbrian (Tyne Tees) Division which was carrying out the actual assault there on D-Day. Numerous detailed aerial photographs and a large-scale model of the area awaited their arrival and were studied. The personal message for all troops which General Montgomery had prepared was read out.

Entertainment had also been arranged for the troops in the marshalling area. There were cinemas and community singing (very popular in those days), and the

21 ARMY GROUP

PERSONAL MESSAGE
FROM THE C-IN-C

(To be read out to all Troops)

1. The time has come to deal the enemy a terrific blow in Western Europe.
The blow will be struck by the combined sea, land, and air forces of the Allies —
together constituting one great Allied team, under the supreme command of General
Eisenhower.

2. On the eve of this great adventure I send my best wishes to every soldier in the Allied
team.
To us is given the honour of striking a blow for freedom which will live in history;
and in the better days that lie ahead men will speak with pride in our doings. We
have a great and a righteous cause.
Let us pray that 'The Lord Mighty in Battle' will go forth with our armies, and that
His special providence will aid us in the struggle.

3. I want every soldier to know that I have complete confidence in the successful out-
come of the operations that we are now about to begin.
With stout Hearts, and with enthusiasm for the contest, let us go forward to victory.

4. And, as we enter the battle, let us recall the words of a famous soldier spoken many
years ago: —

> "He either fears his fate too much,
> Or his deserts are small,
> Who dare not put it to the touch,
> To win or lose it all."

B. L. Montgomery

General
C.-in-C.,
21 Army Group.

6 June 1944.

Monty's D-Day message.

well-known comedian Tommy Trinder was the star of one of the many ENSA concerts which had been put on. The weather had been hot and sunny in May, but the spell of good weather broke on Sunday the 4th June, the day before the invasion was to take place. There were high winds, it was cold and it poured with rain.

The invasion was put off for 24 hours and the assault on the Normandy beaches took place on Tuesday the 6th June in weather which was only slightly better than the previous day.

It was still dull and rainy (though not as windy) on Friday the 9th June when the Lincolns left the marshalling area for Newhaven, where they embarked on infantry landing ships. The trucks and Bren gun carriers set off from London docks where they had been loaded onto ships, although not without difficulty. Whilst the war-weary but cheerful East Enders had put out flags, bunting and banners ('Good luck lads') in their bomb-damaged streets and had come out of their homes to offer tea and sandwiches to the troops, the dockers refused to work overtime to complete the loading. They just clocked-off when it was time to go home and the loading had to be completed by seamen using the ships' derricks.

*   *   *   *

Field-Marshall Gerd von Runstedt, who commanded Hitler's troops in the West, had never lost a battle. In 1939 he had commanded the troops which had encircled Warsaw. The following year he had simply by-passed the French army in their fixed defences of the Maginot Line and driven straight for the Channel. He had directed the German army across the Ukraine to the Crimea in 1941. He had retired at his own request in November 1941 in protest at Hitler's plan for a winter campaign in Russia, but had agreed to come out of retirement the following year to become Commander-in-Chief in the West. By 1944, he was 69 years old.

Von Runstedt now faced a defensive problem for a change, and it was a difficult one. The Germans had to defend 2,000 miles of coastline, stretching from the north of Norway to the French Mediterranean coast. There just weren't sufficient troops to defend all this vast coastline in strength, and he didn't think that this was desirable anyway, for it would tie down too many troops in fixed positions (like the French in the Maginot Line) leaving too few as mobile reserves to deal with any outflanking movement. He was determined not to make the same mistake as the French.

So von Runstedt approached the problem by accepting that Allied landings couldn't be prevented. Certainly he would hold vulnerable points of the coast in strength—like the mouths of the Somme and the Seine, the major ports, and particularly the area around Calais where he (and everyone else) thought that the invasion was most likely to take place. But he would hold back his armoured divisions and mobile infantry, send them to wherever the Allied troops had landed and then drive them back into the sea. His requests for more troops were ignored, but eventually Hitler sent Field-Marshall Erwin Rommel to inspect the defences from Denmark to the Spanish border and report back.

Rommel was far from impressed by what he saw. He didn't agree with von Runstedt's basic assumption that landings couldn't be prevented and the plan to hold back the mobile armoured divisions. This was perhaps surprising coming from Rommel, for he was a leading exponent of mobile, tactical warfare, flinging his panzers around with speed and imagination wherever there was a tactical opportunity.

But Rommel had come to terms with the fact that the Allies now had overwhelming superiority in the air. He realised that it would be difficult—perhaps impossible—for von Runstedt's armoured reserves to move anywhere in daylight against the fighter-bombers of the Allies. Tactical mobility was now dictated from the air. So Rommel felt that the decisive battle would have to be fought on the beaches. The Allied troops would have to be prevented from landing and driven back into the sea before they had time to build up their strength. He told Hitler that von Runstedt's plans would have to be changed and that he was the man to do it. Hitler agreed. Although von Runstedt still remained the Commander-in-Chief in the West, Rommel was given responsibility for the critical area from Holland to the Loire.

Rommel, an inspired leader of men, set about his task with energy and imagination. Underwater obstacles were built—tetraheda, dragon's teeth and logs with spikes and mines which would blow up or hinder landing craft before the Allied troops even reached the beaches. Millions of mines were laid on the beaches. Coastal batteries were roofed and walled with concrete to give better protection from bombs and shells, new pillboxes were built, more barbed wire erected. Every man, even cooks and clerks, had to dig trenches which they were expected to occupy and defend. Gaps in the sea walls were blocked with concrete, anti-tank ditches were dug. Rommel gave orders that these measures were to be carried out not just in the Calais area but also in Normandy which had so far been rather neglected. He moved some of von Runstedt's reserve of mobile infantry to the beaches. Not far behind them the armoured divisions moved forward so that they could be brought into action almost immediately, for Rommel thought that the first twenty-four hours would be decisive. The outer crust of coastal defences would have to be strong enough to hold out until the armour moved up. He said that it was more important to have one panzer division in the assaulted sector on D-Day than to have three there by D plus 3. 'We must stop the enemy in the water,' Rommel declared, 'destroying all his equipment whilst it is still afloat.'

So from February 1944 the fortifications on the French coast were hastily reinforced and the new underwater obstacles put in place. The most strongly defended area was around Calais, for von Runstedt was convinced that the Allied invasion would take place there and the Allies went to great lengths by clever deceptions to confirm this false impression.

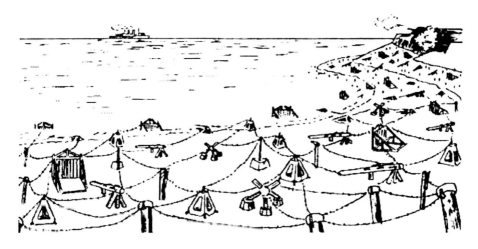

Before and after.

Rommel drew these pictures to illustrate his idea of what D-Day would be like. He wrote: 'The main defence zone on the coast is strongly fortified and well manned. There are large tactical and operational reserves in the rear'.

Rommel agreed that the main Allied attack would be around Calais but he thought that there might also be a strong diversion in Normandy beforehand. It was Hitler, with his uncanny intuition, who got it right. A month before the invasion took place he told his staff that the *main* Allied landings would be in Normandy. More troop reinforcements were sent there immediately, some from the Eastern front where the thaw in April had temporarily halted the Russian advances. Nevertheless, when Allied troops landed in Normandy no German troops were moved from the Calais area for weeks, for von Runstedt and Rommel might have been correct after all.

The Allies had watched the recent build-up of German defences in Normandy with some alarm when it became obvious that Rommel's intention was to defeat the invading army on the beaches. General Montgomery's answer was to land the troops at half-tide, short of the mined obstacles which threatened to do so much damage to the landing craft. As this meant that the troops would be under considerable fire from the Germans before they were in a position to fire back, Montgomery decided to use armour, Major-General Sir Percy Hobart's AVREs (Armoured Vehicle Royal Engineers) or 'funnies', in the very first wave.

Between the wars Hobart had developed advanced ideas about the use of armour, ideas too outrageous for the die-hard generals who, incredibly, still had cavalry regiments with lances—mounted on horses—serving overseas as late as 1941. The British see people with flair as threatening and get rid of them. Hobart had finally been driven into retirement in 1940 and was a corporal in the Home Guard when Churchill rescued him and gave him the opportunity to put his imaginative ideas into practice.

Hobart's menagerie of 'funnies' included flail tanks which could beat pathways through minefields, Churchill tanks with turret-mounted mortars which hurled a projectile called 'The Flying Dustbin' to demolish concrete pill-boxes, tanks without turrets which unfolded ramps for other tanks to climb over, tanks with bridges to span craters and ditches, tanks which laid hessian carpets over soft land (or logs which laid a longer-lasting rough road), tanks which could bulldoze wreckage out of the way and amphibious DD (Duplex Drive) tanks. DD tanks were specially adapted Shermans which, fitted with a flotation collar and twin propellers, could swim ashore.

The 'Flying Dustbin'.

Montgomery was under no illusions about the difficulties facing the Allied soldiers. When he presented his final plans three weeks before D-Day he forecast that Rommel would use his tanks well forward 'to try to Dunkirk us' and then counter-attack. When this failed, Rommel would then try to rope-off the Allied troops, containing them in a narrow bridgehead. It was vitally important for the Allies to gain ground rapidly and pour in troops before the Germans could bring up their mobile reserves. Armoured columns would have to penetrate inland—deeply and quickly—on D-Day to hold off the enemy until we could build up strength. The Allied soldiers would have to be sent 'seeing red.' 'Nothing must stop them,' Montgomery declared. 'Nothing.'

Despite all the preparation, intricate plans and the many hours of training and rehearsal, it was only to be expected that things would go wrong on D-Day, for it was an extremely complex operation, involving thousands of aircraft and ships and tens of thousands of men. Things were made more difficult by the poor weather. Low cloud and high winds made things difficult for gliders; some broke their towropes and others had difficulty in finding the landing zones. Pathfinder paratroops, scattered by the high wind, had to light their flares where they were, and this resulted in the main body dropping wide of the mark, some being carried even further away by the wind.

At Omaha beach the plan to land the armour in the first wave went disastrously wrong. The Americans had turned down the offer of Hobart's 'funnies' except for the DD tanks and they relied solely on them to blast a way ashore and clear the way for the infantry. But the sea was so rough that some of the tanks weren't launched from their landing craft, whilst the others were launched almost four miles from land. Some sank as soon as they left the landing craft and others sank on their way in. Only two reached the shore. Although warships shelled the German defences, the visibility was poor and the dust and smoke soon made it impossible to pinpoint targets. Bombers arrived but, worried about hitting their own troops, dropped their bombs behind, not on, the Germans. Landing craft carrying the cold, wet, sea-sick infantry hit the mined obstacles in the water and the soldiers who made it to

The petard, which fired the 'flying dustbins'.

Two of Major-General Hobart's 'funnies'—a petard to fire 'flying dustbins' followed by an armoured vehicle carrying a brushwood fascine. The bundle could be quickly released to fill a gap—such as a ditch—so that tanks and other tracked vehicles would be able to cross over easily.

the beach came under murderous fire from the Germans.

It was a different story on the Americans' other beach, Utah. The German coastal batteries didn't open fire (their radar had been jammed) and they had been bombed by RAF Lancasters during the night. Then three hundred American bombers arrived to continue the bombing and two battleships, two cruisers and some destroyers shelled the German strongpoints from the sea. The lee of the Cotentin peninsula sheltered the wind which was causing so much trouble further along the coast. Most of the DD tanks, launched four miles out, made it to the shore in time to support the first wave of infantry. Luck was with the Americans, for due to an error in navigation they landed a mile away from the beach where they were supposed to attack and in front of a less well defended sector. Engineers arrived to clear the mines and bulldozers shifted the obstacles on the beach. Men, tanks and vehicles poured through the gaps and by one o'clock they had linked with the paratroops who had landed during the night.

Because of the rough sea, the tide took some of the Canadians' landing craft several hundred yards through the heavily-mined obstacles in front of Juno beach but despite that the casualties were light. Although they were half an hour late, most of the Canadian infantry found that the AVREs hadn't arrived. But with bold determination and help from some DD tanks which were launched only 800 yards off-shore the Canadians managed to break the crust of the German defences. At one stretch of the beach there were no tanks, but the infantry only had to run the length of a football field from their landing craft to the cover of the sea-wall. Unfortunately there was a heavily-armed German strongpoint there and one company lost half its men in the short dash for the sea-wall. A flak-ship came to the rescue, almost running aground as it poured fire into the German defences. Despite all these difficulties the Canadians made remarkable progress and when night fell they were seven miles inland and had linked with the British 50th Division which had landed on Gold beach.

The waves were four feet high off Gold beach and it was decided not to launch the DD tanks but to land them directly behind the infantry. But the AVREs of Hobart's 79th Armoured Division were already ashore when the first infantry arrived. The Germans had ensured that their gun positions were extremely well protected by thick concrete walls against bombardment from the sea—but this meant that their guns couldn't fire out to sea. So the Germans had trained the guns on the section of the beach between the high-water mark and the sea-wall and they were confident that any infantry which tried to land there would be massacred before guns and tanks could be landed to support them. They hadn't reckoned on the infantry landing at half-tide *behind* the armoured 'funnies' which flailed their way through the minefields, smashing concrete obstacles and positions. Passages were cleared through the underwater obstacles and the exits off the beach so that more troops, guns and transport could be landed and moved through. By the end of the day the beachhead measured about six miles square.

The 2nd Battalion of the Lincolns—one of the two regular battalions—landed on Sword beach. The DD tanks and 'funnies' had already arrived as planned. Three exits off the beach were soon cleared and within two hours troops had moved a mile and a half inland. The 2nd Lincolns didn't lose a man during the landing. But the tide continued to come in much further than expected and the AVREs weren't able to demolish and shift all the underwater obstacles. Troops, guns and tanks continued to pour in on the cluttered beach. Soon it was impossible to move. It took hours to sort everyone out and further landings had to be stopped until the middle of the afternoon. This was unfortunate to say the least, for the men of the 3rd Division who landed on Sword beach faced the daunting tasks of not only linking with the airborne troops who were holding a bridgehead east of the River Orne but also of capturing Caen. To make matters worse, it was known that the 21st Panzer Division was in the Caen area. Speed, as Montgomery had been at pains to point out, was essential, but one of the brigades dug in as soon as they had

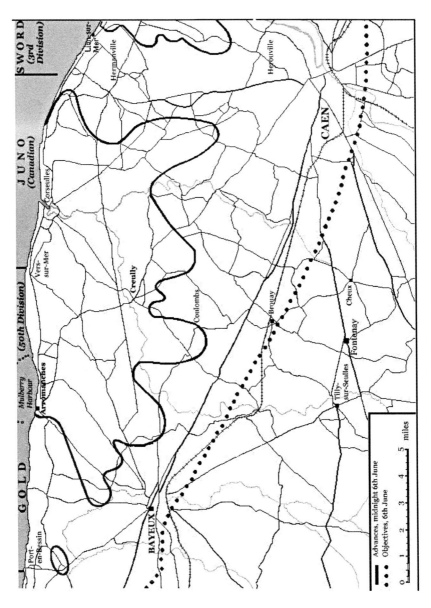

Map 5. The progress that had been made by the end of D-Day.

got through the German coastal defences. There were still some who hadn't grasped the concept of mobile warfare and whose minds continued to work at an infantryman's pace. Vital momentum was lost. Elsewhere, the three infantry battalions which were to thrust towards Caen were assembled and ready to go by eleven o'clock, but their supporting tanks and guns were still in the traffic jam on the beach. In the end they had to set off to see how far they could get without them.

The link was made with the airborne troops, but it was weeks before Caen finally fell. Although the Allies had not made the progress which had been hoped for on D-Day, their achievements in the face of the appalling weather conditions had been remarkable. In one respect the weather had helped them, for although the Germans were expecting the invasion to happen at any time they were caught unprepared, thinking it impossible for landings to be made in such atrocious conditions. When he had heard the weather report the previous day, Rommel went home to spend the day with his family.

The 49th Division—the 'Polar Bears'—was the 'follow-up' division to the 50th Division which had made the assault on Gold beach on D-Day and so it seems a little surprising that the Lincolns didn't embark from Newhaven in their landing crafts until shortly before midnight on Friday the 9th June, almost four days after D-Day. Indeed, Montgomery had hoped that the 7th Armoured Division—the famous Desert Rats—would be able to thrust aggressively to Villers-Bocage, a town almost twenty miles to the south, 'to knock about a bit' on D-Day before the Germans had time to react. The 4th Lincolns should have landed on D+1 when the carrier and mortar platoons were supposed to move quickly to Villers-Bocage to support the 7th Armoured Division. The plan had obviously gone awry, possibly because of the weather and the traffic jams on the beaches which had delayed the unloading of troops, ammunition and equipment.

The Lincolns were part of a huge convoy. When it began to get light the men started to realise just how immense an undertaking the invasion operation had been. Bombers and fighters constantly flew overhead and the nearer they got to France the more ships they saw. There were hundreds of vessels of all kinds—assault craft, tugs towing sections of the 'Mulberry' harbour, freight ships and warships. Battleships were firing shells at some target miles inland. There seemed to be hundreds of barrage balloons. At Gold beach the men gazed in awe at all the wreckage—landing craft, tanks, trucks, guns, all cluttered up with the remains of the German underwater obstacles. Knocked-out concrete gun emplacements were leaning to one side. The men gathered their equipment and cycles as the landing craft carrying Battalion headquarters with 'A' and 'B' companies somehow found a way through, bumping and shuddering its way over the sandbanks right up to the beach. A 'dry' landing! Lieutenant-Colonel Barclay congratulated the skipper, a young naval lieutenant. 'Yes, and now I've got to get the bloody thing off again', he grumbled in reply.

A 'dry' landing—except for one poor chap who has fallen in! Troops arriving in France, some with bicycles.

The 4th Lincolns set foot in France around midday on Saturday the 10th June, 1944. Marshalls and Military Police hurriedly directed them off the beach—'this way', 'up that track', 'follow those signs'—and the men were soon pedalling their way to their assembly area, passing troops and airmen and all kinds of vehicles. They came across more wreckage—ruins of buildings, burnt-out trucks and pieces of discarded equipment strewn about. One or two of the French people who gazed accusingly as they passed by seemed sullen. The Germans had brought a measure of prosperity to these Normans. Some of their daughters had married them, and now their villages and houses were being blown to pieces by the Allies. There was the sound of the odd shot and shells landing in the distance and many of the men nervously wondered what was in store for them all.

From their assembly area, a grass field with a few tents, the Lincolns cycled to Coulombs, about six or seven miles inland, to an area where the rest of the 49th

Division were assembling. It was pouring with rain and they all got soaked. They threw their bikes on a heap and never saw them again.

There was a problem straightaway—there was no sign of the battalion's advance party who should of course have landed earlier. In fact, the advance parties of the entire division hadn't arrived. Because of a cock-up somewhere they were still on a ship which had lain at anchor off the coast for two days waiting for permission to land. They finally joined the battalion the following day, Sunday.

The carriers and transport had travelled separately. One of the carriers slipped into the sea as it was being landed and all the gear of the men travelling in it was saturated when it went under. Private Davey had to borrow some PT shorts until he could get himself re-organised. The carrier was rescued and thanks to effective water-proofing was able to rejoin the rest. The carriers, the anti-tank platoon's guns and the vehicles eventually arrived at Coulombs, so that by the evening of Monday the 12th June the battalion was up to full strength.

It was during that night, the 12th/13th June, that the first V1 flying-bombs were launched. Hitler had actually given orders for the bombs to be launched immediately on the afternoon of D-Day as a shock reprisal, but most of them were dispersed in dumps all over northern France and Belgium and almost every railway line had been bombed by the RAF. There were over sixty launching sites, most of them in the Calais region, and they were ordered to fire a salvo so that they would all land in London at the same time, followed by another salvo every hour until dawn. But only seven of the sites were ready for action, the crews were inexperienced and the equipment was unreliable. The Germans managed to launch ten bombs and only one of these reached London. During the last fortnight of June however two thousand flying bombs were launched, not towards the south coast ports, crowded with troops, tanks and other equipment as Rommel had requested, but at London. As a result, the fastest fighters had to be kept in England and half the Allied bombing effort had to be diverted from supporting the troops in Normandy to bombing the launching sites.

Hitler still clung to the belief that if the Allied invasion failed and his secret weapons succeeded (the V2 rocket was next), then he could negotiate a separate peace in the West. Rommel and von Runstedt still believed that the Normandy landings were a feint, an attempt by the Allies to draw the German forces away from the heavily-defended Calais area before making a second landing—their main effort—there. And now that the flying-bombs were being launched from that region they thought that the Allies would certainly be motivated to make their second landing there very shortly. So the German troops in northern France stayed where they were. Churchill assured Eisenhower that the Allied strategy should not change on account of the flying-bombs. London would take it, as she had taken the blitz.

It was also on Monday the 12th June that the 22nd Armoured Brigade of the Desert Rats made their drive for Villers-Bocage. They entered the town the following morning. The leading tanks went a further half a mile the other side of the town whilst a company of infantry which was following in half-tracks halted along a tree-lined road and the men got out of the vehicles to have a smoke. Suddenly a German Mark VI (Tiger) tank appeared from nowhere. Tigers were the largest, most up-to-date and heavily-armed tanks in Normandy. They weighed seventy tons and carried the huge 88mm gun which could knock out a tank at a range of 2,000 yards. The Tiger came right down the line of British half-tracks and calmly knocked them out, one by one, and then took on a dozen tanks of the regimental HQ further behind and destroyed them too. Within a matter of minutes twenty-five British armoured vehicles were blazing furiously. The British tanks which had gone forward out of the town were now isolated and they too were knocked-out by early afternoon.

The Desert Rats were ordered to withdraw, for it was obvious that some of von Runstedt's mobile reserves had arrived. The 21st Panzer Division was still fully engaged in and around Caen, but to the west—towards Bayeux—Panzer Lehr and the 12th SS Panzer Division were now facing the Canadians and British. They were formidable opponents. Although 'Lehr' means 'training', this was not an outfit of recruits, but of the men who had been *doing* the training. It was the best equipped of all the panzer divisions in the German army but, ordered to move during daylight, had lost five tanks and almost a hundred half-tracks to Allied fighter-bombers before they even reached the front around Tilly-sur-Seulles. The troops of the 12th SS were fanatical brain-washed Nazis, the pick of the Hitler Youth.

Panzer divisions were designed to attack, but here they had been drawn into defence. Now that Rommel's armour was fully committed against the British in the Caen-Bayeux area it would be easier for the Americans to advance further west, and this had been Montgomery's plan all along.

On Tuesday the 13th June the 4th Lincolns, now up to strength, were ordered to relieve the 6th East Yorkshires who had landed on D-Day as part of the 50th Division. They moved to a sector of the front line about a mile and a half north-east of Tilly and started to dig slit trenches. During the campaign, the Lincolns were to learn that digging was a very important activity and that the most vital pieces of equipment after their rifles or Sten guns were their spades.

At a nearby farmhouse one of the officers bartered some paraffin for Camembert cheese and wine. They were in 'bocage' country—woods, orchards, and tough hedgerows on steep banks along winding, narrow lanes. There were strongly-made farmhouses and barns made of stone and where there were no hedges there were stone walls. The hedges were so thick and had such deep roots that even bulldozers and tanks couldn't shift them. This meant that the tanks couldn't move across the fields but were confined to the narrow lanes—so narrow that they were unable to turn round. This was extremely unfamiliar territory, particularly for the 7th Armoured Division which had been used to the wide open spaces of the desert. All this made the bocage ideal country for defenders.

Many of the men in the 4th Lincolns were about to go into action against the enemy for the first time and mixed with the feelings of nervousness were thoughts about how they would react when they came face to face with Germans who were intent on killing them. Would they be able to face the ordeal and resist the natural inclination to run away? Would they really be able to kill a German—another human being—in cold blood? Many stomachs churned at the thought, but even a split-second's hesitation in pulling the trigger might well be fatal.

The Lincolns had to leave their positions temporarily on the morning of the 14th June whilst the RAF bombed nearby Tilly, and when they returned they were on the receiving end of some shelling and mortar fire. This was their first experience of being fired on by nebelwerfers, the Germans' six-barrelled, electrically-operated mortars which fired 15-cm rockets. It was very frightening and the men pressed their bodies into their slit trenches. The nebelwerfer, or 'Moaning Minnie' (because of the dreadful noise it made), was the weapon the troops came to fear the most.

Tilly-sur-Seulles.

93

Staying above ground was certain death and for a time the men clung to the vicinity of their slit trenches, their ears open for the scream of an approaching shell. Gradually, they began to distinguish from the noise which shells were likely to fall nearby and those which weren't and they became less nervous, but for the rest of the campaign they would still subconsciously keep their ears open for the dreaded sound of an approaching shell.

The pioneer platoon made themselves busy laying mines and during the next few nights patrols were sent out to the tiny village of Les Hauts Vents and to the Parc de Boislande. Many of the men were involved in these patrols, which gave them some experience of the front line. It was an anxious, frightening business. Small groups of men were sent off in the dark, sometimes two or three miles into the enemy area, in an attempt to build-up a complete picture of where the Germans' positions were. The Lincolns had their first casualties, including one or two men who were killed.

The nights were of course very short in mid-June and the dusk 'stand-down' was around 11pm whilst the dawn 'stand-to' was shortly after 2am. This meant that no-one got much sleep. German snipers were also a bit of a nuisance and it wasn't easy to locate them. It wasn't a good idea to fire at them as it revealed your position and then down would come the mortars. The men soon learned to keep their heads down. Even so, the Lincolns' position came under fire from shells and mortars but it was nothing compared with the battering which the Germans at Tilly were receiving from the Royal Artillery, and from Royal Navy warships lying off the coast.

On the morning of Thursday the 15th June, the Lincolns were ordered to reconnoitre the village of St Pierre, about a mile to the north-east of Tilly, to find out if there were any Germans there. If there weren't, the village was to be occupied. This was the Lincolns' first action in France, they were nervous and it didn't turn out very well. 'A' Company under Captain Flint, with one section of mortars under Sergeant Stan Masters, were sent with the carrier platoon and they

Captain John Flint (later Major, DSO MC)

94

arrived at the village at half-past eleven. Lieutenant Morley, who was leading one section of carriers, found that the main street was blocked by a British tank which had been knocked out, took a wrong turn and drove almost as far as Tilly along a road which was covered by German anti-tank guns and infantry. The leading carrier was hit, killing the driver, and Lieutenant Morley was taken prisoner. The following carrier—on a bridge—saw what had happened, reversed quickly, went out of control and crashed through the stone parapet into the river. Luckily, the crew survived. The rest of the carriers moved back but they came under accurate mortar fire which caused more casualties and knocked out five more carriers. The other carrier section, led by Captain Dick Newsum, had found the right road but came under fire from some German tanks in a wood about half a mile away. A shell exploded immediately above Captain Newsum's carrier, killing the driver and wounding the platoon sergeant. Leaping on the back of the artillery's Forward Observation Officer's carrier, Captain Newsum yelled at the other carriers to get out.

Meanwhile, 'A' Company had reached St Pierre and were digging-in when Captain Flint heard over the radio that the carrier platoon was in trouble. Shortly afterwards battalion headquarters ordered him to withdraw under cover of a smoke screen directed by the Forward Observation Officer of the 69th Field Regiment.

By this time, some of the men from the carriers had reached 'A' Company. Sergeant Beddard and Corporal Britton felt fairly sure that some of the carriers which had been abandoned when the men had taken cover hadn't been hit and were probably still in running order. It was decided to have a shot at getting them out.

Calling-up support from the 69th Field Regiment's 25-pounders, two platoons moved down the road, Lieutenant Ron Golding's 7 Platoon on the right and Lieutenant Philip Fowler's 8 Platoon on the left whilst Lieutenant 'Tubby' Walker's 9 Platoon stayed behind to hold the fort. 8 Platoon was just forming up to move forward when one or two mortar bombs hit the area, killing Private Wright—'A' Company's first casualty. Under a smoke screen, the two platoons made their way along a hedge and then it was only necessary to nip across a small field to another hedge to get within fifty yards of the carriers which were out in the open. Sergeant Hutchinson and Corporal Britton each ran to two of them under fire, started them up and drove them back like bats out of hell, chased up the road by German mortar bombs. Private Fish, who had only joined the Lincolns a few days before leaving England, said he could drive and volunteered to get the next carrier out. He sprinted out under German fire, covered by fire from 'A' Company's platoons. Unfortunately, Private Fish had selected one which wouldn't start and he had to sprint even faster all the way back again.

'A' Company began to make their way back, with the Germans in a very bad temper. Private Bayes was badly wounded and had to be left, but he was found by another regiment which went in the following day and was soon recuperating in a hospital in England. Altogether ten men had been killed in the Lincolns' first action with the Germans, including Sergeant Fred 'Tiny' Peacock who had only been married for a few weeks. Fred was a huge man who took (as he used to say) a 'tight twelve' in boots; he was from the St Giles area of Lincoln as were several of the others who had been killed.

Fred's brother, Ted, was in the mortar platoon and was anxiously looking for him as the men came back. He kept going up to those who had returned asking: 'Has anyone seen our Tiny? Have you seen our Tiny? Can you tell me what's happened to Tiny?'

After a while Ted sought out Private Jack Hardy, also from St Giles, and said quietly: 'Our Tiny isn't coming back, you know.'

'I know, Ted,' Jack said quietly. 'I'm really very sorry, lad.' There wasn't much more he could say. The deaths, so soon after landing in Normandy, had shaken many of the men. These had been their friends, even before joining the Territorials, and it was difficult—impossible—to believe that they were now dead. Apart from the sorrow at losing a friend, it also brought home to the men the grim realisation—perhaps not fully appreciated before—that they really were facing very great danger and that there would be more deaths to come.

The Lincolns had also lost almost all of their carriers in the skirmish and Captain Newsum later had to take a party to the beach to collect replacements. Dick Newsum, who was married earlier in the year, lived opposite St Peter-in-Eastgate church in Lincoln and before the war had worked in the family's well-known joinery business both at Gainsborough and on Carholme Road, near Lincoln race course. His near neighbour, Sergeant Beddard, who lived at the 'Morning Star' pub in Greetwell-gate (his wife, Joyce, was the daughter of the landlord, John Smith) was killed in action a fortnight later. Sergeant Hutchinson lived in Portland Street in Lincoln and had joined the Territorials in 1938 aged seventeen, Corporal Britton was from Luddington and Private Fish was from Leeds.

The Hallamshires had taken the village of Audrieu the previous day and the KOYLI took Cristot, a couple of miles to the north-east of St Pierre, on the 16th June. The KOYLIs were given massive support. Cristot had already been bombed and shelled for two days and the KOYLIs moved through the cornfields with the tanks of the 24th Lancers and the guns of the 55th Anti-tank Regiment. There was an immense bombardment from the artillery and from Royal Navy warships, whilst RAF fighter-bombers flew overhead. Despite this, the KOYLIs were heavily mortared when they approached the village.

Later on the same day, 'B' Company of the Lincolns under Major Pattin occupied and held the hamlet of Les Hauts Vents. The hamlet wasn't important in itself—it was no more than just a few houses—but the position was wanted as a base. A patrol sent out by 'B' Company came under heavy mortar fire and Lieutenant Gaunt, the second-in-command of the anti-tank platoon, was killed. He had enlisted as a private at Horncastle in April 1939 and although he'd not been detailed he'd volunteered to go with the patrol. Private Baker, also from Horncastle, was wounded and died a day or two later. Lieutenant Francis, from Langrick, was wounded and Private Arthur Wink was killed. Lieutenant 'Tubby' Walker was taken prisoner a few days later when out on patrol.

On Saturday the 17th June, the 6th Duke of Wellingtons of 147 Brigade attacked Le Parc de Boislande, a formal park and woodland surrounding a chateau half-way between Cristot and Fontenay le Pesnel. The Hitler Youth SS were well dug-in and hid until the British tanks had passed, opening fire on the following infantry at short range. The Dukes finally managed to clear the wood but had many casualties. Worse was to come. The following day the Germans shelled the woods heavily and in the face of a ferocious counter-attack with infantry and tanks there were more casualties. Many of the badly shaken Dukes withdrew and reached their sister-regiment, the 7th Duke of Wellingtons, who were waiting to advance beyond the Parc de Boislande towards the village of Fontenay. The 7th Dukes were honour-bound to restore the position and their counter-attack on the 12th SS was successful.

The battalions of the 49th Division were gradually being introduced to battle in turn and it was obvious that although the men were well-trained they were raw. The troops facing them, the 12th SS (Hitler Youth) Division, were not only highly-trained and experienced but fanatical Nazis. The 6th Dukes had 230 casualties over the two days in Le Parc de Boislande, including all of their company commanders—a severe blow to a close Territorial Army battalion. Only forty per cent of their officers were left. The heart was taken out of them and their morale sank even further when their Commanding Officer was sent back to England. They went into action one more time. Everything went wrong. The newly-arrived second-in-command was killed and twelve hours later his replacement ran over a mine and was seriously wounded. The unlucky 6th Duke of Wellingtons were withdrawn into reserve and by the beginning of August had returned to England and been disbanded, the men later providing reinforcements for their 7th Battalion.

Meanwhile, there had been another casualty. Andrew Dunlop, the brilliant young Brigadier of 146 Brigade—who had a fine war record and had won a DSO in the desert—had been looking pale and strained and on 19th June he had to be sent home because he'd had a nervous breakdown. The CO of the KOYLIs, Lt-Colonel 'Johnny' Walker, took over command of the brigade.

There was more bad news. The weather had been kind to the British at Dunkirk but it now seemed to favour Hitler. It had been bad enough on D-Day, but an unforecasted storm of almost unprecedented fury for the time of year suddenly sprang up from nowhere. The furious storm, the worst in June for forty years, went on for three days. Supply convoys in the Channel had to turn back, ships and other craft were dashed ashore off the beaches and two and a half miles of roadway for the Mulberry harbours which were being towed across the Channel were lost. Worse still, the Mulberry harbours, still under construction, were badly damaged—so much so that work on the one in the American sector had to be abandoned altogether. By the time the storm ended there were eight hundred craft of various kinds on the beaches, stranded until the spring tides in July could float them off. Half of the valuable tank landing craft had been damaged or beached. There was five times the damage to shipping than the Germans had caused on D-Day.

It was very serious. Stores, transport and reinforcements couldn't be landed. The stocks of ammunition were dangerously low. The arrival of Lieutenant-General O'Connor's much-needed VIII Corps was delayed; half of the men were on board ships in the Channel and had to stay there until the weather had cleared. Because of the low cloud, activity in the air was severely limited, although a few supplies were flown in. For a time it seemed that the very existence of the Allied forces in Normandy was in great danger. Attacks which had been planned were now out of the question, and the lull not only gave the Germans a breathing space but the opportunity to gather a formidable force. The 1st SS Division, on its way from Belgium, passed through Paris, the 2nd SS reached St Lo and the 9th and 10th SS which had been withdrawn from the Russian front had reached France. But they were having to make long—and very slow—journeys by road because the RAF and USAAF had smashed all the railway lines.

Rommel still had the 12th SS (Hitler Youth) and Panzer Lehr Divisions in the area however. Although somewhat battered by now, they fought with a fanatical determination and it was clear that a major operation would be needed to shift them. Not only that, it was essential for Montgomery's plan for the German armour to be drawn into battle on the front of the British 2nd Army around Caen so that the Americans, further west, could more easily take the offensive.

Time was short. Montgomery decided to launch an attack, code-named 'Epsom'. VIII Corps, which had now arrived, would make the main attack between Tilly and Caen on the 26th June. The 15th Scottish Division, followed by the 43rd Division would establish a bridgehead across the River Odon and the 11th Armoured Division would cross the River Orne and take the Caen-Falaise road. To protect the right flank of the 15th Scottish, the 49th (Polar Bear) Division would have to capture the commanding ridges around Rauray the previous day.

The 49th Division, supported by the Sherman tanks of the 8th Armoured Brigade, was to attack early on Sunday the 25th June to allow VIII Corps to pass through and approach Caen from the south-west. Major-General Barker's plan was to attack on a two-brigade front—146 Brigade on the right and 147 Brigade on the left—supported by the Shermans and a massive barrage from over 250 guns of the artillery and the Royal Navy.

The 4th Lincolns were on the extreme right of the three infantry battalions which were mounting the attack. They had the Hallamshires to their left, who in turn had the 11th Royal Scots Fusiliers from 147 Brigade on their left. The attack was to be in three phases. Firstly the Juvigny-Fontenay road would have to be captured. Once this had been done the KOYLI would move through to capture Tessel Wood, followed finally by the Hallamshires who would go forward to take up a position to the south of the wood. The Lincolns would be attacking Bas de Fontenay, on the western outskirts of Fontenay village.

Because of the storm the operation had to be postponed four times, but good advantage was taken of the time and briefing was extremely thorough. Everyone was completely in the picture, not only about the role of the battalion in its first major action but also what he was individually expected to do. Careful and thorough recces were carried out, there were numerous aerial photographs available and an accurate sand model of Fontenay was made and studied. The battalion rehearsed forming up for a night attack. Lieutenant-Colonel Barclay's policy of vigorous patrolling certainly paid dividends, for a lot of useful information was obtained, particularly after the Tilly-Fontenay road had been crossed several times. From this it appeared that Bas de Fontenay was held by a depleted German battalion, and aerial photographs confirmed this.

The Germans showed signs of being jittery. On one night they sent up white flares and there was considerable small arms fire; sometimes there were red and green flares, followed by mortar fire. Meanwhile, the RAF were now active again and bombed targets west of Fontenay which the artillery had indicated for them by red smoke.

The 50th Division had fought their way into Tilly a few days earlier but there was a gap of over a mile between the village and the exposed right flank of the Lincolns. It was likely that the Germans would counter-attack at this point. As the Lincolns were themselves the right flank of the whole of the 49th Division, it was vitally important for the success of the entire operation for them to capture their objective—the main road between Juvigny and Fontenay on a frontage of 700 yards at the western outskirts of the village—and then hold on

Map 6. The area of the attack at Fontenay.

99

at all costs.

During Saturday the 24th June the 4th Lincolns were told to get as much rest as possible before the attack, due to take place in the early hours of the following morning. Shortly before midnight, the Intelligence Officer, Lieutenant Den Cooke, left with his men to tape the start line. It was fine, but very dark. The battalion started to form up. A squadron of tanks from the 24th Lancers rumbled forward, the noise drowned by crashes from the artillery. The difficult move in the dark went perfectly and by 0315 hours everyone had taken up their positions on the start line. The assault was to be made by 'D' Company under Major Barlow-Poole on the right with 'A' Company under Captain Flint on the left. 'C' Company under Major Jack Staniland and the Shermans of 'A' Squadron of the 24th Lancers were responsible for protecting the open right flank, whilst 'B' Company under Major Pattin was in reserve. 'A' and 'D' Companies each had an assault section of pioneers and both they and 'C' Company had a section of 3-inch mortars. The Lincolns were also supported by the 25-pounders of the 69th Field Regiment, a troop of anti-tank 17-pounders , a troop of self-propelled anti-tank guns, a section from the 294th Field Company of Royal Engineers, heavy (4.2-inch) mortars and machine-guns from the 2nd Kensingtons and a section from the 146th Field Ambulance.

The thorough preparations had made the men confident. They knew what they had to do and they knew about the support which they would get from the tanks and the artillery. Yet now that they were actually lined up on the start line, waiting and (despite the ration of rum which had been issued to fortify them) everyone felt scared for they realised that however well things turned out some of them would soon be dead. Perhaps the waiting was the worst part for some. Zero hour ('H-Hour') came at last. It was almost dawn and visibility was about two hundred yards. There was a devastating crash as the combined guns of eight Field Regiments, four Medium Regiments and the big guns of the Royal Navy opened fire, and the Lincolns moved forward. With over 250 guns there was one gun for slightly less than ten yards of the division's frontage—more concentrated than even the famous barrage put down at El Alamein. The sky was ablaze and the deafening noise stunned the ears.

It was a 'creeping' barrage. The guns fired five hundred yards in front of the start line for twelve minutes, and then lifted one hundred yards every four minutes. Enemy positions which had been located beforehand were shelled and smoke was also arranged to screen the high ground to the south and west. The Kensingtons had the task of mortaring an orchard for the first twenty minutes and then the village of Juvigny from H + 30 to H + 60.

The distance from the start line to the objective, the Juvigny-Fontenay road, was just short of a mile. The first 1000 yards were down a gentle slope through fields of wheat which were just coming into ear, but the rest was more difficult—bocage country of orchards and woods, thick hedges and several stone farmhouses and outbuildings. A stream which ran across the frontage, just short of the objective, would probably be no problem for the infantry, but crossing places would have to be found for the bren gun carriers and anti-tank guns.

To begin with all went reasonably well, but then the unexpected happened. There was an early morning mist lying at the bottom of the slope and this quickly became heavily laden with the smoke from the intense barrage. The Lincolns found that the fog became thicker with every step they took until finally visibility was down to only two feet and they couldn't see the man in front of them. The commander of a Sherman tank said later that he couldn't see the end of his gun. Platoon commanders had to take compass bearings. To make matters worse no-one could hear shouted orders because of the din from the barrage. Platoons began to lose touch with each other. One platoon in 'A' Company, advancing too quickly, had to turn to the right to avoid our own barrage, got lost, and eventually ended up with 'C' Company.

Although it was a wonder that any Germans had survived the barrage there was some mortar fire and a little shelling and Spandau fire seemed to come from all directions at waist height, ripping off the cornheads. It was very frightening. The Germans couldn't possibly have seen what they were firing at. This was literally 'the fog of war'!

'D' Company came up against a party of Germans in the thick hedges and woods of the bocage. Bearing in mind the CO's orders that the assault companies were to push on at all speed to their objectives 'without being distracted by attractive side-shows', the men of 'D' company were in no mood to let the Germans stand in their way. There was some fierce and determined hand-to-hand fighting through the thick hedges and woods for a brief spell (Lieutenant Stainton personally accounting for several Germans) before 'D' Company pressed on. There was a little delay because of the fog and the smoke but they managed to penetrate the German lines by skillful compass readings and they reached their objective before the enemy realised it, without any losses.

Meanwhile, 'A' Company had also moved forward. Buildings loomed up out of the mist and a platoon was dropped off to deal with any Germans still in them. They found several who were dead and took six bewildered prisoners, a half-track and a motor bike and sidecar. Two of 'A' Company's platoons reached their objective before daylight and now that they had joined 'D' Company the code word denoting that the Juvigny-Fontenay road had been reached by both assault companies was transmitted. The message reached battalion headquarters, but then there was silence. There had been problems with communication throughout the action, and it was later found that 'A' Company's wireless set had been destroyed by a mortar bomb, whilst the thick woods had 'screened' 'D' Company's set.

This posed a problem for the Commanding Officer as he could neither see nor hear anything and wasn't sure whether to call up 'B' Company, the reserve company who were to mop up and then plug the gap slightly to the rear of the assault companies. Advanced battalion headquarters went forward so that the CO could assess the situation. When they reached the road he decided to move 'B' Company forward on the left through 'A' Company, which had become split up and had had a few casualties.

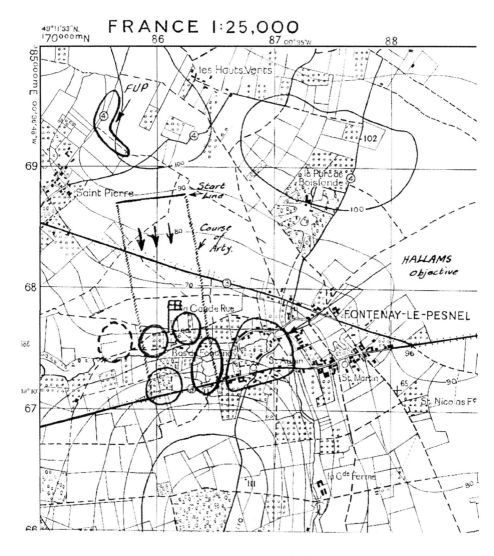

Map 7.   The plan of attack.

Lieutenant-Colonel Barclay, with the bright red scarf he always wore, heavy walking stick and map board, returned to join 'B' Company and inspired them with his determination as they went forward in an extended line, mopping-up Germans from slit trenches and hedge bottoms. Some didn't wait to be mopped-up—one even shouted 'Oi!' to attract Major Pattin's attention and timidly came out of a wood with his hands up, followed by three others. Here and there parties of Germans loomed out of the fog and when the men of 'B' Company were challenged with the word 'Halt!' they just fired and wiped many of them out. Suddenly, out of the mist, a German Mark IV tank appeared and the CO quickly summoned a Sherman and directed its fire onto it. Clearing houses, gardens and orchards on their way, 'B' Company finally reached the road, and after they had found that 'A' and 'D' companies were consolidating their positions, they were sent back a little way to dig in as the enemy would most probably launch a counter-attack.

Meanwhile, 'C' Company and the Shermans on the extreme right were protecting the open flank, and they too took prisoners who said that many of their comrades had left—as they themselves would have done if they hadn't got lost in the fog. 'C' Company's 14 Platoon dug in whilst Major Staniland led 15 Platoon to their second objective a little to the left. Captain Andrews, the Forward Observation Officer of the 69th Field Regiment, directed artillery fire towards the enemy on the opposite slope. They saw two German tanks withdraw towards Juvigny and the 88mm guns of three Tiger tanks kept nosing out of a wood throughout the afternoon but they soon withdrew under shellfire from the artillery and the Shermans of the 24th Lancers who joined in.

Back on the Juvigny-Fontenay road, the artillery barrage had ended, the visibility was improving and everything was very quiet. 'D' Company sent out small patrols, and one led by Major Barlow-Poole came across an armoured enemy half-track. A German jumped out and was taken prisoner and a grenade which was swiftly thrown inside immediately brewed it up. Then six more half-tracks appeared, trying to break out along a narrow lane. Private Sneesby thought quickly and realised that only he could prevent their escape. Although under fire at point blank range, he ran up to the leading vehicle and threw a grenade in the driver's compartment. He was wounded in his thigh and back by automatic-rifle fire from the following half-track, but despite this he whipped-out another grenade and threw it into the rear of the vehicle, killing and wounding the occupants. He then brewed-up the engine with another grenade and blocked the exit for the following vehicles. Private Sneesby then turned his attention to the second half-track. The Germans were so scared by what they'd just seen that they surrendered. Although the other four half-tracks managed to get away they were later found abandoned and were promptly used to evacuate casualties. Private Sneesby accounted for the death or capture of ten Germans and was entirely responsible for preventing the escape of the six half-tracks and their thirty occupants and he later received the

Distinguished Conduct Medal. Later, 'D' Company came across a house with a white flag flying outside, and captured twenty-five stunned Germans from the Panzer Lehr Division who were hiding in a small room. Some men from the 11th Royal Scots Fusiliers who had become lost in the fog arrived in 'D' Company's position, having apparently stumbled all the way through the Hallams (on the Lincoln's left) without coming across anyone.

The job of the Captain Dick Newsum's carrier platoon had been to ferry ammunition up to the rifle companies after a make-shift bridge had been put over the stream. The mist had cleared but the carriers couldn't be seen by the Germans as they were parked behind a high hedge. Just then an ambulance arrived and parked in a gap in the hedge. Although Captain Newsum yelled at the driver to move, it was too late and they were heavily mortared. Dick Newsum was wounded in the leg. 'You need me now, sir, don't you?' the ambulance driver said, rather sardonically. Captain Newsum's exact reply was not recorded, but it was to the point and expressed in rather strong language. Less than a day later he was in hospital in England.

The visibility was improving all the time and now that the Lincolns had reached their objective they were hastily digging-in, preparing for the inevitable German counter-attack. The Engineers and Pioneer platoon feverishly prepared crossing places over the stream so that the vitally important anti-tank guns could come forward. Signallers were busy laying lines out to companies and the men of Lieutenant Cooke's Intelligence section were carefully searching German prisoners as they were brought in. The Medical Officer, Captain MacKay, had set up his Regimental Aid Post in some farm stables and was coolly dealing with a steady flow of casualties, both British and German.

The Lincolns were able to get on with the urgent job of digging-in without too much trouble, but around half-past eleven the Germans opened up with heavy and accurate shell fire from 88mm guns and mortars, particularly on 'C' Company's position. Then they began to fire airburst shells which exploded about thirty feet above the ground, scattering the whole area with shrapnel. These caused more casualties, both killed and wounded, than had been sustained during the attack. Things got much too close for comfort and the headquarters and forward platoon of 'C' Company had to move elsewhere. It was hotting up everywhere now, the German shelling both intense and frequent. They had set up observation posts along the upward slope ahead and had a fine view of the Lincolns' positions. The Germans seemed ready to strike, but the Lincolns received magnificent support from the gunners of the 69th Field Regiment. Directed by their Forward Observation Officers, they hit back furiously and the counter-attack never came. Each gun of the 69th Field Regiment fired several hundreds of rounds that day.

In an orchard, the mortar platoon were getting their mortars into position. Circular pits, two or three feet deep, had to be dug and the mortar placed in the centre. Suddenly all hell broke loose. Shells and mortar bombs fell all around them and the men dived into the pits for cover. It was the most intensive barrage of mortar and artillery fire which the men would experience in the whole campaign. A mortar bomb landed in the pit which Fred Illing was in. Driver Tomblin took the full force of the bomb and was killed, but his body shielded Fred and the rest of the men and they were unhurt. Captain Waters and Sergeant Huddlestone were on the outside of the pit shouting something or other, but then another mortar bomb burst where they were standing and they were blown to bits. Rubble and stones trickled into the mortar pit, followed by Captain Waters' spectacles, still intact. Arthur Turner, the ornamental plasterer from Bradford and now a sergeant, took charge and yelled orders to get out of the orchard fast, as they had obviously been spotted and were sitting ducks. He then tried to reorganise the platoon into a unit capable of fighting again. But seven men in the mortar platoon had been killed and these included the Platoon Commander and four NCOs. Two other NCOs were amongst the further five who were wounded, so the loss to the platoon was devastating. Although Lieutenant Paulger of 'B' Company was the reserve mortar platoon commander, Sergeant Turner was asked a week later if he would agree to being immediately commissioned in the field to take charge of the platoon. He asked if he could think about it overnight and when the men in the platoon urged him to accept (perhaps on the grounds of 'better the devil you know...' thought Sergeant Turner), he agreed. But first, he had to be interviewed by the Brigadier and then, the following day, by Major-General Barker himself. Major Don Stokes went with him and was very supportive and helpful, briefing him on the sort of questions which he would probably be asked. Arthur became a Second Lieutenant and five months later he was a Captain.

And so the Lincolns succeeded in reaching their objective in their first major action. In managing to achieve their objective and consolidate their position they established a firm base for the 49th Division. There had been many acts of quiet bravery in the fog, the dust, the noise and the confusion of the battle. A German who had pointed a pistol at Private Dodson, an unarmed stretcher-bearer from Boston, was taken prisoner by him and later, whilst under fire, he carried a wounded man half a mile to safety. He was awarded the Military Medal, but sadly lost his life at sea when on his way home to England a few weeks later.

But perhaps most important of all was that the battalion as a whole had shown a determined fighting spirit. And most of them had survived. The men were relieved that they had come through the ordeal, had been tested in battle and had upheld the best traditions of the Lincolnshire Regiment. They were proud when they received Major-General Barker's praise: 'The Battle of Fontenay was the Fourth Lincolns' battle.' Sadly, fourteen men had lost their lives, including Captain Sparks, the second-in-command of 'D' Company. Some of the sixty-four men who had been wounded died later. One or two men had lost their nerve and were extremely ill with 'battle exhaustion'—shaking all over and, in one case, unable to speak. The only thing to do was to get them away before too many of the others saw them.

The mortar platoon.

Although he hadn't been wounded, Corporal Sid Hall from Horncastle had to be admitted to a Canadian hospital because he'd been deafened whilst furiously firing his 3-inch mortar. Ironically, he *was* wounded by shrapnel later when a German plane bombed the hospital. He was sent back to England and, bearing in mind Monty's promise, thought that he would be getting off when the hospital train carrying the wounded arrived at Lincoln, where there was a military hospital. Sid gathered his things together but the train didn't stop. It passed straight through Lincoln station and he ended up in a hospital in Aberdeen.

At around mid-day, the KOYLIs passed through the Lincolns' positions with the object of taking Tessel Wood about a mile away, up a gentle slope of cornfields. The artillery put down a barrage as they advanced and, supported by the Shermans of the 24th Lancers and guns from the 55th Anti-tank Regiment, they managed to beat off a counter-attack when they reached the wood.

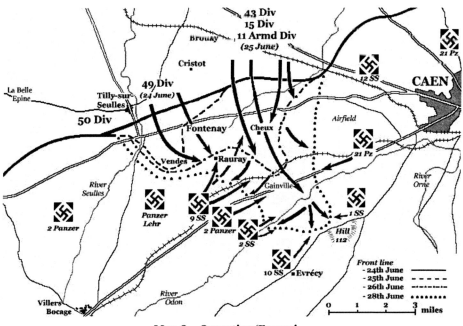

Map 8. Operation 'Epsom'.

Meanwhile, the 11th Royal Scots Fusiliers of 147 Brigade were having problems in their difficult job of clearing the enemy out of the village of Fontenay. Many of their men had got lost in the fog and those who were left were coming up against the Hitler Youth, which had quickly been reinforced by two companies of 21 Panzer. The Germans had fortified some of the houses and there was hand-to-hand fighting in the streets. The hold-up delayed the 7th Duke of Wellingtons who were due to pass through the Royal Scots and advance towards Rauray. In the end, the 7th Dukes, two troops of the 55th Anti-tank Regiment, five platoons of the 2nd Kensingtons, a squadron of the Sherwood Rangers and the 'funnies' of the 82nd Assault Squadron of the Royal Engineers (which hurled 'flying dustbins' at houses which contained Spandaus) had to help to clear Fontenay and it was 11.00 pm before the village was finally taken. Even then, a determined detachment of Hitler Youth still held on in the eastern part of Fontenay and in a wood just outside the village. It had been a very frightening and exhausting day for all the British troops.

Operation Epsom started as planned the following morning, Monday the 26th June, but because the high ground around Rauray had not yet been taken, the right flank of the attacking 15th Scottish Division was unprotected and the Germans were able to pour mortar bombs, shells and machine-gun fire into the advancing Scots. There was no support for them from the RAF either as it had started to rain heavily during the night and the bombers had been grounded by the bad weather.

The Polar Bears of the 49th Division renewed their attacks on the area around Rauray. The 12th King's Royal Rifle Corps and the 24th Lancers attacked towards the village of Tessel-Bretteville but had to pull back in the face of heavy resistance, the 1st Tyneside Scottish and the tanks of the Dragoon Guards found themselves trapped in the bocage and the 7th Dukes and the Sherwood Rangers, moving forward from Fontenay, found the Germans waiting for them and had to withdraw. All three attacks had failed. In the afternoon the 7th Dukes, led by the Sherwood Rangers and supported by the artillery, tried again and this time managed to get to within 1000 yards of Rauray. But it was 9.00 pm before the 11th Durham Light Infantry passed through them and reached the outskirts of the village. The Germans had dug-in very deeply. The DLI and the tanks advanced into Rauray the following morning, but the Shermans were no match for the Germans' huge Tiger tanks. The armour at the front of these fearsome tanks was seven inches thick. Armour-piercing shells simply bounced off them even at very short range and unless a shot managed to hit the weak spot just below the turret-ring the only way of putting Tigers out of action was to try to get a shot at the sides where the armour wasn't quite so thick. A whole troop of Shermans was put out of action and the 11th DLI finally had to take Rauray with fixed bayonets. A little further to the west the Hallams marched by night through the KOYLI to get within 300 yards of Vendes.

The 4th Lincolns were now holding a position around La Grande Ferme, a large stone farmhouse half-way between Fontenay and Tessel-Bretteville. To their left, the 1st Tyneside Scottish were ordered to advance to Tessel-Bretteville and then to the small wooded village of Bretteville, about half a mile south-west of Rauray. They took their first objective but then met very strong opposition. Their casualties were heavy and 'D' Company of the Lincolns were placed under their command to protect their right flank as they fell back. The following day the Lincolns moved to Tessel-Bretteville to take over the positions of the Tyneside Scottish. They were not sorry to move, as the Germans had located their battalion headquarters and it was being shelled quite heavily. By this time eighteen of the Lincolns' twenty-eight sergeants had either been killed or wounded.

Advancing through a cornfield.

Tessel-Bretteville had been a pleasant village in orchard country with a number of attractive stone buildings, but it had now been wrecked by shell fire. The rain continued (at times it was torrential) but at least the wet damped down the appalling stench of the dead cattle and horses—and dead Germans who had not been buried. In Fontenay, a dead German was splattered all over the road, tanks and trucks driving over the flattened remains.

By Thursday the 30th June, VIII Corps, which was making the main attack in Operation Epsom, had sustained 4,000 casualties and was struggling to make progress. Although the 11th Armoured Division had crossed the River Odon and established a bridgehead there were fears that they might be cut off. The British troops had expected hard fighting, but the well-led, well-trained and experienced Germans were resisting with ferocious determination. Furthermore, their reinforcements were now arriving. The Tyneside Scottish had come up against the 2nd SS Division at Bretteville, the 1st SS Panzer Division had also arrived and the 10th Panzer Division was near at hand.

Following a Churchill tank.

Rommel had gathered these Panzer divisions together to blast a way through Bayeux to the Mulberry harbour at Avranches. He aimed to split the British from the Americans and destroy the supply line of both forces. Montgomery's attack—which had been made only just in time—had resulted in the Panzer divisions being drawn into a defensive battle instead.

Seven of the eight Panzer divisions then in Normandy were trying to halt the British. The real worth of Operation Epsom was not so much the ground which had been gained as the frustration of Rommel's plan to drive a wedge between the Allies—and the weakening of his Panzer divisions by both the RAF and by intense and accurate shelling from the artillery and the warships lying off the coast.

Tragedy struck the 4th Lincolns during the night of 30th June/1st July. Two sentries were on watch in the front line and had orders to shoot anything that moved the other side of a track a few yards ahead. Whether or not they issued a challenge or whether it was because of their inexperience and nervousness cannot now be known, but they shot dead Major Jack Staniland, the Officer Commanding 'C' Company, who was doing the rounds of forward positions. Some reckoned later that Major Staniland had forgotten the password 'Mix' to the challenge 'Tom'. Others said that with the best of intentions he used to creep up to sentries to see if he could surprise them (to stress the danger and importance of their job). Major Staniland, a small, friendly, kindly man, much respected by the troops ('he was like a father to us') had been a Territorial officer for many years and was in command of 'D' Company when the war started. He was greatly missed. The sentries were exonerated from any blame by the CO who said that it had been a very unfortunate accident and that they had only been doing their duty.

Sherman tanks approach Rauray.

The Germans launched an attack just before 7.00 am on the 1st July in an effort to cut off the bridgehead over the River Odon. After a period of intense mortar and shellfire, the Germans attacked under cover of a smokescreen between the 4th Lincolns and the 11th Durham Light Infantry and particularly the Tyneside Scottish who were to the left of the 11th DLI. It was a strong attack by infantry of the newly-arrived 2nd SS with over seventy tanks (mostly Panthers) of the 9th SS.

'B' Company (Major Pattin) bore the brunt of the attack on the sector held by the Lincolns. 'Steady boys, keep steady. Hold your fire' yelled Sergeant Baggley, who came from Fulbeck Heath, near Grantham. Then, as the Germans were almost upon them, Sergeant Baggley yelled 'Fire', and his section opened up with Brens and a Piat mortar, normally an anti-tank weapon. The Germans fell under the bullets of the Brens. A bomb from the Piat hit a tree and exploded, and it had the same effect as an air-burst shell, the shrapnel killing and wounding several Germans in one go. Some of 'B' Company's positions were overrun by the Germans but they were successfully counter-attacked by 'C' Company. The Germans who were following behind were now being heavily shelled and mortared. 'A' Company of the 7th Duke of Wellington's were brought forward and came under command of the Lincolns to strengthen their left flank. The Germans made further attempts throughout the morning and early afternoon to infiltrate the British positions. The fighting was particularly heavy in the sector held by the Tyneside Scottish, who had over a hundred men killed and a further three hundred wounded and missing. Because of the weather the RAF was unable to fly, but the artillery and the naval guns fully made up for their absence. The Germans couldn't get through the devastating screen of fire which was being flung at them. 'Crocodile' flame-throwing tanks were used for the first time to clear enemy machine-gunners and snipers from the hedgerows where they were hiding. Tanks of the Sherwood Rangers and 24th Lancers and the anti-tank guns of the 55th Anti-tank Regiment (the Suffolk Yeomanry) came into action and knocked out almost forty German tanks, mostly Panthers. The German attacks became weaker during the afternoon and by 6 o'clock in the evening the battle was over. The troops of the 49th Division had held firm, were still in their original positions and had given the Germans a bloody nose. Sadly, thirteen men from the 4th Lincolns were killed, eight more lost their lives the following day and a further four died of their wounds.

The German losses were in fact very heavy. They were stunned. Whilst Lord Haw Haw on the German radio coined the phrase 'The Polar Bear Butchers' (which subsequently inspired the 49th Division's Christmas card), von Runstedt now realised that the war was lost. Speaking to him on the phone that evening from Hitler's headquarters, Field Marshall Keitel cried in desperation: 'Whatever can we do, what can we do?'

'Make peace you fools' replied von Runstedt. He was immediately replaced by Field Marshall von Kluge and went back into retirement.

*   *   *

The Polar Bears stayed more or less where they were for the next few weeks. An officer of the Tyneside Scottish, wounded in the battle on the 1st July, crawled into the Lincolns' sector, having been in no-man's land for two days. Patrols were sent out into no-man's land (the CO of the 4th Lincolns, Lieutenant-Colonel Peter Barclay, was more active than most in this respect) and unfortunately there were some losses, including Lieutenant Morrill from 'C' Company and Captain Wallage who was the officer commanding the Pioneer Platoon. In bright moonlight, Lieutenant Fowler's platoon discovered six Germans, fast asleep, in a dug-out. They threw grenades and fired Sten guns at the Germans but during their withdrawal an enemy machine-gun opened fire and killed two men, including Lieutenant Fowler. Lieutenant Odom of 'B' Company had a narrow escape when leading a patrol. They found an enemy outpost and for a moment he and a German stood facing each other before they both opened fire with automatic weapons. Lieutenant Odom's life was saved when a German bullet hit the two extra Sten gun magazines which he was carrying in his breast pocket.

All battalions received reinforcements and replenished their stores and equipment during this period. They took turns to move back from the front line for a welcome break from living rough, eating out of cans and sleeping and hiding in holes in the ground, sometimes dusty, sometimes muddy. The 7th Duke of Wellington's arrived on the 11th July so that the Lincolns could have a few days rest at Ducy Ste Marguerite. There was a mobile shower unit here and each man was given a towel and new underpants as he emerged. There was a cinema and an ENSA show and parties of men visited the historic city of Bayeux, where they had the unusual wartime experience of being able to buy unlimited amounts of butter and cheese. On the 16th July the Lincolns were sent up to the line again to relieve the Hallamshires at Tessel Wood.

Quite a number of the men in the German army were of other nationalities who had been pressed into service. Two Polish deserters turned up in the Lincolns' sector with the news that the village of Vendes was now unoccupied. Vendes had been very heavily defended a few days earlier when the KOYLI and the Hallamshires had mounted an unsuccessful attack which had resulted in appalling casualties. Patrols were sent out and the following day, the 18th July, the Lincolns walked into Vendes, occupying it without resistance. The enemy withdrawal must have been carried out in a very orderly manner for only one German was found there, and he was dead. There was nothing left of the village. Vendes had been bombarded for almost four weeks and was in ruins. There were dead cows and horses and outside the village there were the bodies of the men who had been killed a few days earlier. It was a very moving scene. The stench was dreadful.

Somewhat to their surprise, the Lincolns were relieved again by the 7th Dukes and returned to the rest area at Ducy Ste Marguerite, having only left there a few days earlier. Cross-country runs, discussions on current affairs and 'Brains Trusts' were organised. Unfortunately, there was some heavy rain and apart from spoiling the rest period the dusty roads became axle-deep in mud. So it was with difficulty that the Lincolns moved on the 26th July from Ducy Ste Marguerite, not to any of their previous sectors, but to Démouville in a completely new area, to the east of Caen.

*   *   *

There had been something of a stalemate in the first half of July. The British (and some of the Americans) seemed to be trapped in the bocage countryside. A month had gone by since the invasion and Caen (which Hitler had insisted should be held at all costs) had still not been taken. In the end, Bomber Command had to be called in, and on the evening of the 7th July a strong force of Lancasters and Halifaxes dropped over 3,000 tons of high-explosive and fragmentation bombs on the city. There were many French casualties. Most of the Germans escaped the bombing, for they were outside Caen, in the villages which the RAF hadn't attacked in case any of the bombs fell short and dropped on our own troops by mistake. At dawn the next morning, I Corps attacked with three divisions. Part of the plan was for an armoured column to race through the town and seize the bridges over the river. This wasn't a very bright idea, for not surprisingly the streets were blocked with mountains of rubble from the ruins of the buildings which had been bombed. Bulldozers had to be sent for to clear a way. By the time Caen had been occupied and the armoured column had finally managed to reach the river, every bridge had been blown. The Germans were still there, in strength, on the far bank.

The Germans still hadn't moved any troops away from the Calais area, but reinforcements were now arriving in Normandy, some from southern France and even as far away as the Russian front. The Allies began to fear that their bridgehead would become sealed-off. Eisenhower was one of many who became very anxious. Even Montgomery was worried when the Germans started to move some of their armoured formations towards the American sector and he realised that he would have to keep them busy by mounting a large-scale attack around Caen. The Americans were planning a major attack from their sector on the 20th July (Operation Cobra) and Montgomery decided to mount a huge offensive two days earlier from the east of Caen, where the countryside was open and more suitable for tanks than the bocage. The two Allied offensives, he assured Eisenhower, would set the Normandy front aflame.

In the British and Canadian offensive (Operation Goodwood) three armoured divisions with massive air support would advance to gain a firm bridgehead over the River Orne. This powerful attack would draw the Germans to the east just as the Americans were ready to break out in the west. But what the British intelligence staff had failed to appreciate was that the area Montgomery proposed to attack was the most heavily defended in Normandy. Rommel, believing that the Allies intended to make another, stronger, landing in the Calais area thought that he could prevent this if he tied up the British around Caen. Thus both Generals, Montgomery and Rommel, each believed that they were tying up the opposition.

It was impossible to conceal the build-up of such a massive number of tanks, guns and men and the Germans were on full alert for the attack. Rommel toured his defensive positions the day before the British attack and on his way home his car was attacked by fighters. The car crashed into a tree and Rommel, unconscious and seriously injured, was taken to a nearby village called, ironically, Ste Foy de Montgommery.

Operation Goodwood started at dawn on the 18th July, when for three hours the RAF and the US Army Air Force dropped thousands of tons of bombs on the German troops. It was the most massive air attack in support of ground forces that had ever been made. Then the artillery took over and put down a creeping barrage as the tanks rolled forward. Good progress was made for a time, but the momentum was lost when the tanks came up against a screen of 88mm guns. German tanks and troops which hadn't been bombed (they were positioned deeper than had been realised) moved forward quickly to take command of the high ground, out of range of the British 25-pounders which had not yet been brought up. Air support from rocket-firing Typhoons was hampered because their control post with the forward troops had been put out of action. The 11th Armoured Division tried to push forward and lost almost 130—over half—of its tanks, but Major-General Erskine's 7th Armoured Division (the Desert Rats) was slow in coming into action and shortly afterwards he was sacked, as was Lieutenant-General Bucknall, the commander of XXX Corps. The Germans moved more troops up during the night. It rained on the 20th July, the battlefield became a quagmire, the armoured divisions withdrew and Operation Goodwood was over. Montgomery was criticised, for Goodwood was seen as a failure. Nevertheless, a bridgehead had been established east of the River Orne but, of even greater importance, the Germans had diverted two Panzer Divisions which had been on their way to the American sector to the Caen area. On the British and Canadian front there were still seven Panzer Divisions and four heavy tank battalions. The Americans, about to break-out in Operation Cobra, had only two Panzer Divisions and one Panzer Grenadier Division facing them, and this was what Montgomery had intended all along.

The 20th July was an important day for another reason. There was an unsuccessful attempt to assassinate Hitler. A number of senior German officers had plotted to take over and try to negotiate a separate peace with the Western Allies. Hitler miraculously survived, but even if he had been killed it would have made no difference. The Allies would not have agreed to separate peace terms. Indeed, there would be no peace terms at all. The Allies were firmly committed to Germany's unconditional surrender. The war in the west would go on until Germany was crushed.

The Americans had to postpone the start of Operation Cobra because of the poor weather but at last the sky cleared on the 25th July and the offensive started. The Germans were defending road junctions, for Allied tanks had only been able to travel along the roads as they couldn't get through the hedges of the bocage to move over open countryside. What they didn't know was that an American tank sergeant called Curtis Culin had invented the 'Rhinoceros', a gadget to cut through the hedges. Sharp steel teeth welded about two feet from the ground onto the front of a Sherman tank bit into the banks, loosened the earth and cut the roots of the hedges. The Sherman could be through to the open fields with hardly any loss of speed. Sergeant Culin demonstrated his invention to his captain who immediately showed it to his general, and the result was that field workshops hastily welded 'Rhinos' to the front of as many Shermans as possible. The steel for the teeth came from the obstacles which Rommel had installed on the beaches.

*   *   *   *

After Operation Goodwood the 49th Division moved to new positions east of Caen to relieve brigades of the 51st Highland and 3rd British divisions. The Polar Bears now found themselves part of I Corps, which had itself just become part of the 1st Canadian Army under Lieutenant-General Crerar. The 1st Royal Leicesters had now joined the division to take the place of the 6th Duke of Wellington's Regiment.

The village of Démouville, where the 4th Lincolns were now positioned, was a dreadful place. It had been totally ruined and it was hard to imagine that the inhabitants of this (and many other French towns and villages) would ever be able to rebuild it again and return to a normal life. It was also an extremely uncomfortable position. The Lincolns were just in front of a lot of heavy artillery (5.5-inch) and 25-pounder field guns which had been assembled; there was a solid mass of armour to their right and in the rear there were scores of supply vehicles of all descriptions and some workshops. All of these were very attractive targets for the Germans and they were frequently shelled and mortared by the terrible 'Moaning Minnies'. To their considerable surprise, the Germans dropped flares at night and they received visits from the Luftwaffe which bombed and strafed them with cannon fire. Throughout the campaign Second Lieutenant Turner had always shared a slit trench with his friend Sergeant Stan Masters but after a close shave when a bomb had dropped very near to them he realised that if they were both put out of action there would again be no-one to lead the mortar platoon. They were to make separate arrangements from now on.

To make matters worse there were hundreds of thousands of mosquitoes which plagued the life out of everyone. Some men were badly bitten, their arms and legs so swollen as to be almost useless, and they had to be sent to hospital as casualties. Men also started to go down with dysentery.

After five wretched days at Démouville, the 4th Lincolns were ordered to move to Sannerville, north-west of Troarn. Here, on the 1st August, they took over from the 2nd battalion of the Lincolnshire Regiment which had been in Normandy since D-Day. It was the first time the two battalions had come across each other during the campaign.

In the west, the Americans had gained more ground than even they had expected. When they came across a German road block the Rhinos simply cut a by-pass through the hedges and swept on. Now it was the German tanks and anti-tank guns which were unable to leave the narrow lanes of the bocage and they were sitting targets for Thunderbolts patrolling overhead, controlled by an officer riding with the leading tanks. On Tuesday the 1st August, the US Third Army became operational under their outstanding general, George S Patton. He didn't intend to hang around.

Although the German generals wanted to withdraw east to the River Seine to establish new defences, Hitler insisted on driving his army in the opposite direction, westwards, in an attempt to cut-off the supplies of Patton's rapidly advancing troops and to reach the coast at Avranches. Patton had already captured Avranches and his tanks were now speeding across open countryside, virtually unopposed, eastward and to the south of the Germans, who were moving to the west. Allied troops were now to the north, west and south of the Germans and it was obvious to everyone except Hitler that they could be trapped. But the German generals were scared of arguing with Hitler, for the trial of those who'd been involved in the assassination plot had started. To disagree with Hitler in the mood he had been in since the assassination attempt might well have been interpreted as treason.

Because Hitler had moved much of his armour westwards, the Germans were now weaker in the east, in the Caen area, although they still had over a hundred 88mm guns there. The jaws of the trap would close if Lieutenant-General Crerar's 1st Canadian Army, which had now taken over the sector east of the River Orne, could break through from Caen to Falaise whilst most of the German armour was still west of the Orne.

The 2nd Canadian Division and the 51st Highland Division under the Canadian Lieutenant-General Guy Simonds were given the job of making the thrust for Falaise, code-named Operation Totalize. The Polar Bears of the 49th Division, now part of the 1st Canadian Army, would follow-up later and cover the left flank. Simonds, who had flair and imagination, decided to attack at night. Columns of tanks, some with flails, would penetrate the forward German strongpoints. The infantry would ride behind in carriers and then attack the second line of defences under cover of darkness. There would be no preliminary artillery bombardment, although the RAF would bomb the German defences on both flanks.

An hour before midnight on Monday the 7th August the RAF bombed targets marked by flare shells and half an hour later the columns moved either side of the main Caen-Falaise road behind a creeping barrage. Despite a great deal of chaos in the dark, a German smoke screen and the dust raised by a thousand armoured vehicles and the barrage, the 51st Highland Division—on the left of the main road—were three miles inside the German lines by dawn. The Canadians, on the right, met stiff resistance on their western flank but they had taken all their objectives by mid-day. The Germans' defences had been cracked for relatively small cost.

The next phase was to be the break-out by the 4th Canadian and 1st Polish Armoured Divisions but unfortunately neither had been in action before. They didn't crack on and by-pass the few German strongpoints, as Simonds had ordered, but stopped to deal with them and between dawn and nightfall they had only advanced three miles. And then, instead of pressing on during the night, they took up defensive positions. The initial advantage which had been gained had been lost. The Germans organised a line of defence along the River Laison on the 9th August and although the Canadians advanced nine miles the following day they were still seven miles from Falaise. The swift break-through had not been gained.

The 4th Lincolns hadn't been required to do much at Sannerville during the first week in August except patrol after dark. They were on the receiving end of shellfire every now and then but little damage was done and although on one day some mortar fire wounded six men, things were relatively quiet. A Russian deserter came through the lines of 'B' Company followed a day later by three more. Private Fisher, a sniper, captured two prisoners-of-war. A shooting match developed between patrols one night and although Private Robinson was killed the Germans lost three men killed and one wounded. Early in the morning of Monday the 7th August enemy harassing fire killed Lance-Corporal Grant. Later in the day, 46th Commando in their green berets arrived to take over the position and the Lincolns moved to Bourguébus. There had been a recent fierce tank battle here and 88mm guns and 'Moaning Minnies' were still active in the vicinity. An 88mm gun hit the battalion headquarters, killing two men and wounding the adjutant, Captain Corben.

The Lincolns only stayed for a couple of nights at Bourguébus for Operation Totalize had now begun. Following-up the main attack, they moved south on the 9th August to a large wooded area called Star Wood, by-passing the village of La Hogue which had vanished following the bombing when Operation Totalize had started a couple of nights earlier. Nothing was left.

The plague of mosquitoes was even worse at Star Wood than at Démouville. They seemed to thrive on anti-mosquito cream and more men had to be sent back for treatment. The battalion was shelled from time to time and two men were wounded. Two deserters from the 981 Grenadier Regiment came to give themselves up. On the 11th August, a German counter-attack was beaten off by the Royal Scots Fusiliers on the left flank of the Lincolns. Although there were only isolated pockets of Germans in the area now, there was still mortar fire and air-burst shelling every now and then.

On Sunday the 13th August the 4th Lincolns moved further south to Conteville, where they took over from the 2nd Seaforth Highlanders. Major Donald Stokes TD was in command of the battalion (Lieutenant-Colonel Barclay had gone to Luc-sur-Mer for a day's rest with Major Blackstone, the Officer Commanding the Support Company). He and a small group were standing in a road when suddenly a couple of 5cm Granatwerfer grenades arrived. His batman, Stan Dawson, dived for a ditch by the side of the road and was seriously wounded when they exploded. Major Stokes was blown to pieces and died instantly. The whole battalion was shocked and saddened at his death, for he had been with the Lincolns since 1922. Born in Lincoln, Don Stokes had become a very well-known figure in the city during his short life. He was not quite 40 years old. Married and with a five-year old daughter, he had worked in the family business of R W Stokes and Sons Ltd. The coffee shop and café is still there on High Bridge, Lincoln. He had been elected to represent Castle Ward on Lincoln City Council as an Independent, but had resigned his seat on the outbreak of war in 1939. He was a founder member of

Lincoln Rugby Club and had been the captain for a number of years. Cheerful, gallant and popular with all ranks, Major Stokes was a fine upstanding man, a born leader of men. (He had in fact been Mentioned in Dispatches for personally leading his men to safety in Norway). There wasn't a man who had a bad word to say about him—indeed there were some who almost worshipped him. No-one had ever worked harder for the battalion either in peace or in war and there is little doubt that had he lived he would have eventually commanded the battalion. The senior of the Territorial Army officers, Major Stokes *was* the 4th Lincolns and somehow things would never seem quite the same again. It was more than a great loss, it was a tragedy.

Captain Den Cooke (the Intelligence Officer) and Captain Knight (the Second-in-Command of 'B' Company) were also wounded by the same shell and there had

Major Don Stokes and his daughter, Rosemary.

to be a hasty reshuffle of responsibilities. Major Barlow-Poole, a regular officer and the son of the vicar of Horncastle, became the Second-in-Command of the battalion and Major Pattin moved from 'B' Company to 'HQ' Company. Captain Hardcastle took over 'A' Company when Major Flint was transferred to 'B' Company.

The Canadians launched another attack towards Falaise at noon on the 14th August and they occupied the town two days later. By this time the tanks of Patton's XV Corps were only fifteen miles away to the south. Patton wanted to go on to close the gap, but was stopped by his boss, General Omar Bradley, in case his troops collided with the British and Canadians. Patton merely saw that they were in his way. 'Let me go on to Falaise and we'll drive the British back into the sea for another Dunkirk,' Patton pleaded. He was sent off in the direction of Paris instead.

The 4th Lincolns were now broadening the breach which had been made down the Caen-Falaise road for on Tuesday the 15th August they moved east to Billy prior to taking the village of Airan, a further three miles east, against slight opposition the following morning. Soon afterwards a carrier-mortar group was sent about five miles to the north-east to try and capture two bridges over the River Laison at Croissanville. 'B' Company and a platoon of 'A' Company joined them at 3.00 o'clock on the morning of the 17th August. They found that the area was heavily mined and that the Germans were resisting strongly with machine-gun fire. Private Simmonds of the Pioneer section supervised the lifting of 15 mines under fire, and he was later awarded the Military Medal for his courage. An attack was launched when the rest of the battalion arrived and although the village was taken the Germans couldn't be prevented from blowing the bridges up. Later it was found that one of the bridges—although it was in a bad state—could still just be used by vehicles.

On the same day (the 16th August) the Canadians entered Falaise and Hitler relieved von Kluge of his command. He suspected him of trying to surrender to the British. He transferred Field Marshall Walter Model from the Russian front to take his place. Von Kluge committed suicide a few days later, leaving a letter for Hitler advising him to end the war.

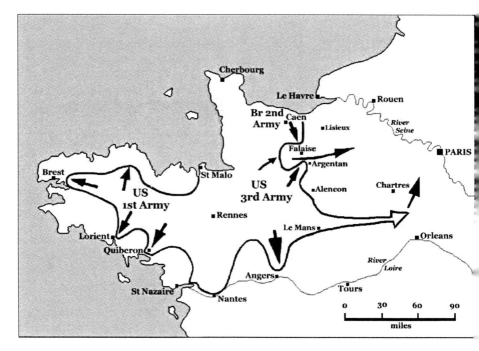

Map 9. Break-out.

120

The Canadian 4th and the Polish 1st Armoured Divisions swept to the south-east on Thursday the 17th August and by the evening were only six miles away from the Americans. Almost a hundred thousand German troops were now squeezed into a pocket and were being pounded by shells and bombs. The whole area was burning, vehicles were on fire and ammunition was exploding. Men fled in terror. Even the Germans who managed to squeeze through the gap soon found themselves targetted by the RAF and US Army Air Force.

The Allies closed in and had joined hands by the evening of the 19th August. What was left of the German armour tried to break out and open an escape route for the infantry, but they were blocked by blazing vehicles and were ruthlessly shelled. But remnants of the 2nd Panzer Division did manage to crash through the thinly-held Canadian line at a village called St Lambert. Major Currie of the 4th Armoured Division won the Victoria Cross for holding his position in the north of the village for six hours with fifteen tanks, four anti-tank guns and less than two hundred men, directing fire from the Canadian guns onto German columns attempting to cross the River Dives. Unlike the Allies, the Germans relied on horse-drawn transport throughout the war and although their armour managed to get through, several columns of horse-drawn transport were shelled as they neared the bridge. The terrified horses stampeded, dragging their loads after them down the steep river bank. Very soon it was choked with heaps of dead and wounded men and horses.

The slaughter in the hell that was the Falaise Pocket was horrific. Ten thousand German troops were dead and a further fifty thousand were taken prisoner. Eisenhower, who visited a day or two later, said that it was literally possible to walk for hundreds of yards at a time, stepping on nothing but dead and decaying flesh. The Germans had lost almost five hundred tanks, their guns and other equipment. Nevertheless, over a period of days more than a third of the Germans had somehow managed to get away and Montgomery was criticised by those who thought he could have closed the gap earlier by supporting the Canadians with reinforcements.

Meanwhile, the 4th Lincolns marched a further five or six miles eastwards on the 18th August and by late afternoon they were relaxing in the cool, refreshing long grass of an orchard in a village twenty miles to the north of the cauldron at Falaise. They didn't have much of a rest, for the Polar Bear Division had orders to get a bridgehead over the River Vie, so they marched another half a dozen miles along twisting tree-lined lanes to the village of le Mesnil-Mauger. By the time the Lincolns got there it was dark, but the road was lit by brilliant parachute flares for, unusually, the Luftwaffe were active and were dropping bombs somewhere to the rear. 'C' Company, leading the battalion, suddenly came under heavy shell, mortar and machine-gun fire. Although it was known that there were no Germans in the village of Mesnil it was found that they were dug-in up slippery steep slopes on high wooded ground on the far side of the River Vie, which ran just outside the village. To get at the Germans, the Lincolns would have to cross the river—or to be more accurate, the river would actually have to be crossed *twice*, for upstream it parted before becoming joined again about a mile further down.

Major Caudwell went ahead and tried to swim the river, which was about twenty feet wide, but it was flowing swiftly because of recent rain and he decided that it would be impossible for the whole company to get across that way. He eventually found a small, rickety footbridge and 'C' Company crossed it in single file, followed by 'B' Company. It was a difficult and slow job in the dark. The Germans sent up green flares and shortly afterwards their bombers arrived, flying low and bombing the approach to the river.

It was then discovered that 'C' and 'B' Companies had only crossed to the island, in-between the two branches of the river, and that it was impossible to go any further. A bomb landed in the middle of a platoon, seriously wounding a sergeant and 32 men, and then a fragmentation bomb landed between Major Caudwell and Captain Ainger, wounding them both. There was nothing for it but to get off the island along the same footbridge.

Meanwhile, 'A' and 'D' Companies had been told by the villagers that there were two other bridges, four hundred yards apart and about three-quarters of a mile away, and they set off down the main road rather than risk getting lost crossing the fields in the dark. Both companies crossed the first bridge and 'A' Company went on to take the second—but then the Germans found them and opened fire, using Bren guns which must have been captured somewhere. It was still dark and the Lincolns were caught between the river and a deep ditch. 'A' Company withdrew and to avoid heavy casualties it was also decided to pull 'D' Company back slightly.

When daylight came, German mortars and snipers made things very uncomfortable for 'D' Company and under cover of artillery fire they were withdrawn to join the rest of the battalion in the village.

The battalion stayed in Mesnil, in pouring rain, for the next two days. The enemy eventually withdrew after the artillery had shelled their positions. All told, the action at Mesnil had been a bit of a shambles—a shambles which had cost eight lives, including that of Captain Metcalfe, the second-in-command of 'D' Company, who was killed when he was hit by a cannon shell.

A church parade was held in an orchard in Mesnil on Sunday the 20th August but a German Observation Officer somewhere must have spotted it taking place for enemy mortars opened up and two men were wounded. There were many orchards and woods in Normandy and they were dangerous places during an enemy 'stonk', for the branches exploded the shells and mortars and showered the shrapnel downwards.

The Tyneside Scottish had a tough time at Mézidon, about five miles to the rear of Mesnil, and there was bitter street-to-street fighting before they cleared the town. The 10th Durham Light Infantry, just to the north of the Lincolns at Mesnil, had managed to cross the river and get to the top of the hill but the Germans mounted a strong counter-attack under a heavy mortar barrage and the Durhams were forced back. By now both battalions had suffered heavy casualties, and shortly afterwards it was decided to disband the 70th Brigade. It was a very sad day for the Territorials from Tyneside, particularly for the 11th DLI which was still at full strength. Old friends were parted when the men were dispersed into other regiments.

The 56th Independent Brigade, comprising the 2nd Gloucesters, the 2nd South Wales Borderers and the 2nd Essex Regiment, replaced the 70th Brigade. This was a regular brigade which, as part of the 50th Division, had landed on D-Day and had taken Bayeux.

Meanwhile, Patton's tanks had now crossed the Seine and were approaching Paris. The Paris police force went on strike and three thousand armed gendarmes and the French resistance—the Forces Françaises de l'Intérieur (the FFI)—seized control of government buildings. By the 25th August hysterical crowds were cheering the tanks of the 2nd French Armoured Division as they rode down the Champs Elysées.

Elsewhere, the Germans were in full retreat and Allied troops—British, American, Canadian, Polish and French—were roaring through pretty countryside which had been untouched by the war. They had problems getting through the towns and villages, for they were cheered by crowds who came out to greet them with flowers, fruit, wine, home-made cider, calvados and even champagne. People tried to get onto the vehicles and—best of all—girls clung and showered kisses. It was not only liberation for the French people, it was also a sort of liberation for the soldiers who had been cooped up for weeks in conditions almost similar to the First World War—ruined shells of buildings, shell-pocked earth, scorched stumps of trees and nightly patrols in no-man's-land. These exhilarating few days when the Germans were on the run became known to all the British troops as 'The Swan to the Seine'. But—as had been shown at Mesnil—there were still rearguard units of Germans around with mortars and Spandaus, ready to fight to the death.

Led by the probing armoured cars of the 49th Reconnaissance Regiment, the Lincolns left Mesnil on the 21st August and, travelling north-east, reached the River Seine, fifty or sixty miles away, just a week later. To the left of the 49th Division, on the coast, was the 6th Airborne Division and to their right there was the 7th Armoured Division and then the 51st Division. On their way, the Lincolns met little resistance until they reached Le Brueil-en-Auge, a village just on the other side of the River Touques about six miles north of Lisieux. There were thick woods on the sharply-rising ground on the far side of the river and 'C' Company and a section of carriers came under heavy mortar and machine-gun fire as they approached. 'B' Company, to the left, found a bridge but it had been completely destroyed and the river was too deep to ford. 'C' Company found the shattered remains of a bridge—just bits of broken timber—and under a smokescreen and covering fire from the supporting tanks and the 25-pounders of the 69th Field

Regiment they managed to cross the river and enter the village, followed soon afterwards by 'B' Company. Parties of Germans tried unsuccessfully to infiltrate back into the village during the night and the battalion came under shellfire throughout the following day, but during the next night the enemy withdrew. Royal Engineers quickly put up a bridge over the river for the tanks, guns and vehicles. The action had cost ten lives and twenty-six men were wounded. Arrangements for the wounded were excellent and the men were quickly brought back to England for treatment. Monty's promise that men would be sent to hospitals near home was still going awry however. Norman Barber, who had been promoted to lance-corporal at Hereford and to sergeant at Kessingland, was wounded in this action and although he was from the Boston area he soon found himself at Tranmere Infirmary. Quite a number of men who were wounded were eventually able to return to the battalion, including Sergeant Barber who rejoined three or four months later.

On the following day, the 24th August, replacements arrived—much needed as by this time the Lincolns were well below strength. The total number of all ranks in 'A' Company, for instance, was down to forty-four. The Lincolns, now in reserve, rested at Le Brueil-en-Auge for the next couple of days and took the opportunity to have baths. Men from the local resistance (the Maquis or FFI) contacted battalion headquarters and a party from 'C' Company was detailed to go with them to round up four Frenchmen who were German sympathisers.

On the 26th August, the Lincolns were on the move again. They crossed the River Risle, where they took eight German prisoners and, with the rest of the 49th Division, arrived on the banks of the River Seine without any further opposition two days later. Most of the battalions in the division had met isolated pockets of resistance from German rearguards on their way. The Royal Leicesters, on the right flank of the Lincolns at Le Brueil-en-Auge, had had to cross the river by means of a rope bridge which their pioneer platoon had managed to erect. The 294th Field Company of the Royal Engineers had constantly been kept busy, clearing mines, filling craters and assembling Bailey bridges across rivers. When they arrived at the Seine there was another problem facing them.

The Seine near Rouen winds in a series of dramatic S-bends and is also tidal. At low tide there is a bore—a tidal wave which can be as high as twelve feet, making it very difficult for bridges to be built. The Engineers managed to build one or two pontoon bridges and, equipped for all eventualities, also constructed and operated large rafts to ferry men and vehicles across the river.

The 4th Lincolns had arrived at the Seine at Quilleboeuf, a small town about twenty miles west of Rouen and on the last bend in the river before it became an estuary. Nearby, about four miles to the east, was a large forest, the Forêt de Bretonne, and it was thought that there were quite a large number of Germans hiding there. On the 29th August the Lincolns assisted the KOYLI in clearing the forest, supported by a squadron of tanks. They met a little resistance here and there, but on the whole the enemy gave themselves up quite easily. The Lincolns took ninety-nine prisoners, including five officers, and the KOYLI took even more. Dumps of equipment and stores had been left in the forest, including trucks and cars in running order, and there were hundreds of horses running loose which had been used to draw the Germans' guns and wagons. It was almost dark by the time the Lincolns reached the northern edge of the forest and the village of St Nicholas on the banks of the Seine. The whole village was burning. The Lincolns took up defensive positions near the village for the night and continued to flush out Germans in the forest the following day when they took another seventy-six prisoners. The men hitched lifts on the tanks and a cameraman from Pathé News furiously turned the handle of his camera as they jumped off to go into the forest. Many of the enemy who were taken prisoner weren't Germans at all. Quite a number were Russians who had been captured earlier in the war and had been 'persuaded' to join the German Army. Some of the enemy came out with their hands up shouting: 'Nicht Boche, nicht Boche', but—who knows—perhaps some of these *were* Germans.

The first thing prisoners lost were their wrist watches. This was the penalty—recognised by both sides—for being taken a prisoner-of-war, and only a fool would take a valuable watch with him to the front line. Next, the Germans were relieved of their ground sheets. These were highly-prized as they were a much better design than the British version, for they could be connected together to make tents.

The Lincolns received a directive from the Divisional Commander, Major-General 'Bubbles' Barker regarding the treatment of prisoners. Apparently he was concerned because he had heard that prisoners were being treated too kindly—almost as guests. This had to stop immediately. It was a good job that he wasn't around when a group of Germans came out of the wood with their hands in the air shouting 'Kamerad', surrendering to half a dozen passing carriers. Private Jack Welch got out of the one of the carriers to stretch his legs and opened a new tin of fifty cigarettes to have a smoke. He noticed that a German who was looking even more bedraggled and sorry for himself than the others was watching his every move and after hesitating for a few moments he offered him a cigarette from the tin. Jack was immediately surrounded by the rest of the Germans, and for a time disappeared altogether. When he emerged, he held the tin up high and slowly turned it upside-down. It was empty.

The road bridge at St Nicholas had been destroyed by RAF Typhoons and some of the Germans had evidently crossed the Seine by boat. They had driven their trucks and cars right up to the river and abandoned them. There were dozens of them. The Germans had been shelled and attacked by the RAF and US Army Air Force, and they had left many dead, both men and horses. There were smouldering tanks, guns and other weapons all over the place. Some vehicles had been neatly parked nose to tail and some were captured intact, but most of them were slewed all over the place, tyres burned and skeletons of what they had once been. In the driving seat of one of the trucks there was a blackened, charred stick of what had once been a man, intense heat having reduced him in size. In a nearby field a party was burying the dead. It really was a terrible scene.

Word went around that every platoon could allow a few men at a time to go through the German vehicles and help themselves to anything they fancied. Booty! Lieutenant Arthur Turner was one of the last to take a look, and there wasn't much left. But he did find a shaving kit in a leather case and he took it to replace the one he'd been given as a 21st birthday present and which had been destroyed at Tessel-Bretteville when a shell had burst over his carrier. A little later he came across a small open vehicle and couldn't believe his eyes when he saw four tins of 50 English cigarettes and three or four bars of chocolate. They must have been captured by the Germans. He quickly stuffed them in his pocket and was walking away, quite pleased with himself, when for some reason he glanced back at the vehicle. It was only then that he realised it was a British jeep and the signs on the front showed that it belonged to the Brigadier. He quickly replaced the cigarettes and the chocolate and hurried away.

During the day (the 30th August) some members of the FFI from Yvetot, a town which was still under German occupation and about six miles to the north of St Nicholas, crossed the river in boats and made contact with the Lincolns. They were delighted when they were given some of the German guns and ammunition which had been found in the forest, and their boats were laden when they made the return crossing over the river. Their leader, Monsieur Rousseau, was quite a character. He was a bit deaf, but he spoke English quite well and he stayed with the Lincolns for a few days as he had useful local contacts and information and could act as an interpreter. He was given a battledress and he set up his FFI headquarters at the battalion HQ at St Nicholas. Before long, he had proudly sewn on some Lincoln flashes—and some 'pips', for he had promoted himself to Captain!

The FFI brought in some more German prisoners on the 31st August and late the following day the Royal Engineers crammed the men of the Lincolns and boxes of ammunition and grenades into ferries and transported them across the Seine from St Nicholas to Caudebec. There was a bend in the fast-running river and the swirling water spun the boats around. Half-way across, the motor on one of the ferries failed and the men had to paddle the rest of the way using shovels. The 4th Lincolns were the first infantry battalion in the whole division to cross the Seine, and an enthusiastic crowd cheered them as they formed up and marched off. The Lincolns were without their carriers and other vehicles, which had had to travel all the way to Rouen to cross by way of a railway bridge. This bridge had been so badly damaged that the drivers thought that it would give way at any moment as they cautiously drove across it. The vehicles joined the rest of the battalion early in the morning of the 2nd September and the Lincolns immediately set off for the village of Gainville, a suburb of the port of Le Havre.

Meanwhile, XXX Corps had crossed the Seine at Vernon. Perhaps mindful of the criticisms he had received about closing the Falaise gap, Montgomery ordered his armoured columns to push boldly ahead, by-passing centres of resistance. In Lieutenant-General Horrocks, the new commander of XXX Corps, Montgomery had just the man for the job. The shattered Germans hoped to form a new line of defence over the River Somme, but on the 30th August, Horrocks ordered the 11th Armoured Division to 'bounce the Germans out of Amiens before they can blow the bridges'. Amiens, on the Somme, was forty miles away, but the 11th Armoured Division drove through the night in pouring rain and arrived at dawn the next day. Three bridges over the Somme were captured intact and the German defence plans were in ruins. Horrocks drove his men on. By the 2nd September the British and two American Corps were on the Belgian border and by the afternoon of the following day—the fifth anniversary of the outbreak of war—the Guards Armoured Division was in Brussels. The 11th Armoured Division by-passed Brussels and by the early afternoon of the 4th September had captured the docks at Antwerp—intact. Montgomery had shown that Patton wasn't the only one who could move armour quickly.

The Germans were now in great trouble. Their Fifteenth Army, on the coast with their backs to the sea, had been cut off. What was left of their Seventh Army had retreated from the Somme only to be captured by waiting Americans at Mons. Hitler had ordered that all available reserves should be sent to face Patton in the Moselle area but now that the Allies were in Belgium they were within striking distance of the Ruhr. Perhaps the war *would* be over by Christmas?

*   *   *   *

Whilst all these exciting events had been taking place, the Canadian Army had been left behind to deal with the Channel ports as Le Havre, Dieppe, Boulogne and Calais had all been by-passed. The huge guns in all of these ports were pointing out to sea as the Germans had assumed that any assaults would come from that direction, and because they were in thick concrete emplacements they couldn't be turned round. There were however quite a large number of guns—including the feared 88mms—in concrete bunkers. Realising the importance of the ports, the Germans had garrisons of ten thousand men in each of them, and they had orders to fight to the last man.

Gainville, where the Lincolns were, was an important German outpost in the defensive lay-out of Le Havre and its speedy capture was crucial for the whole operation. The 4th Lincolns carried out a successful attack at 7.00 o'clock on the evening of Saturday the 2nd September. 'A' Company was on the right of 'B' Company, followed by 'C' and 'D' Companies. There was artillery and mortar support and six-pounder anti-tank guns were ready to be rushed forward as soon as the objectives had been captured. After a good start, 'A' Company was slowed down by thick barbed wire and then 8 Platoon came under heavy Spandau fire and was checked. Despite this, a section under Sergeant Bland pressed on and reached their first objective, but they then came under fire from a Schmeisser machine-gun in some trees ahead. Sergeant Bland rushed the Schmeisser and forced it to withdraw and then, still under fire, took two men to deal with the Spandau which was holding up 8 platoon. He moved so quickly that the Germans were taken by surprise and six of them were taken prisoner. Sergeant Bland was later awarded the Military Medal. Meanwhile, 'B' Company under Major Flint advanced with great dash and by nightfall the Lincolns had secured the village and taken twelve prisoners. More prisoners were rounded-up during the night and many items of equipment, which had been hurriedly left by the Germans, were captured. By the following day the Lincolns were firmly established and had the KOYLI on their left clearing the approaches to Harfleur, and the Hallamshires in reserve in the rear.

Lt-Colonel Barclay was delighted with the battalion's performance and said it was 'a cracking good show all round.' The Lincolns had moved up well and some platoons had been within two hundred yards of the enemy, ready to take over as soon as the artillery's fifteen-minute opening barrage had ended. There had also been excellent close support from Major Richardson's 25-pounders during the advance, which had shattered the German defences.

The attack on Le Havre was to be carried out by the 51st (Highland) Division and the Polar Bears of the 49th Division—both of them British divisions which happened to be attached to the 1st Canadian Army. (In fact, 'Bubbles' Barker later became very indignant when the press and radio put it out that it was the Canadians who had attacked Le Havre.) The 49th Division had 147 and 56 Brigades on the northern side of Le Havre, with the 51st Highland Division to the right of 56 Brigade, whilst 146 Brigade was to the east of the port, facing Harfleur. Those who knew their history (or Shakespeare) realised that this was the second time that British soldiers would be going into battle at Harfleur, for 529 years earlier, almost to the day, King Henry V had led his troops into battle there:

'Work, work your thoughts, and therein see a siege;
Behold the ordnance on their carriages,
With fatal mouths gaping on girded Harfleur.' (*King Henry V—Act II, Scene IV.*)

Henry V would have been astounded had he seen the 'ordnance on their carriages' which was now assembling, for in addition to the usual heavy and field artillery, anti-tank guns and Sherman and Churchill tanks, the infantry was being supported by the biggest collection of Hobart's 'funnies' ever assembled in one place. The approaches to Le Havre were known to be heavily mined and so there were detachments of flail tanks. The Germans also had a large number of concrete gun emplacements, so there were tanks which hurled the huge mortars, the 'flying dustbins'. There were tanks which carried bridges, for there would be craters as a result of shells and bombs. There were 'Kangaroos' (armoured personnel carriers) and 'Crocodiles'—tanks which threw a flame fifty feet forward.

All this equipment had been brought up because it was believed that Le Havre would be a tough nut to crack. It took days to assemble. Whilst they were waiting, the Lincolns, like most of the other infantry battalions, took the opportunity to brush-up on their street-fighting drill, practising until it was perfect, for this was the first time that they would be in action in a town of any size. Everyone, from the generals down, felt anxious about the task which they were having to face.

The RAF arrived at 6.00 o'clock on the evening of Tuesday the 5th September and the men watched the terrible sight of a thousand tons of bombs dropping on Le Havre. From the sea, HM Monitor *Erebus* bombarded the port with 15-inch shells but was then hit herself and had to withdraw. The RAF returned at the same time the following day and this time dropped fifteen hundred tons of bombs. The sky was black with smoke from enormous fires. The *Erebus* reappeared, this time with the old battleship *Warspite,* and resumed shelling the coastal batteries, but once again she was hit and had to retire.

A stream of information was coming in from patrols and the FFI about the enemy's strength and dispositions. During the next couple of days models of the town and the concrete defences were made and studied by all ranks, and officers briefed the men about their objectives and what they had to do. A few German deserters arrived in the Lincolns' sector carrying 'safe conduct' passes printed in German and English which had

Safe conduct pass.

been dropped by the RAF.

Under the signature of General Eisenhower the pass said the carrier was to be well treated and sent back from the front as soon as possible. On the other side it said: 'Why die in the last week of the war? You are between two Allied armies and the sea, and holding out will help no one.' Mention was also made that prisoners got seventy-five cents a day which they could save to buy alcohol and that they were provided with newspapers, wireless sets and games. The terms of the Geneva Convention were also briefly set out.

It rained steadily for two days and the attack was put off. The Lincolns had been outside Le Havre for over a week. Then, on Sunday the 10th September, the RAF intensified their attack and the *Warspite* and the *Erebus* (which had returned yet again) renewed their bombardment and silenced the Grand Clos coastal battery. The Royal Artillery was busy all day shelling enemy gun emplacements. At a quarter to six in the evening the vast army which had gathered to the north of Le Havre moved forward, led by the flail tanks of the 22nd Dragoons. Operation Astonia had started.

The Germans had laid thousands of mines. The flail tanks, detonating some but not all of them, were followed by the Royal Engineers' 'funnies' and then by the tanks. Very soon the rain-sodden ground, already broken up by the bombing and naval bombardments, was churned into a bog. The din was terrific. To the north, the Gloucesters took all their objectives, but the South Wales Borderers on their right had a much harder time because they came across concrete bunkers which were protected by mines and barbed wire. But the 2nd Essex, following up at 10 o'clock, managed to pass through a lane which had been cleared of mines and helped by 'Monty's Moonlight' (the beams of searchlights reflected from the clouds) they too took all their objectives. The Gloucesters pressed forward and by the early evening of the following day were in the centre of Le Havre.

In 147 Brigade, the 1st Leicesters had a relatively easy time, the 11th Royal Scots Fusiliers had a little trouble clearing some strong points and houses and the 7th Duke of Wellingtons, following up in Kangaroos, got off their armoured troop carriers at a bridge captured by the Leicesters and marched into the centre of Le Havre to join the Gloucesters.

To the south, the Lincolns, with the KOYLI and the Hallamshires, didn't start their attack on the perimeter defences at Harfleur until the morning of Monday the 11th September. 'C' Squadron of the 22nd Dragoons' 'Crabs' (flail tanks) led the KOYLI but there were some casualties going through the minefields and flame-throwing Crocodiles had to be used against stubborn German resistance. Nevertheless, the KOYLI succeeded in taking their objectives—well-camouflaged, deep concrete bunkers—by half-past nine.

The Lincolns set off at about noon and passed through the KOYLI. There was an enormous racket from guns of every description—heavy and medium guns of the Royal Artillery, guns firing from tanks, mortars and the machine-guns of the 2nd

Kensingtons. Then came the sound of Spandaus firing at them from some concrete outposts, but the 'funnies' of the 222nd Assault Squadron of the Royal Engineers were quickly in action, firing their enormous, heavy petard mortars—the 'flying dustbins' mounted on Churchill tanks—and from a range of less than a hundred yards put the Germans' extraordinarily-thick concrete bunkers out of action. The blast could be felt half a mile away.

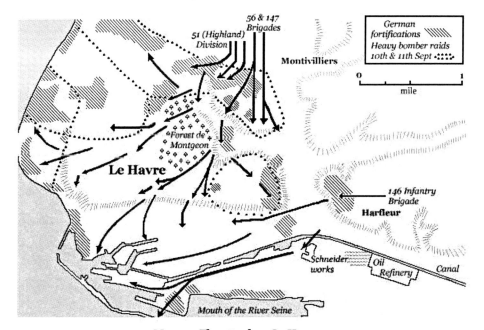

Map 10. The attack on Le Havre.

The men had been told: 'Keep moving. Use the tanks to shelter from any fire from the bunkers—there'll be plenty around. Just keep moving, keep moving'. Crouching, running, firing, stopping, walking, the Lincolns gradually made their way along the lanes which had been cleared in the minefields and through the wire, passing knocked-out concrete bunkers and into Harfleur. They were in the outskirts of Le Havre.

There was an uneasy night. Patrols were sent out and on one of them Major Russell MC (who had joined the battalion to take over 'C' Company after Major Staniland had been killed) was severely wounded. The patrols reported that the road bridges over the railway and the river, which had already been severely damaged by the RAF, had finally been put out of action by German demolition. The Commanding Officer was kept busy throughout the night discussing possibilities with the commanders of the supporting tanks, artillery and 'funnies'.

Eventually a route was found and the Lincolns set off at about eight o'clock the following morning to continue the attack into Le Havre.

A 'crab', flailing a way through a minefield.

Like Lincoln, Le Havre is a town built on two separate levels and they were in the downhill area. The ground rose very steeply on the right-hand side of the main road into the town. Progress was slow, for the road was pock-marked with craters from shells and bombs and there were ruins of houses and buildings to negotiate. The tram lines had been distorted into absurd shapes. Led by the 22nd Dragoons' flail tanks to clear the minefields and the Royal Engineers' petards, the Lincolns advanced slowly, cautiously, stopping, and then moving slowly forward before stopping once more. Again there was fire from Spandaus, but they were silenced following determined assaults with Sten guns and grenades, fire from the supporting tanks, artillery and the 'flying dustbins', which demolished road blocks and barricades. Every strong-point had to be fought for. Suddenly, a Spandau started firing from somewhere behind, the bullets hitting the road just in front of the Commanding Officer's jeep. Luckily, he wasn't in it, but the driver jumped out and tried to take cover by crouching behind a front wheel. By this time the Spandau had singled him out as a target and bullets thudded into the bodywork of the jeep. Others who had taken cover in a shallow ditch by the side of the road watched tensely. Someone had just murmured: 'Poor devil, he's had it,' when the firing suddenly stopped. The German firing the Spandau had been killed. The driver was uninjured but badly shaken and the jeep was a write-off.

The Commander of the Le Havre garrison, Colonel Eberhard Wildermuth, had been badly wounded, and just before noon—in his pyjamas, but wearing his medals—he surrendered. The German garrison didn't surrender 'en bloc', but in small groups when the British troops came within bayonet distance. Two hours later all organised resistance throughout the town had stopped. By this time the Lincolns had passed the Schneider works and had reached the dockyard, which had been mined and demolished by the Germans. They spent the rest of the day rounding-up over five hundred prisoners of all nationalities, some of them very young—so many that the 'walking wounded' had to be put in charge of them. Nearby, the Hallams even captured a submarine.

Ten days had been allowed for the capture of Le Havre, but it had actually been taken in thirty-six hours, the Lincolns having taken a prominent part in the action. The British were relieved (and mildly surprised) that it had been taken relatively easily. The Germans had perhaps not defended as resolutely as had been imagined. Possibly their hearts weren't in it after the pounding they'd received over the past few days from the artillery, the RAF and the *Erebus* and *Warspite*. The Germans hadn't seen 'crabs' (the flail tanks) before, and they'd thought it madness when they'd seen tanks entering the minefields. They were very soon astonished and dismayed by the results. They hadn't come across the flame-throwing 'crocodiles' either, and they thought that they were unfair and 'un-British'—a compliment in a sort of way—and one captured German officer said that all the men in a platoon which had been caught in the open had been burned alive.

But it was found that not all that many Germans had been killed, for they had been sheltering in their concrete bunkers during the air raids and the shelling. As at Caen, the real victims were the French. Several thousand men, women and children had been killed and hardly a single building was left standing.

An officer in the Royal Armoured Corps, Acting Captain the Hon William Douglas Home, had seen what had happened at Caen and he refused to obey an order at Le

Havre. At his court martial some weeks later it became clear that his refusal was symbolic and that he had done it to draw public attention not only to the moral issue of bombing French civilians but also to the unnecessary waste of young lives through the Allies' policy of 'unconditional surrender'. Hitler had also given 'No surrender' orders and thus neither the British nor the Germans had any room for negotiation. Captain Douglas Home knew that Colonel Wildermuth, the commandant of the German garrison at Le Havre, had offered to evacuate the French civilians but this had been refused by the British on the grounds that there was 'no time'. A compromise whereby the French would be moved into a particular quarter of the town which would be notified to the British was then rejected by Colonel Wildermuth.

A flame-throwing 'Crocodile'. The Germans complained that they were 'un-British' and unfair.

William Douglas Home (whose brother, Alec, had accompanied Chamberlain to Munich in 1938 and who was to become the Prime Minister in the 1960s) was clearly concerned about the issue of whether a man's conscience came before orders which he believed to be morally wrong. He said that he hadn't wanted to be a party to what he saw as a war crime. Later, at the Nuremberg trials, the

Germans' defence: 'We were only obeying orders' was not accepted and they were condemned for not refusing to obey orders which they knew to be morally wrong. But this wasn't the view taken in William Douglas Home's case, for he was cashiered and sentenced to twelve months hard labour. Although publicly scorned at the time, Captain Douglas Home had the education (Eton and Oxford), the rank, the social status and the confidence to make a stand and protest about unnecessary killing and destruction. He spoke for many who in their hearts had similar feelings of revulsion and were sickened by the appalling madness of war. He subsequently wrote plays ('The Chiltern Hundreds' and 'The Reluctant Debutante') for the stage, films and television.

A bridge-carrying 'funny', an AVRE (Armoured Vehicle Royal Engineers), at Le Havre.

Nevertheless, war is a ruthless business and Le Havre had not only been taken in less than two days but the British casualties had also been surprisingly light. Only nineteen soldiers had been killed in the whole of the 49th Division and the Lincolns hadn't lost a single man. Over eleven thousand Germans were taken prisoner and they left vast quantities of stores, including Danish butter and cheese (with labels written in English), tinned fruit, chocolate and cigars. The Lincolns captured a warehouse which was full of wine, champagne, brandy and lager. The men didn't think much of the lager, but the two bottles of Martel brandy which every officer, warrant officer and sergeant somehow managed to obtain went down a treat.

The 4th Lincolns left the wrecked streets and houses and the dazed, bewildered, distressed people of Le Havre on the 13th September, the day after the German surrender. They went a few miles to the east, to the village of St Aubin-Routot, for a rest period. For the next few days they played football, had baths and celebrated when the news came through that the Commanding Officer, Lieutenant-Colonel Peter Barclay, had been awarded the DSO and Major Barlow-Poole the Military Cross for their action in the Battle of Fontenay in June.

The Lincolns left St Aubin-Routot on Tuesday the 19th September for Flocques, a village on the way to Dieppe, but they had no sooner arrived when they were ordered to travel towards the general direction of the Albert Canal. They left Flocques early the following morning and set off for Lille, where they arrived the next day at four o'clock in the afternoon after covering over a hundred and fifty miles. They travelled through countryside which had been untouched by the war, and in fact they were the first Allied troops which the French villagers had seen. They were given a tremendous welcome everywhere and the convoy almost came to a stop when excited cheering villagers swarmed round the vehicles presenting flowers, fruit, cider and kisses.

*   *   *   *

So many things happened so quickly in those exhilarating weeks following the break-out of the Allied armies that it's hard to catch up. On the German side, von Runstedt was persuaded to come out of retirement yet again to resume his job as Commander-in-Chief West. Hitler was hoping that his new secret weapons would have a major, perhaps even decisive, impact on the British and following the V1 flying bomb the Germans launched yet another weapon, the V2 rocket, from one of their bases in West Holland. It literally arrived out of the blue and exploded in Chiswick on the 8th September. Thus a new type of weapon was born—the long-range ballistic missile—and there was no defence against it. The Germans had also introduced the world's first jet fighter into the conflict, the Messerschmitt Me 262, and it could have caused serious problems because it far out-paced any Allied aircraft. Fortunately less than 1500 were ever built.

General Montgomery had been appointed to command all the Allied land forces during the landings and until a solid base had been established in Normandy. By the 1st September the Supreme Commander, General Eisenhower, felt that the time had come for him to assume command of all operations himself. Montgomery was still in charge of the British and Canadians and he was promoted to the rank of Field Marshall, but this did little to assuage his disappointment at not being able to command all the Allied armies to the final victory. Furthermore, Montgomery was in favour of striking with concentrated powerful forces on a narrow front (ie *his*) and he disagreed with Eisenhower's strategy which was for *all* the forces to advance on a broad front. Montgomery wanted to win with a single knockout blow, whereas Eisenhower seemed to want to win on points over fifteen rounds. To be fair, Patton had already driven his troops across the River Marne and they were now racing for the Meuse. To stop them would have seemed like madness. And if Eisenhower's broad front stretched the Allies' resources, then Hitler was in an even worse position, for he was kept guessing and he had few reserves left in his dwindling army to restore any major breakthrough along a very wide front.

Meanwhile, on the 15th August, the American VI Corps under Lieutenant-General Patch had landed on the beaches of the French Riviera, west of Cannes. Within a few days they had occupied the ports of Toulon and Marseilles and were striking north up the Rhone valley. They joined forces with Patton's troops near Dijon on the 10th September. But the landing in the Riviera had also been contentious, for whilst Churchill felt strongly that the Allied armies which were already in Italy should have been reinforced instead—to open the way to Austria and the Balkans—Roosevelt just wasn't interested. He didn't want to become involved in Eastern Europe. Moreover, he suspected that Churchill somehow wanted to further British ambitions in that part of the world. Roosevelt not only wanted to curb the British instinct of exerting influence around the world, he was determined that every nation should have independent self-government. The colonial powers would have to give up their foreign possessions altogether, and this included Britain, which would have to give up her Empire. A mistake, for the Russians got to Eastern Europe first. The Americans were to find that for many years afterwards the Eastern European countries were behind the Iron Curtain. *They* didn't have a fat lot of independence.

The Allies had advanced so far by the beginning of September that there were problems of supply. Although the port of Cherbourg had been captured it was by no means fully operational and it was to be late October before Le Havre would be in any shape to help. Most of the reinforcements of men and supplies were still having to come through the one remaining Mulberry harbour and the beaches, and this was now a very long way from the forward positions of both the American and the British armies. PLUTO, the oil pipe-line under the ocean, came in at Cherbourg and although it was being extended inland at the remarkable rate of twenty-five miles a day (over a mile an hour!) many lorries were needed to transport petrol to the thirsty tanks miles away at the front. VIII Corps and much of the British artillery were grounded at the Seine because their transport had to be borrowed to supply the forward troops in Belgium. Neither Montgomery nor Patton was getting the supplies they needed, and this was a further argument for concentrating the Allied effort in either one place or the other and directing all the supplies there.

Another problem was that the Americans had fresh troops and supplies in the States waiting to be shipped direct to the conflict in France and Belgium. Although they were now using Marseilles, what was holding them back in the north was the lack of a deep-water harbour. Eisenhower had repeatedly stressed that Antwerp was desperately needed ('We cannot strike any decisive blow until Antwerp is working') and indeed the docks there had been captured undamaged by the 11th Armoured Division on the 4th September. He would now be able to bring in all the men and supplies needed to carry the offensive into Germany. Or could he? Antwerp, like London, is an inland port, over fifty miles from the sea. The Germans still held both sides of the Scheldt estuary (which was like holding the Kent and Essex banks of the Thames) and they also had powerful coastal batteries which controlled the entrance. The port was useless until the Germans had been cleared from the approaches.

Although the 11th Armoured Division had seized the docks at Antwerp, they hadn't captured the bridges in the northern part of the city, over the Albert Canal. They could have done, but they didn't. Patton would have gone spare. The explanation for this unbelievable lapse was that they didn't know that a further advance north was envisaged. But even if no orders had been given, they had been told to take Antwerp and you would have thought that this would have been interpreted to include the bridges so that the Albert Canal could be crossed without difficulty and a bridgehead established on the other side. The Germans had time to blow up the bridges, were still on the other side of the canal, and the docks were in range of their guns.

But Montgomery's priorities were elsewhere. He had managed to get Eisenhower to agree to Operation Market-Garden, the brilliant and daring idea of seizing the road bridges over the Maas, the Waal and the Neder Rijn with British, American and Polish airborne forces, to clear the way for armoured columns to drive sixty miles north. It would cut Holland in half and isolate the Germans in West Holland, outflank their strong, fixed defences in the Siegfried Line and establish the British army across the Rhine within striking distance of the Ruhr. Montgomery was sure that Eisenhower, seeing the opportunity, would then have to give him the resources to exploit it. It was a gamble, and had it worked Market-Garden might have shortened the war by months, particularly as the German army was in such disarray.

On Sunday the 17th September the airborne forces were dropped to capture the bridges for XXX Corps, which set off from the Meuse-Escaut Canal. By Wednesday the 26th September it was all over. Courageous fighting by American and British airborne troops enabled XXX Corps to reach the southern bank of the Neder Rijn, but not in time to relieve the 1st British Airborne Division at Arnhem.

It was a disaster from start to finish. Yet again, there was bad luck with the weather—particularly fog on airfields in England which delayed reinforcements from being flown in—but the main reason for the failure was poor and muddled planning. The paratroops, who only carried light weapons, should have been landed very close to the bridge at Arnhem to take it by surprise, but it was decided to drop them seven miles away. Not only was the element of surprise lost, but only a few ever managed to get there. The batteries of the radio sets were flat, and anyway were on the wrong frequency, so they wouldn't work, and there was no communication between the units in Arnhem itself or between Arnhem, England, the RAF or XXX Corps. (The war correspondents, particularly the BBC's Stanley Maxted, somehow managed to get their censored reports through however). Determined RAF crews risked their lives when they bravely flew sorties through the flak and accurately dropped supplies according to the plan, unaware that the dropping zone had not yet been captured. The Germans received the supplies. The Officer Commanding the 1st Airborne Division, Major-General Urquhart, got himself cut off and was missing for days. The 43rd Division's advance from the Waal towards the desperate troops in Arnhem was painfully methodical when risks, dash and drive were needed. The Commander-in-Chief of Army Group B himself (Field Marshall Walter Model) happened to have his headquarters at Oosterbeek, a western suburb of Arnhem. Finally, the 9th SS Panzer Division was stationed just north of the town, a fact which was known beforehand but which was lightly dismissed by both Montgomery and the Officer Commanding the 1st Airborne Corps, Lieutenant-General 'Boy' Browning. Ten thousand men had been at Arnhem and over a thousand were killed. More than six thousand were taken prisoner, and half of these were wounded.

Meanwhile, the Canadian Army was still clearing the Channel ports. A lot of Canadians had been lost at Dieppe in 1942 and to their great satisfaction they captured the port without a fight. But it took six days to capture both Boulogne and Calais in similar operations to the one at Le Havre—heavy bombing and shelling—although thankfully the French casualties were not as great as both sides agreed to them being evacuated beforehand. By the time Ostend was captured— also without a fight—thirty thousand prisoners had been taken at a cost of less than fifteen hundred Canadian and British casualties.

But because of the Arnhem operation, Montgomery had not paid a great deal of attention to clearing the Scheldt and years later he was to write that it had been a bad mistake on his part. Although Antwerp is in Belgium, both banks of the Scheldt estuary are in Holland. Three disorganised divisions, the remnants of the German 15th Army which had been cut off, with their backs to the sea, managed to escape from the southern bank. They crossed the estuary in boats, and it took them three weeks for they didn't have many boats and the estuary was mined. If only the British had advanced north of Antwerp they would have been cut off again. The German 15th Army had literally lived to fight another day and they were later able to attack XXX Corps, advancing towards Arnhem, from the west. The failure to clear western Holland—the banks of the Scheldt estuary and then north of Antwerp to cut off the German 15th Army—had indeed been a very 'bad mistake.'

With the Germans in such disarray an Allied amphibious force might at this stage have been able to land at the mouth of the Scheldt without too much difficulty. As it was, the Germans had left a division of war-hardened veterans who had fought on the Russian front on the southern bank. The Canadians couldn't use tanks as the land was flooded and their infantry suffered many casualties before the Germans were finally dislodged. The RAF, the *Warspite* and commandos were used in an amphibious operation to capture the coastal batteries and it took three weeks to clear the estuary of mines. It was to be the end of November before the first convoy was able to enter Antwerp, almost three months after the docks had been captured. If the valiant Arnhem operation had been successful, or if Antwerp had been brought into use much earlier, there might have been a rapid end to the war, with the Western Allies in Berlin. But as things were, the Germans had now gained time to reorganise themselves.

Perhaps the war wouldn't be over by Christmas after all.

Belgium

After staying the night in Lille, the 4th Lincolns crossed the Belgian border at nine o'clock on Friday the 22nd September. They travelled over eighty miles that day until they reached the village of Kessel, south-east of Antwerp, in the early evening. The welcome they received as they passed through the Belgian villages was, if anything, even more enthusiastic than they had received in France. That night, every home in Kessel threw open its doors to the Lincolns.

The 49th Division had been ordered to force a crossing over the Albert Canal and the Commanding Officer of the Lincolns got up very early the next morning to carry out an extensive reconnaissance with the Company Commanders. Then the news came that the enemy had already gone. The following day, Sunday the 24th September, the Lincolns moved forward half a dozen miles in the drizzle to the village of Oostmalle with orders to cross the Antwerp-Turnhout Canal and establish a bridgehead on the other side. The canal wasn't very wide but it looked as if it was going to be a difficult job. The bridge carrying the main road had of course been blown, the surrounding area was flat and so there wasn't much cover, and there were some bends in the canal where the Germans had possibly placed machine-guns.

Joyful villagers greet their liberators. It became a familiar sight as the Lincoln moved through France and Belgium.

141

Some barges on the far side of the canal which might have come in useful had been sunk. In the end it was decided to try to cross the canal on either side of what was left of the bridge. 'A' Company under Major Barlow-Poole would be to the right of the bridge, and 'C' Company under Major Ed Cooke five hundred yards away to the left. 'D' Company under Major Gordon Newsum would then follow on, pass through and go on to establish the bridgehead. 'B' Company would provide a deception to the left. Once the Lincolns were established on the other side of the canal, the Royal Engineers would follow and get to work on building a Bailey bridge for the tanks of the Polish Armoured Division. A daylight attack would probably fail and cause too many casualties so it was decided to attack at night.

When it got dark the assault boats were brought up and placed in position on the canal bank. It was a filthy night. Silently, the Lincolns came forward and formed up in the pitch darkness and driving rain. At one minute past midnight they launched their boats and paddled across the canal. The tension was unbearable. The Germans might see or hear something at any moment and start firing machine-guns at the Lincolns in mid-stream. It only took a minute to cross the canal, but that minute seemed like hours.

There was complete surprise. During the crossing only a few shots were fired by the Germans, mostly on 'C' Company's front. In fact, neither side could see each other in the pitch black. When dawn broke the Germans found to their amazement that the Lincolns had crossed the canal and had infiltrated their positions. There was a little fighting here and there. One of 'C' Company's platoons was unlucky when a small party of Germans came in from behind and, firing blindly, killed four men and wounded six others. Some men who had silently occupied the ground floor of an empty house during the night heard five Germans who'd been asleep upstairs getting up; it was difficult to say who was the more astonished, the Lincolns or the Germans. All told, the Lincolns rounded up ninety-four prisoners, including three officers.

The Lincolns took up defensive positions in their bridgehead. The Engineers arrived and worked at such speed that they had their Bailey bridge up in a couple of hours and by 6.00 am the first vehicles of the Polish Armoured Division were crossing the canal. Elsewhere, the Hallamshires and the Royal Scots Fusiliers had come under intense fire and had been unable to cross the canal and establish bridgeheads in their sectors, so the Lincolns' crossing was the only one that had been successful. Good reconnaissance beforehand had ensured the success of the operation. It turned out to be one of the most important that the Lincolns undertook in the whole campaign—at least three divisions were to cross the Antwerp-Turnhout canal at the bridgehead which they had established. After the war, the battle honour 'Antwerp-Turnhout Canal' was added to the regiment's Colours.

During the morning the Polish Armoured Division poured across the Bailey bridge and later the KOYLI crossed to take a village, Rijkevorsel, slightly less than a mile to the north of the canal. They occupied the village without much trouble, but then the Germans mounted strong counter-attacks throughout the rest of the day and the KOYLI did well to hold on to their positions. They were relieved by the 2nd Essex during the night. Meanwhile, the Lincolns advanced eastwards along the northern bank of the canal after the Leicesters had arrived in the early afternoon to take over the bridgehead.

'A' Company was protecting the left flank, to the north, whilst the rest of the battalion went along the bank of the canal. They hadn't gone very far when they came across some Germans just ahead, so the Lincolns took defensive cover in some brickworks alongside the canal. Perhaps not knowing this, 'A' Company continued moving to the north-east until they found that they were cut off from the rest of the battalion. They had to abandon their transport, carriers and anti-tank guns to take cover in a railway cutting, where they beat off several attacks by the enemy. The Germans then decided to put in a stronger attack. Something had to be done, and quickly. The Artillery's Forward Observation Officer attached to 'A' Company, found that the battery of his wireless set was rapidly getting weaker and in any case he wasn't sure if his map was accurate. He said that it was a risk but he would do his best to bring down accurate artillery fire on the Germans. He saved the day. The gunners were magnificent and the Germans were driven back under a hail of accurately fired shells. 'A' Company finally fought their way out and rejoined the rest of the battalion at the brickworks at three o'clock in the morning.

During the next day, Tuesday the 26th September, the Germans made strong and determined efforts to infiltrate the battalion area in the brickworks but small arms and artillery fire held them off and caused heavy casualties. It was then found that the Germans had occupied a few houses and a cement factory to the west—*behind* the Lincolns. The battalion now had the canal to the south and Germans to the north, east and west. They were in a sticky spot, particularly as they were now cut off from their supplies. An improvised footbridge across the canal was made from half-sunken barges and bits of timber that were lying about, and a few assault boats managed to bring food and some stores, but it was obvious that somehow the Lincolns would have to fight their way out. This was the day, incidentally, that the survivors of the Airborne Division at Arnhem were finally overrun.

On the following morning, Wednesday the 27th September, Lieutenant-Colonel Barclay ordered 'C' Company under Major Edward Cooke to sweep west and north of the battalion's position. 'C' Company made a vigorous attack, supported by artillery and mortar fire and the rest of the battalion. The Lincolns had recently been issued with 'wasps'—flame-throwers mounted on Bren gun carriers. One of these followed twenty yards behind the leading section, who covered the buildings whilst the 'wasp' was fired. A couple of two-second shots were enough to set a building on fire, and the enemy resistance—which up to the time the 'wasp' was brought into action had been strong—suddenly collapsed. The Germans were prepared to face bullets and shells, but not to being burnt alive.

The Lincolns, no longer cut off, continued to meet fierce resistance. These Germans were certainly good fighters. A Spandau machine-gun in the doorway of a factory was causing a lot of trouble. A platoon worked their way round to the left and opened fire, whilst a 'wasp' arrived from the right of another building. There was another Spandau post about twenty yards away from some houses which were also occupied by the enemy and Lieutenant Stainton of 'A' Company sent his Bren gunners to a flank to cover the rear of the houses whilst he led his assault group under heavy fire. He arrived at the front of a house but found that he couldn't force the door open, so he crawled round to the back, hurled grenades through a window and then rushed the Spandau position. Three of the crew fled and were shot by the Bren gunners, whilst the fourth was taken prisoner. It was later found that there were four dead Germans in the house.

Prisoners on their way to collect rations for the rest of their comrades.

Although Lieutenant Stainton's party had been under machine-gun fire during the whole of this action, no-one had been hit. Earlier, Second-Lieutenant Hill of the carrier platoon had been involved in a skirmish against a German machine-gun post. He went forward under cover with three men in a Bren gun carrier and when they were about thirty yards away he jumped out and rushed the Germans before they had time to recover, nabbed six prisoners and then, leaving a man to guard the prisoners, dashed two hundred yards to collect another three who had been a nuisance to him. His youthful audacity amazed everyone, particularly the Germans. Both he and Lieutenant Stainton were awarded the Military Cross.

Elsewhere, the 49th Division was coming up against determined German resistance. The 2nd Essex, at Rijkevorsel, was heavily shelled and had to fight off persistent counter-attacks for two days. The South Wales Borderers had taken over the defence of the bridgehead from the Leicesters and had a desperate struggle to hold on during an assault which lasted for almost four hours. The Leicesters, the 7th Duke of Wellingtons and the Gloucesters joined the Hallams who were having great difficulties in capturing the Depot de Mendicité, a barracks-like building with high walls which was surrounded by a moat twenty feet wide and three feet deep. It was a sort of combined workhouse and asylum and the patients stood around, looking on whilst the battle was raging. Some were killed.

It took two days to clear the Germans out of the place and the Leicesters in particular paid a high price, for seventy men were killed. Many medals were awarded for the bitter action at the Mendicité, including a posthumous Victoria Cross for Corporal Harper of the Hallamshires—the only VC to be awarded in the whole of the 49th Division.

On the 2nd October the 4th Lincolns were ordered to move along the canal bank behind the Poles. There was a left-handed bend in the canal so the Lincolns now found themselves on the west side going from south to north. They approached a place called Ravels, about three miles north of Turnhout, where some Germans were positioned in factories on both sides of the canal. Supported by a squadron of tanks, 'A' and 'C' Companies put in a determined attack on the factory on the west of the canal and soon occupied it. A Belgian civilian appeared and said that there was a tunnel under the canal. As the Germans were still occupying the factories on the other side a patrol from 'A' Company was sent to cover the entrance of the tunnel. They found that the Germans were already there, waiting for them, and they opened up with a Spandau at close range. Luckily the Germans must have been poor shots, for only one man was hurt as the patrol from 'A' Company hastily withdrew. The man who had been wounded dived for a ditch and was pelted with grenades every time he tried to move. Two hours later, covered in blood from five bullet wounds and shrapnel from the grenades, he somehow managed to get back to 'A' Company, and reported: 'Back from patrol, sir'.

The following day, 'B' and 'D' Companies advanced to attack the town of Ravels but after taking twenty-four prisoners found that most of the Germans had gone. The Lincolns stayed at Ravels overnight and then, on the 4th October, they moved forward to chase the Germans but had to wait at Chapel St Jean as the Hallamshires and the KOYLI, under heavy shell and mortar fire, had still to clear the village of Poppel ahead. Delays like this caused tension. Nerves frayed and the men got more and more irritable, so it was a relief when they got the order to get moving again.

The Lincolns advanced from Poppel towards Goirle the next day, supported by a lively squadron of Canadian Shermans whose simple but effective method of protecting the infantry was to shoot at everything in sight, including haystacks. Progress was quite slow, for the road was lined either side with pine woods which took a lot of clearing. Companies took it in turns to lead the way and clear the woods, each company passing through the other so that a fresh company came forward to take on the next bit of this tiresome job. The Lincolns began to come under heavy shelling and mortar fire and enemy resistance stiffened quite considerably when strong reinforcements arrived from the Dutch town of Tilburg. 'A' Company's forward platoon were over a bridge leading into the town and 'B' Company crossed the stream and joined them at dusk. By nightfall, the Lincolns were in all-round defensive positions with the enemy in front and on either side, some only two or three hundred yards away. The men breathed in short, noisy gulps, the slightest sound made them jump and their trigger fingers were nervous. They were pleased when orders were received to withdraw silently during the darkness and make their way to the hamlet of Nieukirk, on the Belgian-Dutch border.

The Lincolns managed to withdraw successfully, but the Germans followed them the next day, the 6th October. In the early morning enemy snipers started to fire from the thick woods nearby and the battalion was shelled. Although little damage was done it was nevertheless all very frightening. A squadron of the 49th Reconnaissance Regiment had still to withdraw to the Lincolns' position, which was just to the west of the main road between Poppel and Tilburg, and the carrier platoon was sent to meet them and to ensure that they weren't cut off. They had almost finished this job when—at two o'clock in the afternoon—the Germans launched a very strong attack, not only on the Lincolns' position but also that of the Hallamshires to the immediate left at Aerle, where they were holding a bridge across a stream which was actually the border between Belgium and Holland.

The armoured cars of the Reconnaissance Regiment were still half a mile away to the right of the battalion and were almost overrun, but 'C' Company, in reserve under Captain Ainger, and tanks of 'B' Squadron of the Canadian Armoured Regiment, quickly mounted a counter-attack and drove the Germans back. For the next three hours, the Lincolns and Hallams were shelled and mortared very heavily and then at half-past five the Germans attacked again. This time their attack was broken up by almost non-stop fire from the 25-pounders of the 69th Field Regiment which Major Nigel Richardson, their Forward Observation Officer, was quickly and efficiently directing. Major Richardson and the 69th Field Regiment had been attached to the 4th Lincolns ever since the days in Iceland.

There was at least a brigade of Germans attacking the battalion and they kept up the pressure throughout the night. The woods which had been cleared were filling up again with Germans and early the following morning they managed to infiltrate the Lincolns' position between two platoons of 'A' Company and the reserve platoon. Once again, it was 'C' Company and the Canadian tanks which came to the rescue and in a swift counter-attack they drove the Germans back. The CO had kept the mortar platoon very close to battalion headquarters and they were firing furiously under his direct control. But the Germans kept pounding the Lincolns with shells and mortars and to make matters worse there was also very heavy fire from Spandau machine-guns on either side of the main road. Most of the Spandaus were silenced by the middle of the morning by the tanks and the artillery's 25-pounders. Second-Lieutenant Arthur Turner, commanding the mortar platoon, was recommended for the Military Cross following this action, but because so many officers had been awarded the MC at Arnhem he had to be content with a Mention in Dispatches instead.

During the morning a company from the KOYLI arrived to take the place of 'C' Company, and the rest of their battalion relieved the Lincolns during the afternoon. The Lincolns were relieved in more ways than one, and thankfully made their way back to the village of Wielde. They had been in action for two weeks and were tired. During that period twenty-two of their men had been killed and more than seventy had been wounded.

The battle at Poppel forest had been a very stiff engagement. It had been a defensive success and much of the credit had to go to the 69th Field Regiment, the Territorial Army gunners from Leeds and Ilkley who had been in constant demand. Speed in bringing down fire was essential and the artillery had once again supported the Lincolns magnificently, immediately and accurately breaking up German attacks and positions in response to Major Richardson's calm and precise directions.

After a good night's sleep, the Lincolns had welcome showers from the mobile bath unit at Wielde and were looking forward to a quiet rest, but during the mid-afternoon they received orders to return immediately to the Poppel area with a detachment from the Free Belgian Forces. But there was little activity here, and it became obvious that the Germans had gone. Patrols found various mines and booby traps around the perimeter of the position and a carrier patrol found a large quantity of valuable electrical equipment—radio transmitters and receivers—which had been abandoned. It was all collected and sent off to the Royal Signals. A message was received from 'Bubbles' Barker, GOC of the 49th Division, congratulating everyone for their efforts during the recent German counter-attack, which now seemed to have fizzled out.

On Wednesday the 11th October the Lincolns were relieved by the Leicestershires and moved to take up defensive positions at Baarle Nassau, a village which was right on the Belgian-Dutch frontier. In fact some of the houses were in Belgium and some in Holland and it was even said that the gardens of some properties were in a different country from the house.

The 49th Division hadn't actually moved very far since crossing the Turnhout canal over a fortnight earlier, but nevertheless a firm bridgehead had been established. To the west, the Canadians were having a dreadful time in the Scheldt and the Polar Bears, dug in defensively, were having to wait until they had managed to clear both banks. The weather may have had something to do with it too, for there was a lot of rain for days on end and tanks would quickly become bogged down in the low-lying marshy ground ahead. There was an occasional skirmish here and there. A small patrol of Germans came across some signallers laying a phone line in the Lincolns' sector but after one of the Germans was killed the rest ran away. Patrols were sent out day and night, the enemy sent over some shells, and snipers killed the occasional German, but generally things were quiet all along the 49th Division's front.

Another German died during the week the Lincolns were at Baarle Nassau—Field Marshall Erwin Rommel. Recovering from the injuries he received when an RAF plane had shot up his car, Rommel was suspected of having been involved in the plot to kill Hitler. He was given the choice of facing a trial in Berlin and being condemned to death (in which case his wife wouldn't have received a pension) or of quietly swallowing a pill and 'dying as a result of his wounds in Normandy.' Rommel chose the latter and was given a state funeral. There were messages of sympathy from Hitler and Goebbels and the eulogy was given by von Runstedt. He hadn't been let in on the secret and really believed that Rommel had died from his wounds.

Holland

'I am constantly hearing of the fine achievements of your battalion,' Field-Marshall Montgomery told Lieutenant-Colonel Peter Barclay when decorating him with the DSO he had won at Fontenay. Afterwards the CO said that this was high praise indeed as the Commander-in-Chief didn't usually get to hear about the actions of individual battalions.

Whilst Monty was decorating the CO—and presenting Major Barlow-Poole with his MC—the 4th Lincolns were taking up new positions. Together with the Hallamshires and the KOYLI they now came under the direct command of the Canadians.

I Corps advanced on the same day that the investiture was taking place. The 4th Canadian Division was on the left, the 49th Division was in the centre and the Polish Armoured Division was on the right. They were heading for Bergen op Zoom, Roosendaal and Breda respectively. The Polar Bears' objective, Roosendaal, was twenty miles away.

The 56th Brigade, supported by flame-throwing Crocodiles, flail tanks, regiments of 25-pounders and medium artillery, and all the heavy mortars they could lay their hands on, advanced four miles on the first day and took three hundred prisoners. The Germans had been taken by surprise and the sheer weight of firepower had been too much for them. The 1st Leicesters in 147 Brigade cut the main Antwerp-Breda road and seized a key bridge just north of a village called Wuustwezel, but the following day they were heavily counter-attacked by enemy infantry, self-propelled guns and tanks. The fighting went on all day and eventually the Germans withdrew, but the Leicesters had suffered over a hundred casualties, including twenty-five dead. It took some time to capture Essen, a long, straggly village just short of the Belgian-Dutch frontier which was heavily defended by the Germans. There was bitter fighting all along the front, but gradually the advance continued. The Germans were, incidentally, from the 15th Army—the ones who had been cut off on the southern bank of the Scheldt but had slipped away in boats in dribs and drabs to the other side of the estuary.

Although the Hallamshires and the KOYLI took part in the advance, the Lincolns stayed where they were because they were receiving reinforcements. Even with the arrival of these new men the Lincolns were still twenty-five per cent short of their full establishment. Men in reinforcement drafts now came from all parts of the British Isles and the battalion had lost much of its 'Lincolnshire' character by now. Although quite a number of the officers and men still remained from the pre-war Territorial Army days, some had been posted to other regiments over the years, some had been wounded and some had been killed. There'd also been some pretty rapid promotions. Tom Adamson from Stickney had been made a lance-corporal in France, a corporal in Belgium and now, in Holland, he was a sergeant.

The children of Southampton did very well during this period. Reinforcements on their way to France and Belgium could only change pound and ten shilling notes into francs, so they tossed their small change to the eager hands of the many children who'd soon got to know about this and gathered round the docks.

The Lincolns were in a small hamlet, Zondereigen, and there were still some Germans around, for there were many forests in the flat countryside in which they could hide. The maps weren't all that accurate because since they'd been printed many of the trees had been felled, so patrols faced difficulties as there were now clearings and tracks in the forests which were not shown. It was hard to move silently because dry sticks crackled when the men walked over them. A small reconnaissance patrol led by Lieutenant Stanion ran into trouble when it was ambushed by some Germans. Only one man returned; Lieutenant Stanion and one of his men were taken prisoner and his sergeant was wounded. Things were generally quiet however, although the Germans sent over a few shells now and then.

On Monday the 23rd October, the 6th and 27th Canadian Armoured Regiments and a Belgian detachment were placed under the command of Lieutenant-Colonel Barclay DSO and together with the Lincolns became known as 'Impforce.' It was on this day that 'C' Company found a German who was laying anti-tank mines. They made him take them all up again before they brought him in. A Belgian civilian reported that there were some Germans in a farm near the village of Ulicoten, and a platoon from 'B' Company under Sergeant Jackson and a troop of tanks penetrated deep into enemy territory to investigate. According to the six prisoners who were taken, the Germans had had many casualties and were so thin on the ground that they were holding the front with just one company rather than at battalion strength. The following day, Second Lieutenant Priestley with a patrol of twelve men and a troop of tanks raided some buildings about a mile in front of the Lincolns' positions. Under cover of fire from the tanks, the patrol rushed the buildings and killed twelve Germans—Sergeant Jackson accounting for at least three—and wounded three others. There were no British or Canadian casualties.

The Germans were withdrawing towards Breda and now that the Lincolns had replenished their stores and equipment they were being brought into action again. Lieutenant-Colonel Barclay was busy organising his 'Impforce'. Lieutenant-Colonel White and his 6th Canadian Armoured Regiment took over command of 'A', 'B' and 'C' Companies of the Lincolns in a section which was called 'Whiteforce' whilst 'D' Company was placed in 'Gorforce' with Lieutenant-Colonel Gordon's 27th Canadian Armoured Regiment.

'Whiteforce' set off towards Breda, nine miles away, on Saturday the 28th October, leaving 'Gorforce' in reserve on the Belgian-Dutch frontier in the Baarle Nassau area. The Lincolns enjoyed riding on the Canadians' Sherman tanks and fairly good progress was made along the cratered road. 'Whiteforce' was using a minor road instead of the more obvious better road, the tanks making short work of the relatively few pockets of Germans they met here and there along the way. They had a rousing reception from the Dutch villagers as they passed through Ulicoten but the Lincolns had to dismount from the tanks when they reached a crossroads near Couwelaar and they had to come into action to clear a position where they could stay the night. Several violent explosions were heard as the Germans blew up some strategic points but with the help of the tanks the Lincolns made a determined assault and overcame the opposition. But there were still some Germans nearby, and as they kept trying to infiltrate, the night was not a very restful one. Eight men were wounded, including Major Flint, the Officer Commanding 'B' Company, but fortunately his wound was only slight and he was back in action about ten days later.

Captured German self-propelled gun.

In the morning, 'Whiteforce' advanced a couple of miles and took two hundred prisoners and a fully-working 88mm gun. 'B' Company (now led by Captain Golding) and 'A' Squadron of the 6th Canadian Armoured Regiment had a 'pheasant drive' to flush a wood east of Ulvenhout. The Germans were driven west into Ulvenhout, onto the guns of 'C' Company and 'C' Squadron who were still trying to overcome resistance in the village and now found themselves having to solve the difficult problem of dealing with these new arrivals as well. Many Germans were killed, wounded or taken prisoner. Once resistance had ended, 'A'

Company and 'B' Squadron passed through to attack Beiberg and then Ginneken, suburbs of Breda, which the Polish Armoured Division was also nearing from the east. As soon as these villages had been taken, 'Gorforce' came forward and then passed through *them*. A bridge over a river had been blown, but once a tank-borne bridge had been laid there was little further opposition and 'Gorforce' moved to the west to cut off the enemy's retreat route. When 'A' Company jumped off their tanks in the moonlight, they found several frightened Germans cowering in a ditch by the side of the road, one of them with a bazooka only ten yards away from a tank.

On the 30th October, 'B' and 'C' Companies, together with the Sherman tanks, swept a forest at Mastbosch whilst 'A' Company of the Lincolns was transferred to 'Gorforce' at Roskam. Riding on tanks, they took part in an unusual move to close a gap through which the Germans were escaping. What made the move remarkable was that it was not only made through a forest—not good tank country—but also at night. Every third tank was left free of passengers, and firing as they went along the objective was soon reached.

Contact was made with the Polish Division on the right and an American unit on the left. 'Impforce' entered Breda on the 31st October and concentrated in the area of the ancient Bouvigne castle (complete with a moat) which had been used by the Germans as a mess. Over a hundred and eighty prisoners were taken together with many machine-guns and countless rifles and small arms. Much to everyone's regret however, 'Impforce' was disbanded after the extremely successful series of operations which had been carried out with the 2nd Canadian Armoured Brigade. Friendships had been struck between the Lincolns and the Canadians at all levels—platoon/troop, company/squadron and battalion/regiment—and as a result there had been very close co-operation and perfect mutual understanding. Everyone was disappointed that the partnership was being broken up and strenuous efforts were made to keep it intact. Brigadier Bingham, the Officer Commanding the 2nd Canadian Brigade, tried hard to keep the Lincolns permanently as a motorised battalion, but it was no use.

The Lincolns enjoyed a few days rest in the beautiful surroundings of the Chateau Bouvigny on the outskirts of Breda. The trees in the nearby forests were a wonderful colour in the late autumn sun. But it was not all rest, for Lieutenant-Colonel Barclay—whose mind was always on the alert—assembled the men to go through the lessons which could be learned from the most recent actions whilst they were still fresh in everyone's minds. He congratulated everyone for doing an excellent job, particularly the patrols for penetrating so deep into enemy territory. He read out messages which had been received from General Barker and the Officers Commanding the Polish Armoured Division, 146 Brigade and the 2nd Canadian Armoured Brigade, congratulating the Lincolns for the fine work they had done in the past few days. Expressing his thanks for the excellent work which the Lincolns had done on his left flank, the Polish general said: 'It has been a source of deep satisfaction for my officers and men to work so closely with such a fine team.'

The Lincolns capture Hitler (alias Doug Collier).

On Thursday the 2nd November, a ceremonial parade was held in Breda. Dutch and Allied flags were to be seen everywhere and the whole population of the town lined the streets and cheered wildly as the troops marched by. A Canadian army band which had somehow appeared from nowhere played as the troops marched past Brigadier Bingham who took the salute.

It was back to business the following day, when the Lincolns rejoined 146 Brigade at Roosendaal. When they arrived they were placed under two hours notice to move, but they were stood down and had a day's rest and a shower in the mobile bath unit instead. On the 5th November the battalion was ordered to support the KOYLI in taking the village of Klundert, but they were later redirected to the Tonnekreek area when it was learned that the KOYLI had entered the village unopposed. Klundert was however a mass of flames, with houses burning on both sides of the road. The Germans had set fire to the village before leaving.

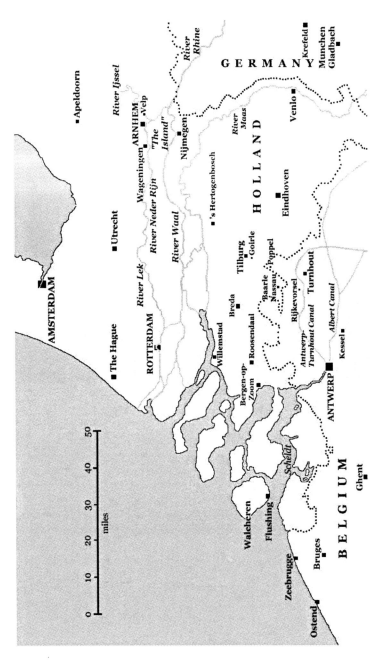

Map 11. Northern Belgium and Southern Holland.

154

The Lincolns advanced in the Tonnekreek area without a great deal of opposition. 'D' Company took two prisoners who turned out to be from the Dutch SS. No-one knew what their subsequent fate was, and to be quite honest no-one really cared. Tonnekreek was the stepping stone to the Lincolns' next objective, Willemstad.

Willemstad was on the southern bank of the River Maas estuary and now that the 56th Brigade had taken the River Mark—a few miles south of the town—it was the only remaining enemy strongpoint south of the river. It had been built as a medieval fortress and still had two moats and high twin octagonal ramparts with bastions sticking out from each corner. The Lincolns crossed the River Mark and made their way towards the town. It was a bleak and desolate scene. The weather was wet and windy, the countryside was flooded and there were deep ditches filled with water either side of the muddy banked-up roads. It was obvious that tanks couldn't be used.

The Lincolns arrived at the outskirts of Willemstad on the 6th November and took up positions east and south of the town, and although they were shelled by the Germans no damage was done. Patrols reported that all the ways into the town were covered by enemy fire and that there was barbed wire around the moats. The next day a small party was sent with a white flag to demand surrender, or failing that, to ask for the several thousand Dutch civilians to be evacuated. The German commander refused to surrender, but he agreed to arrange for the Dutch to leave and in the late afternoon a pathetic procession of men, women and children with a few possessions trudged through the Lincolns' positions.

After an artillery bombardment which did a lot of damage to the town but didn't kill any Germans, 'A' and 'D' Companies advanced into Willemstad early the next day—to find no-one there except five deserters. All the Germans had slipped away after the Dutch civilians had left and they had crossed to the other side of the estuary. They had left a few booby-trapped vehicles but had been in such a hurry that they had also left behind a great deal of carefully packed loot.

The carrier platoon patrolled for several miles along the south bank of the River Maas but found nothing and then handed over to the 18th Canadian Armoured Car Regiment which was responsible for a section of the coast. The Lincolns then returned to Roosendaal to enjoy a few days rest, an ENSA show, a cinema, showers and warmth. Sunday the 12th November was Remembrance Day and there was a church parade during which prayers were said for the fallen, the wounded and those at home. Later, a football match was arranged with the local Roosendaal team which the Lincolns won 5-4.

An exercise in crossing a river by night was held prior to the Lincolns moving, with the rest of the Polar Bears, on Tuesday the 14th November. They travelled a long way and were now back in Belgium at Hamont, a village about twelve miles south of Eindhoven on the Dutch-Belgian border and west of Venlo. The 49th Division had now been transferred from I Corps (which was still with the Canadian army on the extreme left of the front) to XII Corps which, with VIII Corps to its left and XXX Corps to the right, was preparing to advance to the River Rhine.

'A' Company enter Willemstad and pass a German gun.

Another gale in the Channel had seriously affected supplies coming into Cherbourg and the Mulberry harbour, and had re-emphasised the importance of opening the deep-water port of Antwerp. Clearing the Scheldt had thus become a priority after the Arnhem operation but it turned out to be much more difficult than Montgomery had anticipated. Tiresome though it was, the job had to be done and this meant that for the moment any action to attack the Ruhr had to be shelved.

The Germans thus gained valuable time to reorganise the remnants of their shattered army in defence of the Reich. In hindsight, the Allies might have done better if they'd used their resources to clear the Scheldt quickly instead of using them in the operation to take Arnhem. But they hadn't, and so it could be claimed that the bold but failed bid to take Arnhem had, ironically, actually prolonged the war instead of shortening it as had been hoped.

Searching for Germans in Willemstad.

But the Germans had left!

The massive coal and steel areas of the Ruhr were not far over the German border—tantalisingly close to the Allied armies. Once they had been captured Hitler would be in great difficulties. Eisenhower had to some extent modified his 'broad front' strategy (everyone attacking everywhere) because he'd accepted that there were simply not enough resources for a general offensive all along the front. This now extended from the Maas estuary on the coast of Holland to the French-Swiss border which the 6th US Army Group (the US 7th Army and the French 1st Army) had now reached from the South of France. American troops had even been left in the South of France in case the Germans still in Italy tried to break the supply line from Marseilles. Eisenhower agreed with Montgomery's view that the major effort of the Allies should be to capture the Ruhr and that it would take two armies under one man to do it.

Montgomery wanted Eisenhower to let him have the 9th US Army so that he could get on with the job. But Eisenhower had a problem, for if there was to be a concentrated thrust for the Ruhr he would have to limit the amount of supplies to Patton, further south. Eisenhower knew that Patton (and probably the American public) wouldn't stand for it if he had to be halted just so that Montgomery could capture the Ruhr. So Eisenhower decided that the two armies would have to be American and that they would be commanded by General Omar Bradley. The broad plan was that the 1st and 9th US Armies would cross the Roer river and make for the west bank of the Rhine at Krefeld, Cologne and Bonn. The British 2nd Army under Lieutenant-General Sir Miles Dempsey would attack from the Nijmegen area—only half a dozen or so miles from Germany—and advance south between the Maas and the Rhine. The Allies would then be on the west bank of the Rhine all the way from Arnhem to Bonn. The Rhine would then be crossed by the 1st Army south of Cologne and by the 9th Army north of Düsseldorf. Patton's 3rd Army would only advance as and when supplies became available.

This plan had been agreed in mid-October. General Omar Bradley, in command of the US 9th, 1st and 3rd Armies, had commanded a Corps under Patton in Sicily but the roles had since been reversed and Patton, a forceful man, now found himself under Bradley. In early November he managed to convince Bradley that it would only take him three days to get to Metz and the Saar from the Nancy area and then he could advance to the Siegfried line.

Patton's troops attacked on the 8th November. It had poured with rain for three days and it was still coming down in torrents. Tanks got bogged down if they tried to move off the roads and because of the weather there was little air support. Patton's troops were trying to advance on a broad front of thirty miles instead of making a concentrated attack on a very narrow front. After a week of heavy fighting, the Americans only managed to advance fifteen miles and in that time they had used up a considerable amount of ammunition.

On the 16th November, 2,500 British and American bombers accurately dropped almost ten thousand tons of high explosive as a prelude to the attacks made by the

US 1st and 9th Armies. The weather was wet here as well, fields quickly became quagmires when the tanks tried to move and the artillery found that there was a shortage of ammunition. The 9th Army reached the River Roer, the first of their objectives, by the end of November but it was to be another fortnight before the 1st Army arrived. The infantry had slogged their way through the mud for almost a month to advance eight miles, and their casualties had been heavy. The Germans had moved their 6th Panzer Division west of the Rhine and Bradley felt that he couldn't now send his troops across the flooded Roer river in case they became cut off and destroyed.

Further north, Montgomery was still building up his strength and hadn't yet mounted the British attack.

*   *   *   *

The 49th Division was ordered to advance towards Venlo, a town which was only three or four miles from the Dutch-German border. The weather was vile and the flat countryside was waterlogged. After a couple of days of Company training at Hamont (which included digging trenches in the dark!) the Lincolns were getting ready to move at half-past ten on the morning of the 17th November when orders were received to stand down. The 51st Highland Division had already taken the battalion's objective. The CO took his senior officers on a reconnaissance to have a look at their next objective and after they had returned Major Gordon Newsum, the Officer Commanding 'D' Company, decided to go back and take another look. He was killed by a shell.

Gordon Newsum was yet another of the 4th Lincolns' pre-war Territorial Army officers to be killed. He had served with the battalion throughout the war and his death was a great shock to everyone. He had been in the family timber business of H Newsum, Sons & Company Ltd at both their Gainsborough and Sheffield branches and had joined the Territorial Army in February 1939. He was a member of the Lincoln Rugby Club and was the treasurer (and a good bowler) for the Lindum Cricket Club. Gordon Newsum, who was 29 years old, had got married in July 1941 whilst on leave from Iceland and had a daughter who was just over a year old.

The Lincolns had a tiresome day on the 18th November, being ordered to stand down until twelve noon and then until six o'clock in the evening. This latter order was then cancelled when orders were suddenly received to move at short notice, and by the following morning they had relieved the Argyll and Sutherland Highlanders in the Panningen area and had started to dig in. This was yet another tiresome day for, after six hours of digging, the positions were just about complete when to their utter disbelief and dismay they were ordered to move forward another half a mile. Although the language which had greeted this order was both colourful and strong, the Lincolns were pleased in the end that they had had to move, for the positions they had just left were heavily shelled. A very strange thing happened that night. Lieutenant-Colonel Barclay was having a meeting with his senior officers when a fully-armed German soldier suddenly arrived unannounced out of the dark and butted in on the conference. He calmly took a seat at the table, joined the meeting and contributed some useful information.

On Monday the 20th November the Lincolns advanced towards the town of Maasbree with a squadron of tanks from the 44th Royal Tank Regiment. 'C' Company, in the lead, very soon came across the enemy (the 21st Paratroop Regiment) who were defending the main road west of Maasbree with determination. 'C' Company attacked under cover of artillery fire and managed to reach their objective, a triangular-shaped wood. There were some casualties, including Lieutenant Humphries who was killed by artillery fire. 'B' Company under Major Flint was then pushed through to the crossroads just outside Maasbree. It was heavily defended as three roads into the town converged there. It was a shocking day. It was raining very heavily and one by one the tanks 'bellied' in the boggy countryside, so there was a shortage of fire-power as the ever-forceful Major Flint inspired 'B' Company forward. There was little cover and after a hard struggle and a few casualties 'B' Company managed to establish itself astride the crossroads, beating off a counter-attack which the enemy launched with about twenty men soon afterwards. 'A' Company moved up to the left flank of 'B' Company to ward off any threat from the north, whilst 'D' Company were ordered to a position from which they could counter-attack an enemy assault on any of the other three companies. During the night, very successful patrolling was carried out by both 'B' and 'C' Companies which yielded some very useful information about where the Germans were located.

During the following day the companies moved forward, but it wasn't easy because they were under fire from enemy mortars and self-propelled guns. By nightfall they were firmly established in positions, poised for the attack on Maasbree. Lieutenant-Colonel Barclay gave a final briefing to his officers. Because there was an area of flat open country to be crossed it was decided to put in a night attack. The battalion would infiltrate into the near edge of the town during the night to gain a foothold and then, as soon as it began to get light, they would start clearing the enemy from the town itself. Patrols which had been sent out earlier reported that the way seemed clear. 'A' and 'D' Companies moved off in the dark at a quarter-past six, the silence broken by clatters and curses as men tripped over things like telegraph wires which had come down. But the Germans had withdrawn and by half-past seven they had reached their objectives on the far side of the town.

Somewhere a German Spandau fired tracer vertically into the air and this was obviously a signal to their artillery to bring down defensive fire. For a time there was some heavy shelling which fell to the west of the village but it was too late and the shelling missed the battalion altogether. The operation had gone so slickly that 'B' and 'C' Companies had left and were already in the town. By eight o'clock in the morning Maasbree had been completely occupied and the anti-tank guns and mortars were in positions in case there was a counter-attack. The whole operation had gone like clockwork. After five months campaigning all the cogs were well-oiled and the 4th Lincolns were now a highly-competent and experienced regiment. The Hallams passed through on their way towards Blerick, a suburb on the west side of Venlo. Maasbree had not been as damaged as some villages, but a few houses had been shattered and one or two civilians had been killed as a result of the shelling. Nevertheless the people of Maasbree came out of their cellars to find that the Germans had finally gone, and they wept tears of joy.

There was some more spasmodic shelling throughout the day, but after a German deserter had been handed over by the Dutch resistance the Lincolns went back into reserve. The wet weather and the heavy, tracked vehicles had played havoc with the roads and for a day or two the Lincolns had to provide working parties to do road repairs. On Saturday the 25th November however they relieved the Hallams in front of Blerick. There was mild surprise and excitement when they heard that during the three days the Hallams had been there, they had been shelled by Germans—from the Siegfried line. So Germany really was only just a few miles away now!

'A' Company went forward and took up positions on the fringe of some woods overlooking the wide River Maas (the same river as the Meuse in France). In front of them were some strong positions which the Belgians had originally built as a defensive line, facing east, towards Germany. The unfortunate Germans, who had the wide Maas behind and the 49th Division before them, had now reversed these positions so that they were now facing the British to the west, but it was soon found that there were only a few Germans there. The Lincolns carried out several successful patrols and 'C' Company captured four talkative prisoners who revealed the strength of the Germans defending Venlo and the location of their headquarters. Occasionally the Germans sent over a few shells and a solitary plane flew over and gave a burst of cannon fire, but no-one was hurt. Lieutenant Daykin, Sergeant Guest and the pioneer platoon did some exceptional work when they cleared all the mines in front of the battalion and found out where the Germans had placed their barbed-wire defences, some of which were incomplete. Lieutenant White led 9 Platoon of 'A' Company in a successful fighting patrol at eight o'clock on the evening of the 28th November against five German positions which were closely connected by trenches. Although the Germans opened fire straightaway, the platoon dashed through a gap in the wire to the enemy trenches and dug-outs under the covering fire from the rest of 'A' Company which Lieutenant White had previously arranged. A German with a Schmeisser machine-gun fired at Lieutenant White at point-blank range, but he missed. Lieutenant White didn't. This seemed to take the heart out of the Germans in three adjoining posts and they surrendered, but he was fired on from the fourth position, twenty yards away. Lieutenant White killed three of the Germans with grenades and rifle fire and wounded the fourth as he ran off. The whole thing took less time than it takes to tell. Altogether, four Germans were killed, two were wounded and twelve were taken prisoner. There had been no casualties in 9 Platoon and Lieutenant White, who at one time had been the Company Sergeant Major in 'A' Company, was awarded the Military Cross. Later, the CO cited this raid as a perfect example of a successful, well-planned raid by a fighting patrol and he singled out the mortar platoon for special praise for their accurate fire just prior to the attack.

Sergeant Newton also led a patrol from 'C' Company against some Germans in a farm building over half a mile away to the west. During the day he had carried out a daring reconnaissance and had found a route between two minefields and a gap in the barbed-wire. When it got dark the patrol crept silently forward until they were challenged and then fired upon by a German sentry. Sergeant Newton charged and dragged the sentry out of his trench by the scruff of his neck. After three of the sentry's comrades had surrendered, Sergeant Newton rushed more German posts until the whole area was cleared. Again, there were no casualties and Sergeant Newton was awarded the Military Medal for his skill and courageous leadership. The German post was deliberately left unoccupied and 'C' Company had a lot of fun when they watched the consternation of the four Germans who arrived at the post to relieve their comrades, only to find that there was no-one there. Altogether, 'C' Company took the post three times and then left it empty in the hope—always fulfilled—that more Germans would arrive and provide more sport.

But the Lincolns didn't get the opportunity of being amongst the first British troops to set foot on German soil, for the 2nd Seaforth Highlanders from the 15th (Scottish) Division arrived to take over their positions at Blerick on the 29th November. By the evening the Lincolns were on their way to Nijmegen. The Polar Bears of the 49th (West Riding) Division were under the command of the 1st Canadian Army once again and were relieving the 50th Division which had landed on D-Day and was returning to England. They had been given the job of garrisoning 'The Island'.

Although Montgomery later claimed that Operation Market-Garden had been 'ninety per cent successful' it was nothing of the kind. It had been a one hundred per cent failure, for the sole purpose of the whole operation had been to get across the Rhine. It makes one wonder whether Lieutenant-General 'Boy' Browning had fully grasped this, for he said beforehand (not at the end, as in the film): 'Perhaps we are trying to go a bridge too far.' All that had been won after so much courage and effort was a long, narrow salient which led nowhere, for the Rhine, that wide, formidable obstacle to entering Germany, had still to be crossed.

Just inside Holland the Rhine divides into two branches. The northern branch, the Neder Rijn, (the Pannerdens canal) flows north-west until it joins the River Ijssel at Arnhem where it then turns west. Further downstream it becomes the River Lek. The southern branch of the Rhine flows west, past Nijmegen, and also later receives another name, the River Waal. In between these rivers is the area which became known to the troops as 'The Island'.

Nothing could be more desolate. This really was the 'Low Country'. There were huge banks to keep in the water of the swollen rivers which flowed well above the level of the flat, surrounding countryside. The roads were also banked. Because of all the rain and the low-lying, flat countryside the whole area was squelching under water, despite the large number of land-drainage dykes. It was still raining, and it was cold for it was now December. Arnhem, still occupied by the Germans, stood above the level of the area and as they had good observation any movement at all had to be done by night.

There had been heavy action during the vain attempt to reach Arnhem and there were wrecks of tanks, trucks, guns and any amount of other equipment still strewn about. The unoccupied, damaged houses and cottages had been reinforced with sandbags and had become defensive positions. It was all a very depressing sight.

The Germans sometimes sent over some shells during the night, but it was impossible to dig trenches for they immediately filled up with water. And then, if things weren't bad enough, the Germans blew up the dykes of the Neder Rijn to the south-west of Arnhem on the 2nd December, at a moment when the rivers were exceptionally high, and flooded the whole area.

As someone pointed out, it wasn't 'No Man's Land' which now separated the two armies, it was 'No Man's Water'. To avoid their forward units becoming isolated the Allies had to move their troops back from the villages just south of the Neder Rijn to higher ground to the south, between the two rivers—the 'Island'. The Germans re-occupied these villages—Driel, Randwijk and Heteren—and no doubt they were as fed up with the miserable conditions as the British.

To begin with, the 4th Lincolns were spared these cold and wet conditions, for they stayed in Nijmegen, a pleasant well laid out town but which had been severely damaged by bombs and shells, particularly in the area of the bridge. The Lincolns were billeted in a warm and dry school whilst they had two weeks training. There were also ENSA shows and a cinema, and they played football matches against two artillery units. By this time, one or two men who had been wounded were returning to the battalion, including Sergeant Norman Barber of 14 platoon who had been wounded in France in late August.

The Germans attacked the 7th Duke of Wellingtons outside the straggling village of Haalderen at three o'clock in the morning of the 4th December. There was heavy fire from mortars and machine-guns and they managed to get through the forward positions. But the 25-pounders of the artillery put down some tremendous fire and the 11th Royal Scots Fusiliers arrived to put in a counter-attack. It was all over within a matter of a few hours and almost two hundred Germans were taken prisoner. One of the men from the Dukes was awarded the Military Medal for keeping his Bren gun in action for four hours after being wounded.

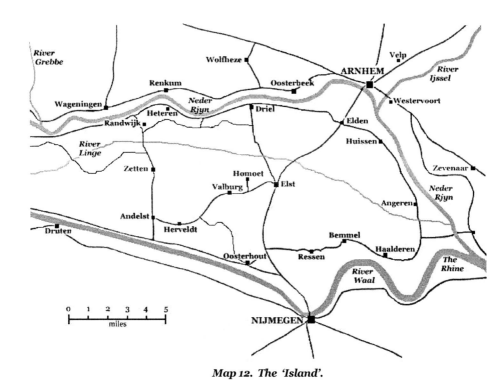

Map 12. The 'Island'.

Major-General 'Bubbles' Barker had been promoted to command VIII Corps and the new Officer Commanding the 49th Division, Major-General MacMillan, visited the Lincolns on the 5th December, followed the next day by Brigadier Gordon who had just taken over 146 Brigade.

There was frost at night and there was snow early in December. On Thursday the 14th December the Lincolns, now rested and fit, left Nijmegen and crossed the River Waal to the Divisional Reserve area at Ressen where they relieved the Hallams. Most of the area was under water and, in addition to checking the rise and fall of the water level every two hours, there was a lot to do. Defensive positions had to be improved and perfected, there was wiring to be laid and there were patrols and sniper sweeps. Flying bombs destined for London or Antwerp roared overhead and caused some excitement at first, but after a time everyone got used to them. It all seemed a bit unreal. Supplies were brought up in DUKWs– two and a half ton amphibious trucks shaped like a boat. The men were issued with gumboots and patrols waded through the water or paddled in assault boats.

The battalion had now been issued with a large number of these flat-bottomed canvas-sided boats and Lieutenant-Colonel Barclay, hearing someone say that the battalion should now be called 'The Royal Lincoln Yacht Club', got into the spirit of things and organised a regatta.

Every platoon selected a crew for the event. The course started on the top of a hedge and circled some telegraph poles along the road before returning to the start line. The Commodore of the regatta (the CO) flew his flag from a DUKW. Bookmakers shouted the odds and had a busy afternoon. Number 18 (Spilsby) Platoon from 'D' Company were the winners. The shouts and yells of the spectators were so loud that they must have puzzled the Germans, for they shelled the course heavily—fortunately after the event was over and everyone had left.

The whole area was flooded throughout the winter.

Although Lord Haw Haw and 'Mary of Arnhem' announced over the wireless that the 'Polar Bear Butchers' would be annihilated over the festive season, the attack on the 7th Dukes early in the month was the only major action on the Island throughout December. On Christmas Day however the Lincolns were at Bemmel in reserve and had just enjoyed a turkey dinner when battalion headquarters was suddenly shelled. Private Showler was killed and Captain Corben and three others were wounded.

On the day after Boxing Day a patrol led by Corporal Watson of 'C' Company delighted the CO when they gave an exciting running commentary over their telephone. The patrol was occupying a house when, at about eight o'clock in the evening, a German patrol arrived and entered the house next door. Corporal Watson, in touch with his company commander by phone, watched and waited. Presently, the Germans left the house and Corporal Watson told his men to hold their fire until they got nearer. He was also whispering the events over the phone: 'They're coming. They're thirty yards away, now twenty, now ten. Their leading man is walking over a plank bridge into the house. They're seven yards away.' A pause and then a shout to his men: 'Let them have it.' A voice came from the darkness: 'Yankee soldier, don't shoot.' After a while Corporal Watson reported that three Germans had been killed and three wounded. Two escaped and the three wounded men were brought back for treatment.

Towards the end of the month the Lincolns relieved the KOYLI at Haalderen, the place where the Germans had attacked the Dukes earlier in the month. Haalderen was directly under the path of flying bombs which were obviously being launched from a site not far away, and on one day 158 were counted as they passed overhead. On New Year's Eve, 'C' Company destroyed an enemy mortar team to bring the year to a close.

But there was some alarm at midnight on New Years Eve when the Germans sent up Verey lights of many different colours, followed by bursts of Spandau fire. When this was followed by the sounds of laughter, singing and a trumpet playing it was realised that the Germans nearby must have got hold of some drink and were having a very happy New Year.

*   *   *   *

There was stalemate on both the Western and the Eastern fronts—for the Russians had also been halted—and Hitler reminded his generals that he still held more territory than at the start of the war. The defensive victories at Arnhem and Antwerp had not only prolonged the war into 1945 but had put fresh heart into the Germans. These boosts to their morale—and the dread of the 'unconditional surrender' which would be demanded if they lost the war—rallied the German people, just as Dunkirk had rallied the British. In fact Eisenhower, realising that Roosevelt's unfortunate stipulation of 'unconditional surrender' was likely to prolong the war and cost unnecessary loss of life, asked if some modification might be found, but he received a negative answer from Washington.

Although the production of petrol and of Tiger tanks had fallen dramatically following strategic bombing raids by the US Army Air Force on synthetic oil plants and the Henschel works at Kassel, the output of most other German arms and ammunition rose to unprecedented heights in the last quarter of 1944. The Luftwaffe now had more fighters than at any other time in its history, but they were grounded because of the shortage of both pilots and petrol.

The call-up age in Germany was lowered from seventeen and a half to sixteen and thousands of men in reserved occupations, shopkeepers, university students and convicts were also conscripted. These, and drafts from the Navy and the grounded Luftwaffe squadrons, produced well over half a million men. Their training, by experienced officers and NCOs, was so simplified and concentrated that a new division could be created in just six weeks. All the new arms and ammunition which were being produced went to these new troops. The precious petrol was used to train new pilots. By the beginning of December, Hitler had thirty-four new divisions in reserve and the Luftwaffe had the pilots for their fighters. It was a remarkable achievement. Von Runstedt was astounded. He was to receive orders which were even more astonishing.

Hitler was convinced that he might still be able to obtain a compromise peace if he could inflict a crippling blow in either the east or the west. He chose the west, for the front was not as wide as in the east and he might be able to capture a significant objective with smaller forces. Besides, it was nearer and less precious petrol would be used. He chose December because bad weather would probably ground the Allies' aircraft and he chose Antwerp as the objective. Re-capturing Antwerp with a strong force would not only deprive the use of the port for Allied supplies, it would isolate the British and Canadians in the north from the Americans further south. The British would give up in despair and the Americans, deprived of the deep-water port, would face starvation. 'Antwerp?' gasped von Runstedt when he heard the news. 'We should get on our knees and thank God if we even reach the Meuse'.

Hitler was in fact repeating the plan he had used so successfully in 1940. The attack was even being launched through the same place, the Ardennes. Then, he had succeeded in isolating the British from the French. The only difference now was that he was aiming for Antwerp instead of the Channel. Part of the plan was to attack from northern Holland, recapture Breda and pin down the British once the Panzers had crossed the Meuse. This time there would be no Dunkirk.

The Germans attacked through the Ardennes on Saturday the 16th December and caught the Americans by surprise. This sector was only lightly held by the Americans, for, just like the French in 1940, General Bradley thought that the Ardennes with its steep wooded hills was unsuitable for open warfare. He had not been too worried about it as he could soon nip any German attack by using Patton's troops to the south and the 1st and 9th Armies from the north.

But he had not reckoned on the strength of the enemy attack. Moreover, he was slow to react. Reserves were not even alerted to move until the evening of the second day, and by that time the Germans were twenty miles into Belgium and heading for the Meuse. The Allies had been dealt a sharp blow and had been sent reeling back. They just couldn't believe that the German army—on the point of collapse—could be making such a powerful attack.

It was very serious. But with the typically positive attitude which is such an admirable characteristic of Americans, Eisenhower told a meeting of his generals that he only wanted to see cheerful faces around the table and that the German thrust should be seen as an opportunity. Nevertheless, in the north the 6th SS Panzer Army had captured a large petrol dump, caught the Americans on the move at Malmedy crossroads and had raced on towards Malmedy. Some of the German units hadn't known what to do with the prisoners they'd taken, so they shot them. When the news of this leaked out it produced a furious reaction from the Americans and their soldiers fought with increased determination. Further south, the 5th Panzer Army almost reached St Vith but then ran into an American division's tank destroyers and artillery and was forced south towards Bastogne. Bradley ordered General Hodges to send some of his divisions from the north to St Vith and General Patton to swing part of his 3rd Army towards Bastogne. Patton at first objected, but then cheered up. 'What the hell', he said, 'we'll still be killing Krauts.' Meanwhile, Eisenhower's reserves were speeding towards the front in every truck and jeep they could find and Montgomery, watching events with interest, moved British troops into position behind the Meuse. Both he and Eisenhower were determined that the Germans would not cross the Meuse— although Lieutenant-General Horrocks had the romantic notion of letting the Germans cross the river so that the final battle of the war could be won at Waterloo! Because the Germans had driven a wedge between Bradley's armies, Eisenhower placed the Americans to the north of the break-through under the command of Montgomery—much to Bradley's annoyance and resentment.

The Americans at Bastogne held on grimly and managed to beat off a last desperate attack on Christmas Day. On Boxing Day, Patton's tanks arrived and the weather which had grounded Allied aircraft suddenly lifted. In the north, the British 29th Armoured Brigade held the Germans' deepest penetration on the right flank and when the American 2nd Armoured Division raced to join them it was all over. By the New Year, the Ardennes salient—the 'Bulge'—had been flattened out. Hitler's last desperate gamble had failed and it had been a great and courageous American victory.

*   *   *   *

Whilst all these dramatic events had been taking place, the Lincolns, with the rest of the 49th Division, had literally been in a backwater. They hadn't been affected at all by the German offensive and, bogged down on the Island, their life was a boring, wet, cold and thoroughly miserable routine of patrols, sniping and an odd small engagement with the enemy here and there. The Lincolns' positions varied from reasonably sound houses to sand-bagged emplacements either in the open or in ruined and roofless houses. Much to everyone's relief a sniper managed to dispose of 'Spandau Joe', a persistent German machine-gunner who had been a nuisance to everyone. Occasionally German propaganda leaflets arrived by shell and they also used loudspeakers, but no-one could hear them properly.

There was one event which had a great impact on the Lincolns however. On the 4th January, 1945 the Commanding Officer, Lieutenant-Colonel Peter Barclay, took over the command of 146 Brigade whilst the Brigadier went on leave and he, and everyone else, expected that he would return in a few days time. But whilst he was away he was appointed to command the 1st battalion of his own regular regiment, the Royal Norfolks. This was a great blow, for Lieutenant-Colonel Barclay had been respected and well-liked ever since he had arrived to command the Lincolns a few weeks before D-Day. It had been Lieutenant-Colonel de Brisay who had transformed the Lincolns from being very amateur Territorials into a war-time unit, but it was Barclay who had turned them into a professional, efficient and by now battle-hardened battalion. He led from the front, treated his men like human beings, knew his job and never let them down, and almost everyone agreed that he was the finest CO the 4th Lincolns ever had.

Lt-Colonel P R Ashburner (centre).

Barclay's replacement was Lieutenant-Colonel P R Ashburner of the Royal Fusiliers, and he arrived on the 19th January.

A few days earlier, Major Barlow-Poole had also left the Lincolns to become Second-in-Command of the KOYLI and Major Corben took over the command of 'A' Company from him. Captain Francis was appointed to command 'D' Company. By now the weather had got colder and the sleet turned to snow. Night patrols were hazardous because of bright moonlight and it was impossible to move silently as ice crackled beneath their feet. Two patrols were ambushed by the Germans and on one of these two men were killed. The V1 flying bombs were still flying loudly overhead although once or twice the men had to take cover quickly when the engines of dud ones cut out. One dropped two hundred yards away from 'C' Company. In the distance it was also possible to see V2 rockets heading towards the skies and one day the speed of the first jet plane they had ever seen, a Messerschmitt 262, left everyone gasping.

British soldiers were now being allowed home on leave for ten days and names of the lucky ones were picked out of hat. Men could also have 'local' leave—forty-eight hours of sight-seeing in Brussels where they were billeted in good hotels or civilian houses and could visit the 'Monty Club' and local cafés. It was a real break just to experience civilisation again. And after a few weeks enduring the miserable conditions on the Island, battalions also took it in turn to have a few days rest in Nijmegen. The Dutch people threw open their houses to the soldiers (friendships were formed which in some cases were to last for many years) and dances were held in the school where the Lincolns had been billeted in December. Some of the men who had been in Iceland were able to go skating again. The Royal Engineers had built a unit where the men could have a hot bath and they'd also constructed a raft (nicknamed 'The Woolwich Ferry') which operated across the Waal to a scheduled timetable. The Germans had in fact tried to re-capture Nijmegen in mid-January when a Parachute Regiment had crossed the Neder Rijn in boats and attacked the Leicesters at the small village of Zetten, eight miles away. The Gloucesters and then the rest of the 56th Brigade had to be called in to restore the situation. The bridge was often attacked by German bombers and on several occasions they used a strange weapon—an unmanned Junkers 88 bomber packed with explosives with a piloted fighter mounted on top. At the last moment the pilot released the bomber and tried to guide it to its target. They all missed. (Another strange German device was the V1 flying bomb launched from the top of a Heinkel bomber flying over the North Sea. One of these flew over Lincoln at Christmas 1944.)

The Lincolns were based at a number of villages during their stay on the Island. There were extremely slippery conditions at Bemmel, where they were issued with white snow suits, and a thaw which was followed by yet another frost made things even worse. At Druten, a German self-propelled gun shelled the spire of the church and it was swiftly chopped up for firewood by the local residents who were very short of fuel. The depth of the water on the roads was chest-high in places.

On the 17th February, Field Marshall Montgomery visited the Polar Bears at short notice. In some places he told the men to gather round whilst he stood on the bonnet of his jeep and talked to them. He inspected all the men of the Lincolns who could be spared from duty, had a chat to some of them and then gave an informal talk in a village hall. He was very amused at the cries of dissent when he asked the men if they were satisfied with the leave allotment. Montgomery was a good leader, respected and liked simply because he went to the trouble of seeing his men and talking with them.

The Polar Bear battalions had local skirmishes with the enemy and some bordered on the bizarre. One day, three German midget submarines came up the Waal towing logs twelve feet long which had mines lashed to them. Two were destroyed by anti-tank guns and the third one dived and disappeared. Patrolling on foot was impossible and patrolling by night was ruled out because there was a strong, swirling current and underwater obstacles in the flood water, and there were very few landmarks. So boat patrols tended to be sent out at first light or when the weather was misty. It was nerve-wracking, for the troops felt very vulnerable sitting closely together in their slow, flimsy canvas boats—an easy target for the enemy. In the silence, they thought that the splashing of their paddles must surely be heard ten miles away.

In mid-February, an advanced base for patrolling, about fifteen hundred yards ahead of the battalion's position, was set up by men under Lieutenant Hill. The route was all under water and the base—a wooden house—rocked alarmingly in the current.

Fresh milk was almost unheard of. Lt Jim Taylor (in the window, extreme right) watches as Tom Hassall (left) and Sgt Williamson (right) do their best to provide some for 17 Platoon, 'D' Company.

There was a naval engagement when Sergeant Stevens and Privates Howson and Simpson were sent forward another thousand yards in an assault boat to search another house and came across eight Germans in a similar craft.

Sergeant Stevens yelled at the Germans to surrender: 'Kaput, fini' but the Germans opened fire and paddled away as fast as they could. Whilst Howson and Simpson paddled furiously behind them, Sergeant Stevens returned the fire with his Bren until they reached a half-submerged bridge where they got into a concealed position by tucking the boat behind one of the arches. They then let fly with everything they had. Screams and groans were heard and a few moments later there was only one man left in the German boat. He dived overboard and tried to tow the boat behind him but after a further volley he too disappeared. On another occasion, Sergeant Hibbard of 'B' Company took a boat patrol out at dawn under cover of a mist. They moored the boat in the ground floor of a flooded house, crept silently upstairs and spent the day watching twelve unsuspecting Germans in the next house, a hundred yards away. They had to be very quiet and could only talk or have a cough when a V1 flying bomb passed overhead. The Germans had no idea that they were there and moved openly about the house and brewed tea. One of them showed his admiring comrades his new pair of trousers, but they were probably damaged when the RAF was directed onto the house and it disappeared in a cloud of red brick dust. On another occasion a boat patrol from 'B' Company found two Germans in a farmhouse and took them prisoner. They had been sent out a fortnight earlier to find food for their company and had spent the night in the farm. The next morning they had found that the floods had risen during the night and that they were cut-off. They had lived for two weeks on bits of vegetables which they'd found floating around and were very pleased indeed to be taken prisoner.

The Lincolns had to patrol by boat.

Not all of the Lincolns' patrols were successful however. There was an abandoned farm in an area called Groenewoud, south-west of Driel, at the end of a country lane, and at seven o'clock in the evening of the 5th March a reconnaissance party set off to occupy the farm, intending to stay there for three days.

They went by foot as by this time the water level had dropped, but even so it took them a long time to travel the two miles on a dark, rainy night with their equipment and rations and occupy the farm. The Germans had had the same idea. Whilst the Lincolns were in the upstairs rooms organising themselves a German patrol managed to get into the same house unobserved, surprise them, take them prisoner and bundle them off to Driel without delay. Worse was to come. The following evening a line party was sent to lay a telephone line and the Germans, now in possession of the farm, allowed them to get within a few yards before shouting: 'Hands up'. Completely surprised and bewildered the soldiers didn't put their hands up and two men were killed and another taken prisoner. Six of the men managed to return safely. Even now the true situation wasn't appreciated. It was thought that the shooting must have been a terrible mistake made by the original group, for they hadn't been told that the line party was being sent. Suspicions were only aroused after two snipers who had been sent to the farm were unable to get a reply after they had shouted several times. At one o'clock on the morning of the 8th March a combat patrol of one officer and seventeen men was sent to search for the missing reconnaissance party. The searchlights which provided artificial moonlight were switched off and visibility was only a few yards. In the farm, the Germans heard whispered commands outside and didn't answer when one of the men from the combat patrol came near and called out: 'Are you there?' The patrol came nearer and the question was repeated. Then the Germans sent up a flare which showed that the patrol was surrounding the farm and they opened up with machine-guns. The Lincolns returned fire with Bren guns, rifles and a PIAT mortar. A large barn where the Germans had several machine-guns positioned caught fire when some tracer bullets went into the thatched roof and a phospher grenade silenced another position, although the men escaped unhurt. A second barn caught fire. By this time all the German defence posts had been burnt out and they withdrew to the sound of exploding ammunition under cover of an artillery and mortar barrage. Although the Lincolns searched for traces of their missing patrol they found nothing and the mystery of its disappearance remained unsolved until after the war. Surprisingly, there were no casualties on either side.

There were a few more minor skirmishes with the Germans before the Lincolns were relieved by the 2nd Essex on the 12th March. They moved to Oosterhout, a reserve area where they got the opportunity to have a bit of a rest, get cleaned-up and re-equipped. It was spring, there was dry land and after four cold, wet and dreary months, the Lincolns were about to move off the Island at last.

*   *   *   *

New Year's Day, 1944 was an amazing day in the air, for the Luftwaffe launched Operation Bodenplatte (Baseplate), a surprise attack designed to disrupt Allied operations and to buy time for the defence of Germany. Shortly after dawn, eight hundred Luftwaffe fighters and fighter-bombers, brought together from units throughout Germany, attacked Allied airbases and caused considerable damage, destroying hundreds of aircraft on the ground. But they had not attacked all the airfields and, after the initial shock, Allied fighters took off. After the biggest aerial dogfight of the war, scores of German planes were shot down or crashed on their way home. The Allies were able to replace their losses within a few days, but it had been a disaster for the Germans as they had lost well over two hundred precious aircrew.

In the East, the Russian offensive started on the 13th January. They captured Warsaw a few days later. Marshall Zhukov's armies breached a gap a hundred and eighty miles wide and swept into Germany itself. Wrongly believing that it would take the Western Allies at least two months to recover from the offensive in the Ardennes, Hitler rushed fighter planes and at least half of the Panzer Divisions in the West across Germany in a desperate attempt to hold the Red Army and in particular to defend the Baltic coast where crews were being trained to operate the new electro U-boats. Virtually all the output from the factories and repair shops went to the crumbling Eastern front. Strangely, Hitler had hopes that the Communist advance would put the wind up Britain and bring the Western Allies to their senses. He thought that Britain and America would join forces with him against the Russians. 'They entered the war to prevent us from going into the East, not to have the East come to the Atlantic,' Goering agreed. 'If this goes on, we will get a telegram (from the West) in a few days.' Some hope. Churchill, Roosevelt and Stalin were meeting at Yalta.

On the 2nd February, after the most concentrated barrage of the war (over a thousand guns put down more than half a million shells on a seven-mile front) XXX Corps attacked through the Reichswald Forest from east of Nijmegen to secure the ground west of the Rhine. Three weeks later, Lieutenant-General Simpson's 9th US Army, now under the command of Montgomery, and the 1st US Army began crossing the River Roer. By the 3rd March Simpson's troops reached the Rhine south of Düsseldorf and had joined with the Canadian Army north of Venlo. On the 5th March, the US 1st Army reached Cologne whilst Patton's 3rd Army covered almost sixty miles in three days to reach the Rhine further south. Every bridge across the Rhine had been blown—except one. On the 7th March, the 9th US Armoured Division in Lieutenant-General Courtney Hodges' 1st Army reached the hills overlooking the banks of the Rhine at Remagen and saw to their astonishment that the railway bridge was still intact. A platoon raced down the hill in their jeeps and took a prisoner who said that it was due to be blown at four o'clock. It was a quarter-past three. American infantry raced across the bridge at ten minutes to four whilst their engineers cut every demolition cable they could see. A few charges went off and toppled the bridge slightly, but not enough to blow it into the river. The Rhine had been crossed and it had cost the Americans fourteen casualties.

Further south, Patton, egged-on by Bradley, was driving his 3rd Army hard. They crossed the Lower Moselle south-west of Coblenz on the 14th March and four days later Patton's tanks, closely followed by engineers with assault boats, were only six miles from Mainz. Six battalions of Patton's 5th Infantry Division crossed the Rhine by boat during the night of the 22nd March virtually unopposed. By the evening of the 23rd there was a bridge-head six miles deep and seven miles wide and Patton's armour was pouring across on bridges which his engineers had constructed. Bradley was delighted when he received a telephone call from Patton saying: 'You can tell the world that the US 3rd Army made it before Monty has even got started'. Neither of them liked Montgomery very much.

Montgomery, the master of the highly-organised, elaborate set-piece attack, perhaps didn't understand the unorthodox, pragmatic, dash and drive of the Americans, whose generals were told what the objective was and then left to get on with the job. It wasn't (and perhaps still isn't) the British way of doing things.

Montgomery's crossing of the Rhine went according to schedule. There was the usual huge bombardment and heavy air attack before the troops crossed the river during the night of 23rd March in assault craft, supported by DD swimming tanks. Two airborne divisions dropped the following morning and by the 26th March the engineers had constructed twelve bridges. Montgomery had calculated that it would take twenty days to establish the bridgehead, but the enemy opposition was not as great as had been expected (some had been drawn off to Remagen), and an armoured counter-attack was easily beaten off. By the fifth day the British and American forces were ready to break out of a bridgehead thirty-five miles wide and twenty miles deep. Within a week Montgomery had twenty divisions and fifteen hundred tanks across the Rhine.

On Montgomery's right, Field Marshall Model's Army Group had orders to defend the Ruhr as a fortress, but the way to the Westphalian plain and the Elbe was open in the centre. There remained just one problem. To the left the Germans were still in Holland.

*   *   *   *

After four frustrating, cold, wet months, the 49th Division was on the move at last. On the morning of Monday the 2nd April, a dull, windy day, the divisional artillery put down huge barrages as the infantry battalions, supported by tanks and RAF Typhoons, set out to capture the villages and hamlets between Nijmegen and Arnhem which were still occupied by the Germans. The 4th Lincolns set off at noon, 'A' Company (Major Corben) with a troop of tanks leading the way. It was interesting to see at close quarters the enemy positions which the Lincolns had watched from the distance for such a long time. Satisfying too, for the picture of the enemy's dispositions which patrols had built up was found to be entirely accurate.

The Lincolns' immediate objective was the village of Angeren, and supported by heavy and accurate fire from the tanks (and a call to the artillery to dispose of a particularly stubborn pocket of resistance) they arrived there at half-past six. It was decided to press on to the next village of Huissen, three miles away. Perhaps the RAF hadn't been told of this decision because at about seven o'clock Major Flint's 'B' Company, which was now in the lead, was attacked by two of our own aircraft. Two men were killed and seven were wounded. 'B' Company's vehicles were then held up by an undefended road block and a bulldozer had to be called-up to shift it. Meanwhile, 'C' Company passed through on foot and reached Huissen shortly after half-past eight. There were still quite a few Germans in the area and although they seemed bewildered and disorganised it nevertheless seemed rather eerie knowing that they were roaming about in the dusk on both sides of the road. The battalion had to stay very much on the alert all night. Privates Fuller, Jones and Woodcock had been killed and fourteen men had been wounded in the day's operations.

Huissen was less than a mile from the Neder Rjin and the following morning the Lincolns were ordered to cross the river. Shortly after one o'clock 'C' Company had a platoon across, followed ten minutes later by the whole company. The Neder Rjin, the objective of the Arnhem operation the previous September, had been crossed with no opposition! Local people said that the Germans had left that morning. 'D' Company arrived and patrolled north, where they had a good look at Arnhem.

By the 5th April, after an operation which had only taken three days, the whole Island had been cleared of Germans and the Polar Bears received a message of congratulation from Major-General Rawlins, who had now taken over the division from Major-General MacMillan.

The next operation was to take Arnhem. Behind and to the west of the town there were commanding heights, so it was decided to attack from the east. But first, another river, the Ijssel, would have to be crossed. For the next few days there was chaos as troops, assault boats, tanks, artillery, trucks, jeeps and carriers assembled in the triangle between the east bank of the Neder Rjin and the south bank of the Ijssel. Some had crossed the Neder Rjin whilst others came via Emmerich, about twenty miles to the south-east of Arnhem. "Buffaloes" arrived—tracked landing vehicles manned by the Royal Armoured Corps.

Somewhat to the surprise of the Lincolns, they were withdrawn from the bridgehead they had established over the river. They returned to the Island, travelling to the south-west for about eight miles, through Elst to a position just outside Valburg. Although this was a rest area, with ENSA concerts and baths, it was not all recreation, for company training was carried out. The busiest man in the battalion was Lieutenant-Colonel Ashburner, for after a church parade on

Sunday the 8th April he had to go to a meeting at brigade, then he held a meeting with his company commanders before finally attending a meeting at division in the evening.

The bridge over the River Ijssel.

On the 10th April, the Lincolns left for their new location, Zevenaar, a large village across the Neder Rjin, about six miles south-east of Arnhem. Whilst the men got down to more training, the CO and the Intelligence Officer went to yet another meeting at Brigade headquarters. They were impressed by what they heard, for brigade provided some very high quality intelligence which had possibly come from the Dutch resistance in the town. Each enemy unit was listed, together with details of their strength and arms—and even the names of the officer in charge of each company. They learned that there was a Dutch SS regiment in Arnhem, and that although the soldiers were young they lacked training. The rest were of very poor quality. The 46th Machine-Gun Battalion was a "category" unit—soldiers who were physically in a low category with rheumatism, heart problems and even missing limbs. Like the 1071 Grenadier Regiment, many were doddery old men (in their mid-forties!) with a World War One veteran here and there. Everyone had left Arnhem except for the police, firemen and the soldiers. Troops would have to beware of the many mines which had been laid in the town and would particularly have to look out for booby traps—grenades with trip wires which had been left in large numbers in houses and factories.

After a couple of visits from Brigadier Gordon, the Lincolns left Zevenaar for their concentration area, three or four miles away, during the evening of the 12th April. 'D' Company had two casualties when Lieutenant Hurmson and a private were injured by a booby trap. Just after six o'clock the following morning, the Lincolns left for the assembly area at Westervoort, a small village on the south bank of the River Ijssel. The south-east of Arnhem, an industrial area, was just across the river, and the 56th Brigade was already there, having crossed during the night under cover of a bombing attack and a massive and very noisy barrage from the artillery. (Incidentally, the 1st Leicesters of 147 Brigade didn't *cross* the river to reach Arnhem—they came *down* it in Royal Navy landing craft all the way from Nijmegen!)

The Royal Engineers were still busy putting a complete Bailey pontoon bridge into place (it had been prefabricated five miles away and towed down river) so 'D' Company crossed the river in the amphibious 'buffaloes' of the 11th Royal Tanks at eight o'clock, each man carrying as much equipment as possible. They went on to contact the 2nd South Wales Borderers who were already positioned near a railway embankment. The other three companies had all crossed the river by half-past eleven, together with a jeep and five carriers—the CO's, one carrying ammunition, one for the 4.2-inch mortars and two for the Royal Artillery Observation Officers.

'D' Company set off towards the eastern part of Arnhem at noon, closely followed by 'C' Company. It wasn't long before 'D' Company came up against very stiff heavy automatic fire at a cross roads and the Germans started working round to their rear. Captain Francis called for artillery support and very heavy fire was immediately brought down on the cross roads. He ordered his men to occupy and clear a nearby large factory. The road to the factory was through two tunnels under the railway line. The first was passed without any difficulty, but the second tunnel had been blocked by timber which even tanks couldn't shift. The Royal Engineers' armoured bulldozers had to be called up. Several Spandaus were firing down the road and others from the sides of the railway embankment. Nevertheless, 'D' Company managed to find a way into the dim interior of the huge factory only to find that Germans seemed to be everywhere. The factory was a labyrinth of passages, stores, sheds and machines and the roofs were alive with snipers. If a German was killed another one seemed to come from nowhere to take his place. They kept appearing from all sides, and at one time 'D' Company seemed to be surrounded by them. Somehow, they managed to hold out until a platoon from 'C' Company arrived to give them a hand. Meanwhile, the armoured bulldozers had arrived outside and after fifteen minutes they managed to get rid of the roadblock. Canadian Sherman tanks, guns blazing, roared through the tunnel into the factory yard. A sniper fired a burst of automatic fire from one of the factory chimneys but he was dealt with by the Besa of one of the tanks and his body somersaulted to the ground. Although a particularly stubborn pocket of Germans held out until the shed they were in was set on fire by flame-throwers, the factory was occupied by two o'clock with 'C' Company on the ground floor and 'D' Company upstairs. It had been a hard business, for the enemy resistance had been fanatical. One German officer had five bursts from a Bren before he was finally stopped and another man who was wounded tried to throw a grenade at anyone trying to approach him. It was discovered later that the factory, which had a strong garrison, was one of the enemy's key points for the defence of Arnhem and the Divisional Commander paid a special visit to the Lincolns to compliment them on the magnificent way they had fought. Captain Francis and Major Ed Cooke of 'C' Company were both awarded the Military Cross.

'A' Company passed through the factory and was directed to a crossroads and by half-past six 'B' Company, followed by 'D' Company, had reached the heights near Rozendaal on the north-east side of the town. 'C' Company had been left at the factory to make sure there weren't any Germans still hiding there. The Lincolns had broken through the outer crust of the Arnhem defences, allowing the rest of the 146th Brigade to pass through, and had taken 111 prisoners. It had been one of the hardest day's fighting of the whole campaign. Second Lieutenant Burns, Sergeant Stevens (the hero of the 'naval engagement' in mid-February), Corporal Thompson and Privates Fisk and Spain had been killed and forty-nine men had been wounded, including Lieutenant Paulger and Captain Hill.

The intelligence which brigade had provided was found to be a bit inaccurate. They had said that there were only seven hundred and fifty to a thousand enemy troops in Arnhem, but more than sixteen hundred were taken prisoner. A total of sixty-two British soldiers had been killed. Brigade had however been correct about the lack of training of the very young Dutch SS troops. It was difficult not to feel a bit sorry for them when German recruiting posters were seen: 'Join up and your parents will eat.'

The famous 'bridge too far' at Arnhem.

Trucks move carefully over a pontoon bridge at Arnhem.

Temporary bridges at Arnhem.

The following day, the 4th Lincolns mopped-up between Rozendaal and Velp, a large built-up suburb on the eastern edge of Arnhem. 'C' Company, having now searched every part of the factory, moved to the east to clear houses in the built-up area. Four men were wounded during the day and a further 123 prisoners were taken.

One of 'D' Companies platoons became heavily engaged at a crossroads the next day (the 15th April) and for a time were pinned down. Tanks and flame-throwers quickly arrived and after they'd done a good deal of flailing and flaming the problem was sorted out. Although they weren't to know it at the time it was the 4th Lincolns' last action. Many Dutch resistance men from Velp arrived at battalion headquarters throughout the day to give information about what the Germans were doing and where their positions were. But it was the 56th Brigade which attacked Velp that night. Flail tanks led as the 2nd Essex took a hundred prisoners on the north side of the suburb, the 2nd South Wales Borderers forced their way into the centre, and to the south the 2nd Gloucesters took fifty prisoners.

The Lincolns were ordered to pass through 56 Brigade the following morning to take De Steeg, a village about four miles to the north-east. There were a number of roadblocks which held them up slightly and there were some woods to their right which made them cautious but not a single German was seen. The Lincolns reached De Steeg and fanned out to the villages of Rheden and Scherponhof but no

Knocked-out German tank.

enemy troops were seen. The battalion then returned to Velp, where they were enthusiastically greeted and cheered by the excited population.

Half a dozen Germans are rounded up, to the delight of the people of Velp.

The battalion stayed at Velp for a couple of days. Nothing much happened except a Polish deserter (in civilian clothes) and half a dozen Germans were found and taken prisoner. On Thursday the 19th April, the Lincolns moved from Velp to Wolfheze, and as it was about five miles on the other side of Arnhem, they saw for the first time the appalling damage which the town had suffered, both during the recent action and also that of the previous September. It was still smouldering. There were bombed and shelled ruins of buildings, rubble, craters and black smoke everywhere. Royal Engineers were busy clearing mines and white tape marked where they had been. Bulldozers were shifting rubble and every now and then there was an explosion as something was demolished—a mine perhaps, or a damaged building being blown up.

There were further poignant scenes as the Lincolns reached Wolfheze, for this was the area where the 1st Airborne Division had landed in September. There was still a lot of equipment strewn about and a mass of gliders—hundreds of them—some wrecked beyond repair and others in perfect condition. And there were graves too. It was very moving.

Three live polar bears were found in Arnhem zoo. Major-General Rawlins, the Officer Commanding the 49th (Polar Bear) Division, politely declined the offer to have one of them sent over to his headquarters.

The whole family has turned out to welcome the Lincolns in the spring sunshine at Velp.

    *   *   *   *

The war in Europe was coming to an end very quickly. The Red Army took Vienna on the 13th April and they launched their attack on Berlin three days later. In Italy, the spring offensive started on the 9th April, with both the US 5th Army and the British 8th Army aiming for Bologna. After the Allies had crossed the River Po on the 23rd April they met little resistance as they rapidly advanced towards the north, helped by thousands of Italian partisans. Brazilian soldiers attached to the US 5th Army took Turin and Japanese-Americans—not allowed to take part in the war in the Pacific—were the first Allied soldiers to reach the Italian-French frontier.

Now that twenty German divisions had been moved to face the Russians, there was little serious fighting on the Western front. Field Marshall Kesselring was now in charge because von Runstedt had been fired—yet again—after Remagen, but there was little that he could do. Most of the German army in the West was bottled-up in the Ruhr, surrounded and blockaded, and eventually over three hundred thousand men surrendered in a greater capitulation than at Stalingrad. Field Marshall Model shot himself. By the 11th April, Bradley's troops were only fifty-three miles from Berlin. Churchill pressed Eisenhower to get to Berlin before the Russians, not only for the honour and prestige but also for political reasons. There was virtually nothing to stop the sixty divisions which Eisenhower now had at his disposal, but Bradley thought that taking Berlin itself might cost a hundred thousand casualties—'a pretty stiff price to pay for a prestige objective.'

Someone on Eisenhower's intelligence staff had got the idea that the Germans were preparing a National Redoubt in the alpine area of Western Austria and Southern Bavaria. It was believed that Hitler and his gang, with picked SS units, would continue the war from the virtually impenetrable Alps using specially selected and fanatical young men to train guerillas. Eisenhower decided to make a powerful thrust in the centre to link up with the Red Army in the Leipzig-Dresden area and that once this was done his troops would then go south-east to seize the Redoubt before the Nazis got there. Patton was to find that it was all a wild goose chase as the Germans had made no such plans. He could have reached Prague but the Russians objected and he was stopped. The Russians wanted Czechoslovakia as a satellite.

Meanwhile, the Red Army was advancing swiftly along the Baltic coast and it was realised that they could even reach the North Sea, sealing off Schleswig-Holstein (and thereby Denmark and Norway) in the process. It was a close run thing. By-passing any areas of resistance his troops came across, Montgomery drove hard for the Baltic. He reached Wismar and Lübeck with six hours to spare.

On Thursday the 12th April, President Roosevelt collapsed and died suddenly. Hitler and Goebbels saw it as a miracle. They believed that the unlikely Allied coalition between the communist Russians and the capitalist British and Americans would collapse. Once the armies of Russia and the Western Allies had met head on in the centre of Germany they would start squabbling with each other about their zones of occupation. When they started fighting each other the German troops in the north under Doenitz and those in the south under Kesselring would be ordered to draw back to let them get on with it. Perhaps he was almost right, for who knows what might have happened if Patton had taken Prague against the express wishes of the Russians?

*   *   *

The people living in large Dutch cities were on the point of starvation. Those living in the country weren't too badly off, but the winter of 1944/5 had been exceptionally harsh. Public transport had almost ceased to exist and barges hadn't been able to make their way through the frozen canals. There was no coal, no electricity and no wood. Factories had been forced to close for there were no raw materials, and in any case there was no power. So many bridges had been blown that it was impossible to transport food into the cities and people ate bulbs and even family pets to stay alive. It had been what the Dutch people still call to this day 'The Hunger Winter'. By April 1945 the Dutch were down to a diet of three hundred calories a day and even the Germans only had a thousand calories. People were dying of starvation in the streets and the most vulnerable were the children and the elderly. On the 27th April, SS General Artur Seiss-Inquart, the Austrian-born Governor-General of Holland, agreed to an unofficial truce to allow convoys of food to pass through the lines. From eight o'clock the following morning, Germans were not to be fired upon unless they were seen to be taking offensive action.

So whilst the Lincolns in Wolfheze were ordered to clear up and salvage the equipment left by the 1st Airborne Division, some of the other units in the 49th Division became involved in the humane mission of taking food to the Dutch people. Each day, British and Canadian convoys made their way through the German lines to deliver thousands of tons of food at distribution centres. The RAF and US Army Air Force also came over to drop millions of rations. It was a strange, unreal interlude. Surely it couldn't be long now before the Germans gave up altogether?

On Sunday the 22nd April, the Lincolns received a delightful surprise. The band of the 2nd battalion of the Lincolnshire Regiment, which had been in Lincoln throughout the war, had been selected for a six weeks' tour in North-west Europe. For over a week they'd been stuck in a transit camp with the bands of some other British and Canadian regiments, but Bandmaster Williams had somehow wangled a visit by his band to the 4th Lincolns at Wolfheze. The band played at church that evening and then gave a concert which was enjoyed by the troops and the local Dutch people. Early in the morning, four days later, the battalion's transport left Wolfheze to travel nine or ten miles to the north-east to the village of Lunteren and they were followed by all the companies which marched there. The regimental band, still with the battalion, played as the 4th Lincolns proudly marched into the village, where Brigadier Gordon was waiting to take the salute. The Lincolns were still at Lunteren when the news came through that Hitler had shot himself. The following day, the 1st May, the Lincolns moved six miles south, through Ede, to relieve the Gloucesters at a village called Bennekom. There was more good news— the Germans in Italy had surrendered. The Lincolns had only been in Bennekom for two days before they were on the move yet again, this time a couple of miles south to the town of Wageningen. There was no enemy activity at all now and it had been decided to thin out the line.

On the 3rd May, a dull and unsettled day, the Lincolns arrived in Wageningen to find a scene of extraordinary activity. There were a few decrepit German cars and quite a large number of smart British staff cars parked outside a small hotel and there seemed to be an equally large number of staff officers about. A BBC mobile recording van was there as well.

The Lincolns—particularly 'S' (Support) Company—had a grandstand view as General Seyss-Inquart, General Blaskowitz and an officer who looked as though he was the boyfriend of one or other of the German staff, left the hotel having negotiated the surrender of all German troops in Holland to General Eisenhower's Chief of Staff (Lieutenant-General Bedell Smith), Prince Bernhardt of the Netherlands and the Commander of the 1st Canadian Corps. Prince Bernhardt may have felt in a peculiar situation, for he had been born and raised in Germany.

The Germans surrender at Wageningen.

The following day, on Lüneberg Heath, the Germans surrendered all their forces in North-West Germany and Denmark to Field-Marshall Montgomery. On the 7th May, at General Eisenhower's headquarters at Rheims, the Germans unconditionally surrendered all their forces on all fronts. The war in Europe was over, and the fearful menace of Nazi domination which had seemed so real and so near to the British in the dark years up to the end of 1942 was at an end. It was almost unbelievable to realise that all the shooting and shelling, the noise, the dreadful stench of the dead—and the fear—was over at last.

Monday the 7th May was a beautiful spring day, warm and sunny, and it was a day no-one would ever forget. Just after noon, 146 Brigade started to move in their trucks to the outskirts of Utrecht. By half-past two all the men had formed up, the Hallamshire (City of Sheffield) battalion of the York and Lancaster Regiment, followed by the 4th battalion of the Lincolnshire Regiment and then the 4th battalion of the King's Own Yorkshire Light Infantry, the regiments which had fought together all the way from Norway. Other units which had played such an important part in the brigade's battles followed in their transport a detachment from the 2nd Kensingtons with their heavy machine-guns and mortars, the guns of the Royal Artillery towed by their quads and the 49th Reconnaissance Regiment in their armoured cars.

The 4th Lincolns enter Utrecht.

In their best battledresses, with their webbing well blancoed, boots highly polished and their rifles at the slope, the Brigade marched smartly into the centre of the city of Utrecht, led by the band of the Lincolnshire Regiment playing the regimental march, 'The Lincolnshire Poacher.'

They received an incredible reception. Everyone in the city was there. Even invalids were wheeled out into the streets because they wanted to join in the celebrations. The band and the men had the utmost difficulty in moving through the wild, rapturous, cheering crowd, and very soon what had started out as a march became a somewhat slow, erratic procession as the smiling troops almost disappeared under the huge number of ecstatic people who swarmed over them. The people of Utrecht just went mad.

Flowers and bottles were thrust upon the soldiers. Better still, hundreds of girls linked arms with them, kissing them as they struggled through the city. There was never any parade such as this. The carriers, armoured cars and trucks which were following fared no better, children and girls jumping on them in wild delight. German troops, still armed, looked on sullenly and silently, ignored by both the Dutch and the British. The band, which had been swallowed up and lost, finally managed to break a way through the crowd to play 'God Save the King' and the Dutch National Anthem, 'Wilhelmus', before thousands of people who had swarmed in the open square in front of the battalion's Officers' Mess at the Hotel Terminus. It was a very moving moment which would never be forgotten by those who were there.

The following day, Tuesday the 8th May, was officially proclaimed as 'VE Day' and a voluntary Thanksgiving Service was held in the open air, with the band playing the hymns. Almost everyone attended, regardless of denomination, to remember and pray for their friends and to be thankful that they themselves had survived. The men were given the rest of the day off.

In hot and sunny weather, the Lincolns moved off the next day to Maarssen, a village about three miles north-west of Utrecht and on the Amsterdam-Rijn canal. There were still thousands of Germans in Holland and they had received orders to move to concentration areas to be disarmed. The Lincolns established two camps in fields around Maarssen under the supervision of 'B' and 'D' Companies, whilst a third was set up across the canal at De Haar under the Support Company. There was much to be done, for apart from disarming the Germans, they had to be documented and arrangements made for them to be fed. Roads were blocked by hundreds of horse-drawn carts piled with equipment and so many Germans arrived that it was impossible for them to be kept in POW cages. But they were guarded and they obeyed the orders which their officers—acting under *our* officers' instructions—gave them. Gradually, things were sorted out. Firstly (of course) the Germans' wrist-watches were taken from them. Then rifles were placed in one dump, machine-guns in another, small arms ammunition in yet another, steel helmets in one pile, binoculars in another and so on.

The 4th Lincolns march through Utrecht.

The Germans were made to do all the work, but after a day or two most of them were moved to a huge prisoner-of-war cage which had been set up about eight miles away at Hilversum.

Nevertheless, some Germans stayed to do some work, including the removal of some dangerous ammunition from a dump which they blew up under the supervision of the Lincolns' Pioneer Officer, Lieutenant Daykin. Throughout this period the weather was perfect—hot and sunny with just a light breeze. Whilst the Germans worked, the battalion played football matches and a couple of trucks left daily for men to have a day out in Amsterdam and Den Haag (The Hague). The local people organised a dance on the village green and the regimental band gave a concert in the open-air. On Sunday the 13th May some men representing the Lincolns were sent to the 49th Division's Church Parade which was being held in Utrecht cathedral in the presence of the burgomaster and Lieutenant-General Foulkes, the Officer Commanding the Canadian 1st Corps. The rest of the battalion had their own Church Parade at Maarssen.

German soldiers leaving Holland to go home in a landing-craft manned by the Royal Navy.

The following Thursday, the Lincolns handed over to the Royal Winnipeg Rifles and moved back to Arnhem. A party of all ranks under Major Freeman was selected to represent the 4th Lincolns at the Victory Parade, which the Canadian

Army was holding at The Hague on Monday the 21st May, and a couple of practice parades were held. Unfortunately, the spell of good weather had broken by now and the men, and their best battledresses, got soaked as they marched in the pouring rain past Queen Wilhemina, Prince Bernhardt and General Crerar, (the Officer Commanding the 1st Canadian Army). Bandmaster Williams, the senior bandmaster present, was in overall charge of all the bands on the parade, both British and Canadian.

After the CO had presented a shield bearing the battalion's emblem to the burgomaster of Arnhem, the Lincolns left the town, their Canadian friends and Holland on Wednesday the 23rd May. They were on their way to Germany.

To this day the Dutch people talk of their liberation—by the Canadians. Whilst it is certainly true that many Canadians died during the liberation of much of Holland, part of the British Army—attached to and under the command of the Canadian Army—also made a significant contribution. Amongst these were the 4th Lincolns, part of the Polar Bear's 49th Division. Perhaps their contribution is not entirely forgotten, for monuments depicting the Polar Bear still stand in such towns as Roosendaal and Utrecht.

Germany

The 4th Lincolns left Arnhem early in the morning of Wednesday the 23rd May. The weather was overcast as the convoy drove on the first stage of their journey along the familiar road to Velp. A couple of hours later the convoy crossed the frontier into Germany and the men of the Lincolns looked from their trucks with interest as they bumped along the roads. The countryside looked peaceful and pleasant enough, but here and there were scenes of utter devastation, marking some position or other which the Germans had vainly tried to defend in the British 2nd Army's drive to Hamburg and the Baltic. By half-past four, after a drive of almost a hundred miles, the battalion arrived at Glandorf, a small town between Münster and Osnabruck. The war had not seemed to have affected this part of Germany at all. The land was rich with an abundance of produce and livestock and the people were well fed and extremely well dressed. The men's attention was very soon attracted to the excellent silk stockings which every fraulein seemed to be wearing.

News of the arrival of the Lincolns must have travelled fast, for the very next day there was an unexpected and most welcome visitor. Lieutenant-Colonel Barclay arrived, anxious to meet the men he had led from Normandy into Holland and to hear all the news. And then it was discovered that the 2nd battalion of the Lincolnshire Regiment was at Lengerich, a village just down the road, only twelve miles away. Transport was laid on for anyone who wanted to respond to the 2nd Lincolns' invitation to visit them and quite a number of men went, for some had friends with the battalion. The following day, men from the 2nd battalion arrived on a return visit.

But the 4th Lincolns didn't stay long at Glandorf. The Brigade Commander arrived on the 2nd June to outline the battalion's future role to the CO and the following morning they set off in convoy once again to travel sixty miles south-east to Brilon. This was in an area—forty miles west of Kassel—which had been captured by the Americans.

Germany was in chaos. There was no civil government and Montgomery and Eisenhower were having to run things as best they could. The infra-structure in many parts of the country had been completely destroyed—bridges were down, the railways were out of action, sewers didn't work, there was no electricity or gas and many factories were ruined. Factories which were still in working order couldn't get raw materials. Hospitals were crammed with German wounded and there was almost a complete lack of medical supplies. There were thousands of prisoners-of-war who had to be fed, over a million and a half prisoners in the British zone alone. Those who had not been in the SS were now being released at the rate of twelve thousand a day, with priority being given to those who had worked on the land or in coal mines. Many of the men who were being released seemed puzzled, for they had expected to be drafted into units to fight alongside the British and Americans against the Russians.

The Lincolns capture a German flag.

Arrangements had to be made for the Allied prisoners-of-war who had now been released to be returned home. There was the problem of the German concentration camps like Belsen. There were over a million German refugees who had fled in terror before the advancing Red Army and were now homeless in the British and American sectors. In some parts of the Russian sector there were practically no Germans left. Many people, particularly those from the large cities, had lost everything they possessed as a result of the bombing, and were homeless. Many people just had the clothes they stood up in. In the cities there was little food. This was the sad legacy which Hitler had left to the German people.

To add to the problems, there were six million people who had been transported to Germany from all over Europe as forced labour. They were described as 'Displaced Persons'. Temporary camps had been set up for them, where they could live until such time as arrangements could be made for them to be re-settled, although some of the people in the camps were stateless. The camps were all enclosed with high wire and the Americans were guarding a number of them in the Brilon area, but they were now expecting the British Army to take over. This was the future role of the 4th Lincolns which the Brigade Commander had outlined to the CO the previous day.

There were seven camps in the area, each holding several hundred people. Many of them were Russians, but there were also Poles, French, Dutch, Italians, Lithuanians and Jugoslavs. Some of them were women. Battalion HQ and 'A' Company was at Nieder Marsberg, 'B' Company was at Brilon, 'C' Company guarded a camp at Olsberg, 'D' Company was at Bredelar, the Support Company was at Winterberg, the Mortar Platoon was at Medebach and the Carrier Platoon was furthest away at Hallenberg, over twenty miles from Brilon. Military Police also arrived at each of these camps.

The Lincolns moved into the billets vacated by the Americans. It took a little time for them to become adjusted to their new and unusual role. No-one knew quite what to expect. The people in the camps were allowed out during the day, but there was a curfew at night. The wire surrounding the camps was very often cut at night and searches had to be made for the cutters, but they were never found. Not only did Company Commanders become in effect Camp Commandants but they also found that the local Germans saw them as being responsible for the maintenance of public order. The Germans complained about break-ins, stolen cars and rape. Twenty armed Russians were alleged to have stolen food from a farm. A British officer (not from the Lincolns) and a girl were found, killed by a gun; five Russians were arrested. There were also quite a few fights between the different nationalities in the camps which had to be sorted out. Thorough searches for arms were often made in the camps and sometimes weapons were found. A serious fight broke out one day between thirty Italians—some with knives—and five Germans, and men from the Lincolns and the Military Police had to intervene. A couple of Germans who were sweeping leaves were approached by two Poles who asked them for a match, but they didn't have any. When the Poles threatened to shoot them, one of the Germans tried to run away but he was killed by the Poles, who then disappeared.

There were one or two other kinds of incidents. Although the tranquil countryside was very beautiful and seemed untouched by the war, a carrier going along a country road suddenly blew up on a mine and a second carrier which went to the rescue then hit another one. Privates Peat and Donaldson were killed. A German in the locality was arrested for hiding Nazi Party uniforms and insignia, and another one was taken to jail when it was found that he had buried fifty thousand rounds of small arms ammunition in his garden. Telephone wires were cut, and a civilian car tried on three occasions to knock down Royal Signals Don Rs (despatch riders) on their motor bikes. It was known that there were still a few die-hard Nazis around who called themselves 'werewolves'. Was this some of their work?

So far as the men in the 4th Lincolns were concerned the job was over now that the war against Germany had been won. It was easy to forget that the war against Japan was still going on and it came as a bit of a shock when the men heard that some of them were being sorted out to go to the Far East. This mainly affected those who had been called-up relatively recently and who'd joined the battalion as replacements. Towards the end of June seventy-eight men and two subalterns were transferred to the 2nd Lincolns, who were getting ready to go to Baltimore in America on the first stage of their journey to the Far East. Although some of the older men in the 2nd battalion were transferred to the 4th Lincolns in exchange, it was decided to disband 'C' Company. Another change which took place at about this time was that Lieutenant-Colonel E S Scott arrived to replace Lieutenant-Colonel Ashburner as the Commanding Officer.

Fraternising with 'Russian Rose', one of the displaced persons.

The troops in Germany were now getting home leave and 7,500 men were regularly sailing daily between the Hook of Holland and Harwich. Off duty, football and cricket matches were arranged with the KOYLI and Hallams and a sports day was held to select the battalion's representatives at the Divisional Sports which were held later at Winterberg Palace. A canteen was opened by the Belgian Welfare Service at Brilon. Cigarettes were tenpence for a packet of twenty and were used as currency in dealings with the Germans. You could get a reasonably good camera or watch for two hundred cigarettes. Beer was sixpence a pint. Although the currency in canteens was pounds, shillings and pence the men were not allowed to use British currency. When they returned from leave they had to change their money at the Hook of Holland for 'baffs'—British Armed Forces Vouchers—and they received their pay in them too. They were a bit like monopoly money, with notes for pounds, ten shillings, five shillings, one shilling, sixpence and even threepence. Although you were allowed to use British pennies and half-pennies, there were also plastic discs for them as well. BAFVs were issued to prevent the Germans getting hold of British pounds sterling. Needless to say, it couldn't be prevented altogether and troops haggled with the German spivs who stood around in the streets or the cafés. On a good day you could perhaps get almost seventeen marks for a pound sterling. You could apply to have part of your pay paid in marks, but if you were ever found to have more marks on you than were shown in your pay book, you were in trouble.

Field Marshall Montgomery had issued a card to every officer and man about fraternising with the Germans. He explained that if British soldiers mixed freely with the Germans, went to their houses or danced with their girls it would be resented by their own families in England and by the millions of people who had

suffered under the Gestapo. So, for the moment, fraternisation with the Germans was officially banned. At Medebach, the mortar platoon was billeted in some houses next to a factory which was still fulfilling a contract to make socks for the German army. The factory employed around sixty young women. Captain Turner realised that Monty's order would be almost impossible to carry out. 'I don't want to find out that anyone has been fraternising with these girls,' he told his sex-starved platoon. The men understood exactly what he was trying to say, and he never did find out anything...

Captain Arthur Turner.

An all-women military band from the ATS visited and a party of around sixty Russians came and gave a concert of national songs and dances. The officers organised a deer and wild boar shoot, but because the Germans were so short of food it was decided beforehand that three-quarters of anything shot would be handed to the local civilian authorities for distribution to the Germans.

A further draft of men left the battalion to join the 2nd Lincolns, who were now stationed at Ghent in Belgium, and many were sorry to have to remove their Polar Bear flashes from their uniforms. Shortly afterwards the war in the Far East suddenly ended and the 2nd Lincolns were sent to the Middle East instead.

Throughout the summer, the displaced persons gradually left the camps, but then in the autumn it was heard that twenty thousand civilians from the Ruhr were being sent to the Brilon area and it was feared that they probably included an element of trouble-makers. In the end they went elsewhere, but over six thousand homeless people from Berlin and the Russian zone arrived instead.

Christmas 1945 was marred because Private Jones in HQ Company was killed in a truck accident. The Lincolns had a carol service in the Lutheran church at Brilon and the thoughts of most of the men turned to home. After all, the war had been over since May and it was difficult for the men to understand why they were still in the army, let alone Germany, instead of being with their families and friends in Lincolnshire. Most of the Germans who had been taken prisoner were already home.

Monty's 'no fraternisation' order was soon relaxed.

Demobilisation had in fact started. Group numbers had been worked out according to age and length of service and men were placed in the appropriate group. By Christmas men in Group 24 were being demobbed, but although the Territorials in the 4th Lincolns certainly had the length of service, most of them were in later groups because they weren't old enough.

In spring 1946 the 4th Lincolns moved to Gevelsburg, about fifteen miles south of Dortmund. A weekly newspaper, *The Lincoln Imp*, was published for a time, but the battalion began to lose a lot of men all at once, as the Group Number of many of them was the same and they were now being demobbed at last. Private Clarke from 'B' Company was the last man of the original Territorials to be demobbed when he left in April, 1946.

Relaxing in the sunshine at Winterberg Palace.

Saturday the 8th June 1946 was celebrated as 'Victory Day' and there was a huge parade in London in which representatives of all British and Commonwealth Services took part. A special feature was the massed Colours of every British infantry regiment. The Colours of the 1st battalion had been placed for safe keeping for the duration of the war in the vaults of a bank in New Delhi and were still there. The Colours of the 2nd battalion weren't available either, so it was the 4th Lincolns' Colours which represented the regiment on the Victory Day parade in London. In Lincoln, the regiment was presented with the Honorary Freedom of the City. It was hoped that the ceremony would take place outdoors, but it rained and so it was held on the stage of the 'Savoy' cinema instead. The band, under Bandmaster Williams, led the parade but there was some disappointment as there weren't many soldiers present who had served during the war in the Lincolnshire Regiment. The two regular battalions, the 1st and the 2nd, were in the Far East and Middle East respectively and although the 4th and 6th battalions were in Germany and Austria many of the Territorials had by now been demobilised. So most of the men on parade were recruits from the depot, although Major Hastie managed to scrape together a platoon formed for the occasion by men from the 4th Lincolns who were home on demob leave.

The strength of the battalion was indeed now rapidly dwindling as more and more men got demobbed, and in July 'D' Company was disbanded. Shortly afterwards, in Gevelsberg, Germany, the 4th battalion of the Lincolnshire Regiment was disbanded altogether.

And so the 4th Lincolns didn't return as a complete battalion with the band waiting for them at the station for a 'Welcome Home' parade, but came home in ones and twos. There was a homecoming reunion later however at their old depot, the Drill Hall in Broadgate, Lincoln. The Mayor (Alderman F Hill) welcomed almost three hundred of the Territorials who had been mobilised in 1939. Mrs Evelyn Stokes, the widow of Major Don Stokes, presented each of the men with a gift of four pounds ten shillings which had been raised by the Homecoming Fund Committee and a vote of thanks to the Mayor was proposed by Colonel Newton, who had commanded the 4th Lincolns in the early part of the war. After the formal proceedings there was a dance with music provided by a well-known local band, Len Marshall's Dance Orchestra.

*　　　　*　　　　*

These part-time Territorial Army, Saturday Night soldiers, many of whom had joined for a bit of a lark or the chance of a free holiday at the annual camp, had been away from their homes, their families and friends and their jobs for almost seven long years—years when they should have been courting girls, playing sports and going to the pub, enjoying the prime of their lives. Instead, they had suffered humiliating defeat in Norway, cold and discomfort in Iceland and had faced fear and death in France, Belgium and Holland. But they had returned home with optimism, for hadn't the war shown just what the British people could achieve when they all pulled together? Everywhere there was a feeling that a new age was dawning, an age where the newly-established United Nations would ensure that there would be no more wars, an age where a better-educated, more tolerant and classless society would strive towards creating new heights of civilisation. There were hopes—more than hopes—ideals.

That is what all the deaths and the suffering had been about. None would ever forget what it was like. Moving forward in the rain, the thunder of the guns, the dreadful sound of the 'Moaning Minnies', the indispensable spade tucked into the back straps of a pack with the equally valuable enamel mug bouncing up and down, shoulders bent under the load, faces strained. Passing the waiting ambulances whose drivers pretended not to see them, but who saw them all the same. The feeling of fear when suddenly there was the clatter of machine-guns ahead and it felt as though a cold hand had gripped the heart. Then into the battle, men shouting, cursing, crying with pain, some falling...

The total strength of the 4th Lincolns when they had landed in France was around 800 officers and men. During the campaign 557 were wounded—although this figure includes later replacements who were themselves wounded. Some of these young men returned home with lost limbs. Others had wounds which would

199

restrict them from ever living a normal life, prevent them from playing sports or limit their choice of jobs. Some were suffering impaired hearing or vision.

There were those who would speak freely afterwards about their experiences and there were those who would never say anything. All would carry vivid memories of those seven years for the rest of their lives and there would be some who would wake up in the night.

They were the lucky ones, for two hundred and twenty-seven of them never came home at all.

Appendix

The 4th battalion, the Lincolnshire Regiment

Roll of Honour 1939-45

1940
April

21st	Private R S Ballam	Missing, presumed died of wounds
	Private H Prike	Killed in action
	Private R M Smith	Killed in action
22nd	Private G F Roe	Died of wounds
	Private A Toyne	Killed in action
23rd	Corporal F W Tibbs	Died of wounds
27th	Private J Barr	Missing, presumed died of wounds
	Private E Harrison	Killed in action

May

3rd	Private J C Simpson	Died of wounds at sea

June

18th	Private G Humphreys	Died of wounds

July

7th	Private J F C Drury	Died on active service

December

3rd	Regt Sgt-Major G W Bostock	Died (stroke)

1942
January

6th	L/Corporal H Lamb	Died as a result of an accident

February

27th	Private R Giles	Died as a result of an accident

March

11th	Private G W Burden	Died (heart attack)
29th	Private C Coulter	Died

1943
June

3th	Corporal F H Sizer	Died as a result of an accident

November

1st	Private C Bourne	Died
17th	Sergeant E Dunk	Died

1944
June

15th	Private R Andrews	Killed in action
	Corporal G R Baxter	Killed in action
	L/Corporal J Elliot	Killed in action
	Private T S Oakes	Presumed killed in action
	Sergeant F L Peacock	Killed in action
	Private A W Preston	Killed in action
	Private D Thorold	Killed in action
	Private J Waddle	Presumed killed in action
	Private F Wright	Killed in action
	Private J York	Died of wounds
16th	Lieutenant J D Gaunt	Killed in action
17th	Private J T Baker	Died of wounds
18th	Private A G Wink	Killed in action
21st	Private J Halton	Killed in action
	Private R Howells	Killed in action
23rd	Private P Major	Killed in action
25th	Private J A Brewster	Killed in action
	Private C C Carpenter	Killed in action
	Private J Crosby	Killed in action
	Private E A Davies	Killed in action
	Private C Golland	Killed in action
	Private D Hoyle	Died of wounds
	Sergeant D G L Huddlestone	Killed in action
	Private J Hughes	Killed in action
	Private B Lambert	Killed in action
	Private H Petch	Killed in action
	Private W A Settle	Killed in action
	Captain L F Sparks	Killed in action
	Private H C Tomblin	Died of wounds
	Captain D W Waters	Killed in action
26th	Private C Ashton	Died of wounds
	Private R Bailey	Died of wounds
27th	Private J R Bealey	Died of wounds
	Sergeant E Fell	Killed in action
	Private J Haywood	Killed in action
	Private R Hodson	Killed in action
	Private S J Taylor	Died of wounds
29th	Private L Allen	Killed in action
	Private H R Hudson	Died of wounds
30th	Private J Jones	Killed in action
	Major J M Staniland	Killed in action

July

1st	Private F Briggs	Killed in action
	Private W Chadderton	Killed in action
	Private F Cheffings	Killed in action
	L/Corporal R C Dewey	Killed in action
	Corporal H Diamond	Died of wounds
	Sergeant L Guest	Killed in action
	Private S Haithwaite	Killed in action
	Corporal F Hall	Died of wounds
	Private J Hemingway	Killed in action
	Private W W Jackson	Died of wounds
	Private A E Jones	Killed in action
	Private T Morgan	Killed in action
	Company Sgt-Major B H Ringham	Killed in action
2nd	Sergeant W H Beddard	Killed in action
	Private J S Cox	Killed in action
	Private F L Dutton	Killed in action
	L/Corporal S Hanslip	Killed in action
	Private D A Johnson	Killed in action
	Private E Plumtree	Killed in action
	L/Corporal T C Smith	Died of wounds
	Private T T Tyas	Killed in action
3rd	L/Corporal H Havercroft	Died of wounds
	Private W Plant	Died of wounds
	Corporal H Robinson	Killed in action
	Private A Saunders	Died of wounds
	Corporal A C Turner	Died of wounds
4th	Private S Williamson	Died of wounds
5th	Private C W Dodson	Killed in action
8th	Company Sgt-Major F H Grantham	Killed in action
10th	Lieutenant P C Y Fowler	Killed in action
	Lieutenant G H E Morrill	Killed in action
	Private H Warne	Killed in action
11th	Captain W A Wallage	Died of wounds
16th	Private C R Goodchild	Died of wounds
17th	Private G H Drakes	Died of wounds
	Private A Pegg	Died of wounds
18th	Private B Chapman	Killed in action
19th	Private W Belton	Killed in action
26th	Private J L Crockett	Killed in action
	Corporal R B Hibbitt	Killed in action
	Private A Ruddock	Killed in action
27th	Sergeant H Hudson	Killed in action
	Private T H Kelsey	Died of wounds
28th	Sergeant T W Jinks	Died of wounds

August

3rd	Private W E Berry	Killed in action

5th	Private L Spittlehouse	Killed in action
6th	Private J A Robinson	Killed in action
7th	L/Corporal C Dodsoñ MM	Presumed killed in action at sea
	L/Corporal H Grant	Killed in action
8th	Private M Coaten	Killed in action
13th	Major R D Stokes TD	Killed in action
16th	Private L Beardsmore	Killed in action
	Private F Gaflsky	Killed in action
	L/Corporal J H Hill	Killed in action
	Private F J Hutton	Killed in action
	Private D Judson	Killed in action
	Private E L Stuart	Killed in action
	Private J K Turner	Killed in action
	Corporal W E Wilkinson	Killed in action
17th	Private G Maddrell	Died of wounds
18th	Lieutenant J F Metcalfe	Killed in action
	Corporal J E Leaning	Died of wounds
19th	Sergeant W J Baggley	Killed in action
	L/Corporal J E Bradshaw	Killed in action
	L/Corporal R N Hayward	Killed in action
	L/Corporal R Turner	Presumed killed in action
	Private A Walker	Killed in action
	Private E Ward	Killed in action
20th	Private F Hemingway	Killed in action
22nd	Sergeant F A Baker	Killed in action
	Corporal G English	Killed in action
	Private A W B Fowle	Killed in action
	Private F A Hewson	Died of wounds
	Private H Jollands	Killed in action
	L/Corporal T Kendall	Died of wounds
	Private B Pullan	Killed in action
	Private S Rossell	Killed in action
	L/Corporal F West	Killed in action
23rd	Company Sgt-Major A J Parratt	Died of wounds
September		
3rd	Private J Nicholls	Killed in action
	L/Corporal J R Robinson	Killed in action
	L/Corporal G N Wilkinson	Died of wounds
21st	Corporal A H Evison	Died of wounds
25th	Private H R Dawber	Killed in action
	Private R Graham	Killed in action
	L/Corporal R Hiley	Killed in action
	L/Corporal T Kenderdine	Killed in action
	Private G Yates	Killed in action
26th	Private J W Hardy	Died of wounds
	Private A N Hopkins	Killed in action
	Sergeant G Wilson	Killed in action

27th	L/Corporal J Golton	Killed in action
	Private H A Johnson	Died of wounds
28th	Private W Mulligan	Killed in action
29th	Corporal C Chambers	Killed in action
30th	Private J Ambrose	Died of wounds

October

1st	Private J A Lambert	Died of wounds (POW, Munich)
	Corporal L Avison	Killed in action
5th	L/Corporal P Baker	Killed in action
	Private C Drinkall	Killed in action
	Private G H Hancock	Killed in action
	Private W Reynard	Killed in action
6th	Private J E Goodwin	Killed in action
	2nd Lieutenant E A Greenall	Killed in action
	Private H B Howarth	Killed in action
	Private J A Siddall	Killed in action
	Private E H St Ledger	Killed in action
7th	Private R Clements	Killed in action
	Private W B Hollick	Killed in action
	Private L T F Simmons	Killed in action
	Private H Smedley	Died of wounds
	Private H Taylor	Killed in action
	Private F Towle	Killed in action
	Private K Walker	Killed in action
8th	Private J Brummitt	Died of wounds
	Private G Clark	Killed in action
21st	Private L P Cassidy	Killed in action
	Sergeant E Taylor	Killed in action
30th	Private F Kelly	Killed in action

November

5th	Private A T Ivory	Killed in action
6th	Private A R Charsley	Killed in action
	Private A Syson	Died of wounds
12th	Private I Anthony	Killed in action
17th	Private P H Butler	Killed in action
	Major G H Newsum	Killed in action
19th	L/Corporal W L Hopkinson	Died of wounds
20th	Private J H Eatherington	Killed in action
	Lieutenant A D Humphreys	Killed in action
	Private A Hassall	Killed in action
	Private V Hebden	Killed in action
	Private E Mountain	Died of wounds
	Private S Pledger	Killed in action

December

6th	Private F W Rowell	Died (POW)
24th	Private J Showler	Killed in action
31st	Private F Whittaker	Died of wounds

1945
January

5th	L/Corporal W Barfield	Killed in action
8th	Private W B Bates	Killed in action
	Sergeant W Eccles	Killed in action
11th	L/Corporal A G Wilkinson	Killed in action
23rd	Private D Dinsdale	Died (POW, East Prussia)

February

5th	Captain G S D King	Killed in action
24th	Private K W Pocklington	Died (POW, Stalag XXA)

March

1st	Private A L Mann	Died (POW, Poland)
6th	Private J I Hyde	Killed in action
	Private J J McNee	Killed in action

April

2nd	Sergeant H C Bowden	Killed in action
	Private H A Fuller	Killed in action
	Private J G Jones	Killed in action
	Private G A Woodcock	Killed in action
13th	2nd Lieutenant H V Burns	Killed in action
	Corporal S S Cragg	Died of wounds
	Sergeant S Doughty	Died of wounds
	Private C C Fisk	Killed in action
	Private J Greenwood	Died of wounds
	Private E F Spain	Killed in action
	Sergeant W E Stevens	Killed in action
	Corporal R G Thompson	Killed in action
14th	Private S E D Martin	Died of wounds
17th	Private G T Rose	Died as a result of an accident
	Private T W Wilson	Died of wounds
19th	Private G W Thomas	Died (POW, Germany)
21st	Private W A Grainger	Died of wounds
	Private J W Houlden	Died of wounds

July

9th	Private W Donaldson	Killed by a landmine
	Private C Peet	Killed by a landmine

September

14th	Private A Palmer	Died as a result of an accident

December

24th	Private K Jones	Died as a result of an accident

Ranks are those which were held at the time of death, irrespective of whether they were temporary or permanent.

This Roll of Honour is believed to be accurate, although it has been compiled from three sources, all of which differ slightly from each other. Checks have been made in some instances with the website of the Commonwealth War Graves Commission (http://yard.ccta.gov.uk/cwgc/register.nsf.)

The number of casualties in the **49th (West Riding) Division** (the 'Polar Bears') was 1,642 killed, 1,399 missing and 7,751 wounded, a total of 10,792.

Awards

Distinguished Service Order (DSO)
Lieutenant-Colonel F P Barclay MC (Royal Norfolk Regiment, attached to the 4th Lincolns)
Major J O Flint MC

Distinguished Conduct Medal (DCM)
Private G H Sneesby

CSM A E Bilsborrow

Military Cross (MC)
Captain J R Ainger
Major B H T Barlow-Poole
Second Lieutenant J A Bent
Major F E Blackstone
Major E N Cooke
Major J O Flint DSO
Captain R V Francis

Captain R F Golding
Captain E G Hill
Lieutenant S Priestley
Major C E Russell
Lieutenant W J Stainton
Second Lieutenant C F G White

Military Medal (MM)
Sergeant W Bland
Private C A Burrell
Sergeant G E Chambers
Corporal C Cross
Lance Corporal C Dodson
Private W E Firth
Private F W Freeman
Sergeant Green
Sergeant A Greenwood

Private D Grimmitt
Corporal W Higham
Sergeant W Jackson
Corporal H Marshall
Sergeant P Newton
Private R Roach *
Lance Corporal F M Simmonds
Corporal G A Watson
Sergeant E C Ward

Private Roach was later commissioned and won the Military Cross whilst serving with the 5th Lincolns.

Croix de Guerre
Captain D F Cooke

Sergeant L B Britton

Index

Many promotions were made during the course of the war. Ranks, where given, are those held by each man when FIRST mentioned. **Bold italics** indicate photographs.

209